DATE			/

Peasants and Protest

Peasants and Protest

Agricultural Workers, Politics, and
Unions in the Aude, 1850-1914

Laura Levine Frader

University of California Press
Berkeley   Los Angeles   Oxford

University of California Press
Berkeley and Los Angeles, California

University of California Press, Ltd.
Oxford, England

Library of Congress Cataloging-in-Publication Data
Frader, Laura Levine, 1945–
 Peasants and protest : agricultural workers, politics, and unions
in the Aude, 1850–1914 / Laura Levine Frader.
  p. cm.
 Includes bibliographical references (p.).
 ISBN 0-520-06809-2 (alk. paper)
  1. Peasantry—France—Aude—History. 2. Vineyard laborers—France—
Aude—History. 3. Trade-unions—Agricultural laborers—France—
Aude—Political activity—History. 4. Socialism—France—Aude—
History. I. Title.
HD1536.F8F66 1991
331.88′1348′094487—dc20   90-31951
                                                            CIP

Printed in the United States of America
9 8 7 6 5 4 3 2 1

Contents

Illustrations

Tables

Preface

Like many studies of this kind, this book emerged, much changed, from an earlier incarnation as a doctoral dissertation— a study of socialist politics and the revolutionary syndicalist labor movement in a village in southern France. The origins of this work are more personally and intellectually complex. Whether one chooses to recognize it or not, the métier of social historians is an intensely political one. How could it not be? We study the stuff of which politics is made: people, classes, groups, interests, social movements, and social conflict. Politics is everywhere, and as James Baldwin once remarked, even if we are not interested in it, it surely is interested in us. I mean politics in the sense of subject: the lives and struggles of ordinary men and women whose stories have more often than not been left out of the "master texts," and whose social action both included and went beyond the politics of parties and organizations. Politics as analysis: for writing social history entails making sense of social relations and the ways in which men and women have made their way through the contradictions and conflicts that structure their lives.

My taste for social history came from my own history. I grew up in the fifties—years usually associated with the so-called silent generation but that were in fact filled with turmoil in the United States, for those who chose to keep their eyes open. From the grotesque challenges to freedom of speech and conscience by McCarthyism to the beginnings of the civil rights movement in the South, these years were filled with political and social struggles of all kinds. The stories of the trials and troubles of ordinary people that circulated around the dinner table; the social realist paintings and murals of my father that depicted the plight of dustbowl farmers and the unemployed during the Depression; my own work in the sixties against racism, and participation in the movement against the war in Vietnam—all this fed my interest in the ways in which people have for centuries organized and fought against oppression and for social and economic justice. These experiences were the real origin of my interest in the history of class formation, the development of the labor movement, and the heroic age of socialism and revolutionary syndicalism.

At a more specific level, my interest in the vineyard workers of the Aude emerged in a graduate seminar I took with Leo Loubère at SUNY Buffalo. Leo's generous sharing of his own research materials with his graduate students permitted me to start work on some of the questions that have informed this book: why did the Midi become red (we know it wasn't just the wine), and, especially, what was the relationship between the revolutionary syndicalist labor movement and the growth of socialist political parties in what then seemed like an unlikely setting—the vineyards of southern France? In the course of plodding through old newspapers, election returns, and police reports of strikes for a seminar paper on social and political change in the Aude, the Hérault, and the Pyrénées-Orientales, I discovered Coursan. This village at first glance seems like every other village in the vineyard plain of the Aude, with its neat stucco houses, red roofs, and dogs sleeping in the sun. Yet at the beginning of this century the workers and villagers of Coursan occupied center stage in the economic and social shifts that transformed lower Languedoc in the sixty years or so before the First World War. Leo encouraged my interest in local history, nurtured my thinking about these questions, and helped me acquire the tools to begin to answer them. I owe him a great deal.

I am also deeply indebted to the late Sanford Elwitt, who upon arrival at the University of Rochester began advising a young doctoral student who was about to dash off for thesis research in France. Sanford fed my interest in the politics of social history, always pushed me to ask more questions, and gently steered my thinking in more challenging directions. His critical spirit and keen editorial eye enabled me to transform a set of minute details about the economy and politics of a small French village into a doctoral dissertation and, still later, a book. But Sanford's friendship and intellectual companionship were in many ways even more important. I could always count on him to read a draft, offer advice, check out an idea, help me think through a problem, or just listen. His untimely death was a real loss, not only for me, but also for the many others whose lives and work he touched.

Along the way, many other people, through their help, advice, and support, have lent much to this work. The tremendous generosity and warmth of the people of southern France is legend. But it is also true! And my Audois friends deserve all my thanks. In particular, Rémy and Monique Pech have been absolutely central to my work on the Aude. Both their scholarly work on the politics and economy of the Languedoc vineyards and their sharing of the history and culture of their *pays* have given me a look into the social history of southern France that I could never have obtained from libraries and archives alone. For Rémy's generous assistance in interviewing the men and women of Coursan I am enormously thankful, as I am for the opportunity to get to know three generations of Pechs from Vinassan, Aude. Xavier Verdejo, of Cuxac d'Aude, also helped me to see the peculiarities of local politics through his work and knowledge of Cuxac history.

Robert Debant and the staff of the Archives Départementales de l'Aude made my months at the Archives very pleasant indeed. I also wish to thank the staff of the Service de Cadastre in Narbonne, who helped me survive a tortuous journey through the maze of land survey records of Coursan. The Service du Tribunal de Grande Instance in Narbonne allowed me to consult the civil registers of Coursan in 1973. Maître Jean Auger, *notaire* in Coursan, generously brought down from his archives all the wills and records of property transmission I could have wanted and shared numerous and valuable anecdotes about the work of a *notaire*. Monsieur Gilbert Pla, mayor of Coursan, the staff of the Coursan town hall, and indeed the people of Coursan could not have been warmer or more generous with their assistance as I struggled to tell the story of their past.

I am equally indebted to others in Paris and elsewhere. Isabelle Martelly and Pierre Dimeglio generously offered friendship, support, and hospitality throughout the various phases of this project, as did Claude Mazauric; Jean-Paul Socard and Karima Amry gave me the space and peace to finish writing at "La Germenie"; and Jean-Paul Socard and Deke Dusinberre assisted in translating some difficult texts. These last three stretched my mastery of the language with nightly games of Scrabble (in French!). J. Harvey Smith generously shared with me his knowledge of the Midi and of the *question viticole*; as seen in the pages that follow, I have learned much from his work. Members of the Social History Seminars at the University of Warwick and the University of Birmingham (U.K.) listened to and helpfully commented on papers that eventually became chapters. I owe an enormous debt to Ted Margadant, whose close reading of the manuscript helped me to transform a doctoral dissertation into a book; I also benefited enormously from John Merriman's careful reading and encouragement and from Dan Sherman's reading of earlier drafts. The American Council of Learned Societies and the Northeastern University Research and Scholarship Development Fund provided support to enable me to return to France on several occasions; the College of Arts and Sciences of Northeastern University allowed me to take time away from the university to finish the book. Cyrrhian MacRae of the University of Aston (U.K.) typed and typed an earlier version of this work. Nancy Borromey of the Department of History at Northeastern was a tremendous help in the final, rushed stages, as was Susanne McCain, who helped proofread and prepare the index. Sheila Levine and Rose Vekony of the University of California Press expertly and patiently shepherded the manuscript along; Anne Geissman Canright's superb copyediting helped to smooth out the rough edges. Finally (though in no sense last), Stephen Bornstein's support and intellectual companionship helped in innumerable ways to bring this project to completion. He knows how much that means.

Introduction

A tourist driving through the French countryside is immediately struck by the diversity of landscapes, vegetation, and forms of habitation that unfold as one travels south from Paris: the broad, flat plains interspersed with fruit trees of the Ile-de-France; the isolated farms and rolling landscape of the Dordogne; dispersed hamlets nestled among the terraced hills of the Ariège; the flat coastal vineyard plains of the Mediterranean. This patchwork of geography and of varied forms of material life conceals a much more profound diversity, however, one of culture, of politics, and of history—a diversity that recent studies of rural France have repeatedly underlined. If small peasant market farmers in the Var developed communitarian traditions that ultimately led them to embrace socialism before World War I, small landowners and sharecroppers on isolated farms in the Gers to the west turned to Bonapartism after a brief flirtation with democratic socialist (*démoc soc* or *montagnard*) politics in the 1840s; peasants in Brittany, in contrast, scratching away an existence from weak soil, cultivated their religious traditions in the Catholic church and remained solidly conservative through much of the nineteenth and twentieth centuries.[1] Indeed, one is led inevitably to the conclusion that in those rich and vital years of economic, political, and social transformation when the Third Republic was forged, there was not one rural society in France, but several.

On the vineyard plain of the Mediterranean coast the department of the Aude was part of the kaleidoscope of French rural society. But unlike many of the cultures and subcultures of that kaleidoscope in the nineteenth and early twentieth centuries, the Aude straddled both rural and urban worlds. The sophisticated market economy and social relations of production that developed in the vineyards across the eastern half of the department bore striking similarities to those of the industrial, urban world to the north. By the late 1800s and the first decade of the 1900s, the expansion of vineyard capitalism and the emergence

1

of a rural working class led the Aude to experience social tensions similar to those that characterized relations between labor and capital in many industrial centers. The surface tranquility of sleepy vineyard towns exploded with strikes and protests as revolutionary syndicalism and socialism put roots firmly into southern soil. The purpose of this book is to explain how left-wing politics and labor radicalism emerged from a long process of economic and social change during this time.

Most historians who have examined the process of class formation, the rise of socialism among rank-and-file workers, and patterns of working-class protest in nineteenth- and twentieth-century France have turned their attention to the decline of artisans, textile and metal workers, miners, and glass workers in towns and cities like Toulouse, Lyon, Carmaux, Rive-de-Gier, St-Chamond, and Le Cambon-Feugerolles, as well as Paris. In describing the process of class formation that accompanied the development of nineteenth-century industrial capitalism, these scholars—who include Joan Scott, Ronald Aminzade, Michael Hanagan, and John Merriman—have shown how mechanization and new production processes removed artisans' control over work and hiring practices, made traditional skills outdated, drove down wages, and threatened job security, and how socialism and syndicalism helped workers articulate a response to economic and social change and so helped shape the working class.[2]

A few scholars have examined some of these issues in rural France. Leo Loubère's study of radicalism in Mediterranean France has attempted to show how radicalism and socialism developed strongholds among small peasants and artisans throughout the region by offering solutions to peasants' insecurity in the face of economic change and market crises.[3] Jean Sagnes and J. Harvey Smith have chronicled the emergence of a rural working class in areas of vineyard monoculture around the turn of the century in the department of the Hérault. They have shown how vineyard workers mobilized against their declining situation in the vineyards by forming labor unions and striking to defend their rights in the workplace, as well as how socialist politicians built a constituency among these same groups of rural dwellers from the late nineteenth century through World

War I.[4] Tony Judt, on the contrary, has argued that in the Var, where small-scale peasant production dominated the countryside, no rural working class ever developed. Although peasants in the Var suffered from the economic crisis of the 1880s just as peasants everywhere suffered, Judt emphasizes that it was the peasants' interdependence and cooperation, rather than merely their vulnerability to market competition, that drew them to socialism and made the Var a bastion of left politics before World War I.[5]

Finally, some scholars have shown that rural communities provided a welcome environment for the germination of left-wing politics in the tumultuous years between 1848 and 1852. John Merriman, Ted Margadant, and Christopher Guthrie have chronicled the activities of *démoc-soc* political clubs and popular associations among peasants and artisans, and Edward Berenson has shown how popular religion provided a vehicle for left-wing politics in rural France during that time.[6]

With the exception of Sagnes and Smith, none of these writers have focused exclusively on rural workers, the development of revolutionary syndicalism, and labor militancy in the countryside. Moreover, women's contribution to the development of agricultural capitalism and their role in rural protest have been largely neglected as well. Important questions remain about the process of class formation in the countryside and about the nature of rural working-class protest, questions that the present study attempts to answer. Did rural workers experience a process of proletarianization similar to that of industrial workers? Did rural workers organize in the same way as urban workers? Did agricultural workers' protests occur along the lines of urban workers' collective action, as outlined by scholars such as Edward Shorter and Charles Tilly and recently tested by Michael Hanagan?[7] How do we explain the Midi *rouge*? Why did peasants and workers in the Aude gravitate toward radical and socialist politics, and what were the limits of those politics for workers? In the process of answering these questions, this book incorporates gender into the study of class formation by looking at the gender relations of agricultural capitalism, at the place of gender in labor and protest movements, and at the way in which working-class families experienced proletarianization.

As capitalism changed the face of modern France, altering the work process and the social relations of production in towns and cities, it also transformed the countryside between 1850 and 1914. To be sure, in France, over 44 percent of the population still earned its living from the land by the end of the 1800s, and many areas saw the consolidation of small and medium farms over the course of the nineteenth century (the Loire, the Allier, and the Var, for example). At the same time, especially in regions of *grande culture* (cereals, beets, and vines), the gradual concentration of agricultural capital meant that almost 40 percent of the land consisted of large properties of over forty hectares, owned by a mere 4 percent of the population.[8] In poor departments such as the Aveyron, the Corrèze, and the Lozère, the poverty of small proprietors encouraged emigration. In the Aude however, as in much of lower Languedoc, the development of agricultural capitalism took a different course. Neither the consolidation of small and medium landownership nor massive out-migration occurred. Peasants from surrounding regions flocked to this small southern department as large vineyards came to dominate the fertile plains of its eastern half. This study shows how an agricultural wage-earning class emerged through the process of capital concentration, repeated economic depression, and class division. It simultaneously traces the way in which socialism and the revolutionary syndicalist labor movement shaped class identity.

Chapter 1 looks at how an agricultural revolution between 1850 and 1880 transformed the countryside of the Aude from fields of lucerne and wheat, dotted with olive and mulberry trees, into a vast, undulating landscape of vines. By the end of the nineteenth century, the Aude (and especially the eastern plain around Narbonne, on the banks of the Aude River), once considered the breadbasket of southern France, boasted the largest surface area devoted to vines in the region.[9] This agricultural revolution benefited small and large landowners alike, and greatly enlarged Audois villagers' ties to the regional and national markets. It paved the way for an intensive, almost industrial form of capitalist viticulture that employed large numbers of wage laborers. But the Aude did not follow the classic model, according to which capital concentration destroyed small producers. Significantly, in the Aude the development of large-scale agricultural capitalism allowed small producers to survive. Here, much as Smith has found for the Hérault, small farms and vineyards were increasingly subdivided; many workers in the ranks of small growers not only tilled their own land, but they also worked part-time on large vineyards. These two competing forms of capitalist production persisted through World War I. Yet contemporary officials in lower Languedoc who believed that these multiple forms of landownership would assure social and political stability were to be disappointed under the Third Republic.[10]

Chapter 2 shows how economic change and depression in the Aude stimulated the development of the left-wing politics that first appeared in the popular democratic socialist movement of 1848–1852. Later in the century, the same forces that laid the foundations of republicanism during the Second Republic furnished the bases of radicalism at the time of the Commune: the protourbanization of the countryside, the growing market interests of rural winegrowers, and the presence of urban politicians who sought to mobilize rural dwellers in the context of economic downturn. As Chapter 3 shows, the shift to vineyard monoculture and the attendant entrepreneurial mentality made the Aude's economy especially vulnerable to depression. Three major depressions in the late nineteenth and early twentieth centuries—the phylloxera crisis of the 1870s and 1880s, the agricultural depression of the 1890s, and finally the great wine market crisis of 1900–1901, whose aftershocks persisted up to World War I—accelerated the process of capital concentration in viticulture, led to the impoverishment of small landowners and the proletarianization of the vineyard worker, and accentuated class divisions in the countryside. These processes occurred in the Aude in much the same fashion as Smith and Sagnes have described for the Hérault.

It is tempting to apply the urban industrial model to the study of the class formation of rural workers. But as Chapters 3 and 4 show, rural workers forged a class identity from conditions very different from those of the urban world. Whereas proletarianization in cities and factories resulted from the undermining of workers' skill and control via mechanization, speedups, and new techniques of management and payment, in the countryside other factors affected agricultural workers. As in the Hérault, before about 1880 the widespread landownership characteristic of southern vineyard society contributed to the skill and status of landowning workers. By the turn of the century, however, the evolution of vineyard capitalism had eroded the privileged position of vineyard workers, who now shared characteristics both of artisans, with their history of independence and craft tradition, and of the industrial proletariat, with their dependence on wages as their primary source of income. As Chapter 4 shows, part of the process of proletarianization was the acceptance of gendered definitions of work and skill that kept some workers (women) at the bottom of the wage scale. Although working-class families developed strategies to deal with hard times, ironically they aided the development of agricultural capitalism, just as the urban working-class family unwittingly assisted the development of industrial capitalism by allowing employers to profit from the gender division of labor and exploit families' reliance on women's wages. Ultimately, definitions of difference based on gender, skill, and wages divided men and women and weakened labor's ability to mobilize workers in the Aude.

Edward Thompson's oft-quoted insight that "class is a relationship, not a thing," is no less true in the Aude than elsewhere, where class was the consequence of shifting relationships between peasants and workers and the land and between workers and their employers.[11] As those relationships changed, so did class identities. The vineyards of the Aude, then, present a picture of social and productive relations very different from the supposedly homogeneous peasant communities of the Var studied by Judt. In the Audois countryside, the process of class formation occurred slowly, following changes in the structure of the vineyard economy and the vineyard labor force and the emergence of new political cultures.

Agricultural depressions, the concentration of vineyard capital and its social consequences, class division, the marginalization of small vineyard owners, and the gradual proletarianization of vinedressers all paved the way for the development of socialism between 1890 and 1914, a story we examine in Chapter 5. In the 1880s and 1890s, urban artisans, workers, and small landowners looked toward radical and socialist political groups that promised relief from debt and economic insecurity. The story of left politics in the Aude shows how local variations developed on national themes. Whereas radicalism and socialism diverged nationally and became separate political movements by the end of the century, in the Aude the two movements retained a practical political affinity, though differing in theory and public discourse. In addition, Audois socialism developed in distinct ways. Initially revolutionary in their rhetoric, socialists in the Aude grew increasingly moderate in their political strategy and practice during the last years of the nineteenth century and into the early twentieth as they sought to capture the allegiance of downtrodden small vineyard owners. Nor did socialists actively organize rural workers: political parties and unions did not overlap in the vineyards of the Aude, another distinctive feature making the Aude's political and social landscape different from that of the Var or the Cher. Ultimately, not socialism, but revolutionary syndicalism—a product of those same economic changes—seized the forces of class conflict in the countryside.

Vineyard workers forged a political identity from three major factors: (1) the growth of viticultural capitalism and the attendant decline in workers' status, (2) the development of socialism, and (3) the emergence of revolutionary syndicalism in the countryside. Chapter 6 shows how the evolution of viticultural capitalism led to the eventual mobilization of rural workers. Early in the twentieth century, under the influence of the revolutionary syndicalist Bourses du travail, unions composed of agricultural workers, worker/landowners, and small vineyard owners sprang up across the Aude, just as they did in the Hérault, the Gard, and the Pyrénées-Orientales. Between 1903 and 1914 the sound of the tocsin rang throughout lower Languedoc as workers walked off the job to protest wage reductions and the firing of fellow workers and to demand recognition of their unions, higher pay, shorter hours, and contract negotiations. These unions drew their strength from workplace solidarity as well as from workers' material grievances. Community support in densely populated vineyard villages also contributed vitally to class solidarity and served as a weapon in labor struggles. And small vineyard owners, because of both their own ambiguous status and the hostility to large vineyard capital that they shared with workers, supported the rural labor movement as well.

Just as socialism developed in distinctive ways in the Aude, revolutionary syndicalism also emerged as the product of specific local conditions, fierce in its rhetoric and anticapitalist *discours* but more realistic in its pursuit of bread-and-butter aims. Here the workers of the Aude remind us that syndicalism, far from being theoretically consistent, developed and evolved in practice, a product of real struggles and shaped by local conditions. The strike movement of 1903–1914 in the Aude proved that unions could make tangible gains for workers; but the momentum of the movement did not last. Workers left the unions, leaving behind a committed core of activist leaders who attempted to push the rank and file in a more radical direction. This trend, though, which included establishing a distance from socialist electoral politics, was temporarily reversed by the dramatic events of 1907, examined in Chapter 7.

In 1907, small growers and agricultural workers throughout lower Languedoc joined forces with urban workers and artisans in a massive protest movement, demanding government regulation of wine production. This attempt to extricate the southern wine market from nearly twenty years of depression showed that people's capacity for collective action was determined not only by the forces of production in which they were enmeshed, but also by the nature of the winegrowing communities in which they lived. The momentary unity of vineyard villages against the government did not last, however. In the end, the estrangement of the ever more intransigent syndicalist leaders from increasingly reformist socialists was even greater than before. These divisions vividly demonstrate the underlying complexity of a rural society based on two competing forms of capitalist production. The labor movement also declined in the wake of 1907, as radical syndicalists distanced themselves from small vineyard owners, withdrew from the unions, and undermined the unions' ability to undertake future labor struggles.

Analyzing the process of class formation among rural workers and the politics of rural society, then, provides perspective on a number of major issues in the history of French socialism and the history of the French working class: the occasionally fluid definition of class and the changing nature of work and class relations in agriculture; the variations within French socialism in the nineteenth and early twentieth centuries; the relationship between the organized labor movement and socialism; and the nature of protest movements and strike activity in rural as opposed to industrial settings.

Students of peasant societies and economies, especially in Latin America, have used the concept of articulated modes of production to analyze the transition from noncapitalist to capitalist modes of production and also to explain how, in some cases, the two modes of production could coexist.[12] By the 1850s, when this study begins, the economy of the Aude was based in a single mode of production, agricultural capitalism (although, as we shall see, various forms of agricultural capitalism coexisted). At this time, even before the vineyards dominated the Audois economy, an agrarian bourgeoisie had emerged; building large enterprises that operated with wage labor, it had come to prevail in the market and gained control of local politics. The evolution of the Aude in the second half of the nineteenth century, whereby vineyard monoculture became the mainstay of the local economy, did not change the mode of production; rather, it shifted the forms of capitalist production, allowing for the growth of a petty commodity sector—small landowners— along with an unusual hybrid, the laborer-landowner. After 1880 a second shift occurred, involving an increase in the scale of large capitalist enterprises, the emergence of a working class, and the virtual disappearance of the laborer-landowner. The petty vineyard producer persisted, albeit under increasingly difficult circumstances. What interests us here is less the articulation of these forms of production (although that is certainly part of the story of the changing economy and society of the Aude) than the human and political consequences of these shifts, which will help to explain why the countryside of southern France exploded with political and labor radicalism in the years before World War I.

In tracing the evolution of the vineyard economy and the process of class formation among vineyard workers, this study moves among three levels of investigation: the region, lower

Map 1.   France

Languedoc; the department of the Aude; and the workers of a single village, Coursan. By the nineteenth century, lower Languedoc, and especially the Mediterranean coast, was marked by the coexistence of small villages and highly urbanized market centers: Carcassonne, Narbonne, Montpellier, and Béziers. The department of the Aude is an appropriate focus of study for several reasons. Here in the plains of the Aude River, stretching

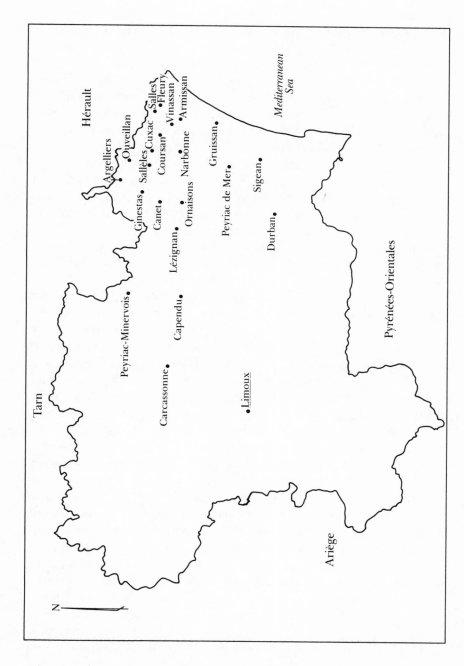

Map 2. The Aude

from Carcassonne to Narbonne and north to where the Aude meets the Hérault, capitalist viticulture was well established by the turn of the century; it therefore provides a good laboratory in which to study the transformation of the vineyard economy. The department is of interest for political reasons as well, for socialism in lower Languedoc owed much to the work of socialist activists from the Aude.[13] The department's left-wing history began in the democratic socialist clubs of the late 1840s and early 1850s and continued through the Third Republic. Moreover, much of the leadership of the region's revolutionary syndicalist movement came from the Aude; the union newspapers *Le Paysan* and *Le Travailleur de la terre* were published in Cuxac d'Aude, and union activists François Cheytion and Paul Ader came from Coursan and Cuxac, respectively. The 1907 winegrowers' revolt began with the founding of the first *comité de défense viticole* by Marcellin Albert in the village of Argelliers, Aude.

The town of Coursan provides an opportunity to test larger generalizations about the nature of class formation and the politics of skilled workers at the local level. As the head town of the canton of Coursan, 7 kilometers from Narbonne (the subprefecture of the Aude) and 650 kilometers from Paris, Coursan stood at the center of the wine-producing plain of the Aude and had strong ties to the regional market economy from the early 1800s. Linked by the main road, and eventually by railroad, to Narbonne and Béziers, Coursan stood on the major trade and transportation routes of the Mediterranean littoral and was in a sense typical of the Mediterranean *bourg*, or urban village. As in many areas of lower Languedoc, moreover, at a time when most of the French countryside was being drained by the *exode rural*, the population of Coursan grew, nearly doubling during the second half of the nineteenth century. Coursan also provides an example of a town where a few large estate vineyards dominated the local economy by the late 1800s. Known for their massive production of common table wine (some estates produced as much as fifteen thousand hectoliters of wine annually), these large "wine factories" shaped the experience of the vineyard working class.

Of course, the vineyard workers of Coursan cannot be taken as representative of vineyard laborers in the region as a whole, or as presenting a model of rural class formation in this period, despite Coursan's similarity to many other Languedocian *bourgs* and villages in physiognomy, economic structure, and class relations. Nevertheless, to the extent that the workers of Coursan shared important characteristics and experiences with other workers (not least because of their major role in the regional revolutionary syndicalist agricultural workers' movement), they permit us to look closely at the rural workers' experience and, most important, to understand how changing forms of agricultural capitalism, political culture, and community helped to form the rural working class and a rural labor movement in the early 1900s.

1

PEASANTS, WORKERS, AND THE AGRICULTURAL REVOLUTION IN THE AUDE

In the twilight of the ancien régime, before the great harvest failures that helped to bring down the monarchy, the *intendant* of Languedoc, Charles Ballainvilliers, wrote to the king, "There is no area in France which can be compared for the abundance of its harvests in grains to the fertile plain of Coursan, although . . . none produces more beautiful wheat than [the plain of] Narbonne."[1] In the mixed economy of the Aude in the eighteenth century, fields of wheat stretched for miles on either side of the Route Royale from Carcassonne to Narbonne and on up to Béziers in the Hérault. Here and there the regular pattern was broken by hectares of lucerne, vines, and olive trees. A variety of small rural industries—most notably drapery—flourished in the small villages that dotted the map of the Aude, providing the protoindustrial economic bases of the hilly west and southwest of the department, around the towns of Chalabre and Quillan.

A century later the physiognomy of the Aude had changed radically. Instead of the gold and buff of wheat and rye broken occasionally by rows of olive trees, now miles of green vineyards prospered under the hot Mediterranean sun in the eastern plain of Narbonne. In the west, the drapery industry was but a shadow of its former self; everywhere, rural industry was now largely tailored to serve the vineyard economy. This agricultural revolution marked the beginning of the Aude's transition to the modern world of capitalist agriculture, with its conflicts and economic crises. It altered the rhythms of the work year, gave birth to a whole series of specialized work skills and new forms of labor, and influenced patterns of landownership in the department. Virtually all social groups benefited from the "golden age of the vine." How and why did that agricultural revolution come about, and how did it affect landownership, social structure, and work patterns in the Aude?

The Aude Before Vineyard Monoculture

The grain-growing economy of the Aude was in part a product of the mercantilist policy of the ancien régime, where governments strictly controlled the planting of vineyards and even fined peasants for planting new vines without government authorization. Once these restrictions disappeared with the revolution of 1789, however, grains continued to dominate the Audois economy for the next fifty years, and vines remained "une affaire de gagne petit," something to bring in a bit of money on the side.[2] In fact, most southern wine never appeared on Audois tables but went off to distilleries in Narbonne and Carcassonne, to produce *eau de vie* and the ⅗ liqueur for which the department was known; these products were then shipped to Bordeaux, Rouen, Paris, and sometimes abroad.[3] Thus, unlike the self-sufficient peasant economies of other parts of France, the mixed capitalist agricultural economy of the Aude was already highly commercial and market-oriented at the beginning of the nineteenth century.

Wheat also brought Audois farmers and merchants important commercial links with the region and with the rest of France. Audois wheat growers regularly exported their surpluses to other Mediterranean departments—the Hérault, Gard, Bouches-du-Rhône, and the Alpes-Maritimes—via the bustling commercial centers of Carcassonne and Narbonne. In either town they could link up with the Canal du Midi, the lifeline by which goods traveled to markets east and west; or they could take their goods by road to the port of La Nouvelle, just south of Narbonne, where they could reach Cette, Marseille, and Toulon by boat. In addition to their agricultural commerce, towns like Carcassonne, Limoux, Montolieu, Cennes-Monesties, and Chalabre, possessed large-scale draperies that also carried on a lively export trade. Finally, small-scale protoindustry, most of it home-based, flourished in Audois villages in the first half of the nineteenth century: forges in the southwest near Quillan; masonry, caskmaking, and carpentry; tailoring, shoemaking, and dress-making. In 1836, the census of Coursan listed four blacksmiths, four butchers, three carpenters and cabinetmakers, two turners, two coopers, two weavers, three locksmiths, three harnessmak-ers, a wigmaker, a miller, and two seamstresses! There was one café in the village.[4] Generally speaking, then, commercial ex-change was central to the economy of large towns like Car-cassonne and Narbonne, as well as to the economy of smaller *bourgs* in the eastern half of the department, such as Coursan and Lézignan.

During the early 1800s, in the period of mixed agricultural capitalism, virtually everyone in most Audois villages owned some land—artisans, tradesmen, shepherds, workers, and even unskilled laborers (Table 1).[5] In Coursan, only foremen (*ramo-nets*) and farmhands (*domestiques*)—individuals who usually came from outside the department—did not make their way into the ranks of landowners in this period. Most propertyholders in Coursan in these years owned tiny pieces of land (less than one hectare). About one-third of the landowners held larger proper-ties of between one and five hectares, and they relied on family labor. Baptiste Rouge, for example, a shoemaker, owned two hectares, which he farmed part-time with his wife, Louise, and their twelve-year-old son. Antoine Hérail, a harnessmaker, his eighteen-year-old son Antoine, also a harnessmaker, and his wife, Claire, worked that family's two and one-half hectares.[6] Ownership of even a small piece of land for most of these people could provide a comfortable supplement to income and a cush-ion against unemployment.

Owners of properties of between six and twenty hectares and larger required wage labor and mules or horses to cultivate their land. Most of these holdings consisted of small parcels scattered throughout the village (*biens du village*), although a few proprie-tors owned large estates of over twenty hectares *en bloc*. These independent property owners dominated the cereal-based econ-omy in Coursan. In Coursan, eight large farms employed local, unskilled wage laborers (*brassiers*) for plowing, sowing, and har-vesting. Not surprisingly, as in all societies in which the owner-ship of land is a major determinant of social status, the owners of these large farms occupied positions of power and prestige in

Table 1. Occupational Distribution of Landowners in Coursan,
Aude, 1851–1911

Occupation	1851	1876	1896	1911
Vineyard worker	54 (20.2%)	153 (26.1%)	80 (12.2%)	91 (15.4%)
Independent small proprietor (*cultivateur*)	30 (11.2%)	61 (10.4%)	76 (11.6%)	58 (9.8%)
Proprietor	21 (7.8%)	75 (12.8%)	109 (16.6%)	85 (14.3%)
Artisan, trades	100 (37.3%)	149 (25.4%)	238 (36.3%)	226 (38.2%)
Other agricultural worker (*jardinier, berger*)	31 (11.6%)	51 (8.7%)	40 (6.1%)	28 (4.7%)
Overseer	11 (4.1%)	30 (5.1%)	38 (5.8%)	34 (5.7%)
Foreman	0 (0.0%)	2 (0.3%)	6 (0.9%)	7 (1.2%)
Farmhand	0 (0.0%)	6 (1.0%)	6 (0.9%)	4 (0.7%)
Professional, village official	21 (7.8%)	60 (10.2%)	62 (9.5%)	59 (10.0%)
Total	268 (100%)	587 (100%)	655 (100%)	592 (100%)

Source: Service de cadastre de l'Aude, Narbonne, "Cadastre foncier de Coursan, 1851–1911."

Note: This table shows only those landowners for whom an occupation was recorded in the land records (a little more than half the landowners in Coursan each year) and only those who were residents of the village (numerous landowners lived outside of the village). Individual landowners have been observed at three points through the Cadastre to trace their landownership, purchases, and sales over time.

the local community, dominating local politics. Men such as Esprit Tapié, André Salaman, and Antoine Givernais from Coursan canton sat on the department Conseil général and on municipal councils and served as justices of the peace and mayors (as did Henri Emmanuel Sabatier and Joseph Hérail, of Coursan). Few of these men actually tilled the soil themselves.

Nonlandowning workers and tradesmen in the previneyard years relied on wages that were barely adequate for subsistence. Although skilled workers like masons and carpenters earned respectable daily wages of between 2.75 and 4 francs, in the late 1840s agricultural workers in the Aude earned only from 1 to 1.50 francs per day (at this time a two-kilogram loaf of bread cost about 20 centimes). Occasionally employers paid agricultural workers in kind with potatoes and beans or gave them meals on the farm. Even worse, male workers in the local textile industry earned only 75 centimes per day, and women 50 centimes.[7] Employers were able to keep wages low because they could rely on these workers' labor all year round and did not need to hire them away from tilling their own land.

The Agricultural Revolution in the Aude

By the middle of the nineteenth century, the economy of the Aude had entered a period of profound transformation. During the Restoration and the July Monarchy, two factors led Audois farmers in the eastern half of the department to put their money into vineyards. First, in the 1820s and 1830s, as the national consumption of wine slowly began to increase, wine prices also rose from late-eighteenth-century levels of 8–10 francs to 20–25 francs per hectoliter. Income from vines could be almost double that from wheat (400 versus 225 francs per hectare). Local farmers became convinced (and they were partly correct) that they could make a fortune within two or three years.[8] Second, state policy, by which Restoration monarchs strove to balance the divergent interests of burgeoning industrial free traders and agricultural protectionists and to prevent a repetition of late-eighteenth-century *crises de subsistance* by insuring adequate domestic grain supplies, favored the transition to winegrowing as well. The sliding scale of import duties established under the July Monarchy clearly favored commercial over domestic agricultural interests, allowing Russian wheat, for example, to sell below the price of French wheat on the domestic market.[9] Although both wheat and wine prices dropped in subsequent years (especially during the nationwide agricultural depression of 1847–1853, hectoliter for hectoliter, wine remained more prof-

Table 2. Comparative Surface Area of Grains and Vines in Narbonne Arrondissement and of Vines in the Aude, 1788–1900 (in hectares)

	1788	1814	1820	1830	1839–1840	1852	1857	1862	1882	1892	1900
Grains	—	—	23,824	20,616	29,595	36,970	17,351	—	—	—	483
Vines	10,111	16,070	—	23,699	26,613	30,587	34,904	—	—	—	69,128
Surface area planted in vines, Aude department	—	—	—	—	—	—	—	81,869	167,488	115,408[a]	

Sources: Georges Barbut, *Etude sur le vignoble de l'Aude (récolte de 1913)* (Carcassonne: Pierre Polère, 1913), 57; Michel Augé-Laribé, *Le problème agraire du socialisme. La viticulture industrielle du Midi de la France* (Paris: Giard & Brière, 1907), 37–38; AD Aude 13M61, "Vignoble départemental, cépages et produits, an XIII–1878"; Georges Barbut, *Histoire de la culture des céréales dans l'Aude de 1785 à 1900* (Carcassonne: Gabelle, 1900), 9; France, Ministère de l'agriculture, *Statistique de la France, Agriculture, Résultats de l'enquête décennale de 1862* (Strasbourg: Berger-Levrault, 1868), 82; ibid., *1882* (Nancy: Berger-Levrault, 1887), 143; ibid., *1892* (Paris: Imprimerie nationale, 1898), 86.

[a]The 1892 decline with respect to 1882 was due to phylloxera; this figure includes newly planted and fully productive vines.

Table 3. Average Yields per Hectare and Prices per Hectoliter of Wine
in the Narbonnais, 1788–1912

Year	Yield (hl/ha)	Price (fr./hl)	Year	Yield (hl/ha)	Price (fr./hl)
1788	12	8	1890	175	15
1845	—	40	1900	147	3–5
1847–1848	30–35	27	1905	45	9
1854[a]	9–11	45–50	1907	55	10
1856–1857	34	30	1908	89	7
1866–1867	40[b]	35–40	1910	41	32
1872	45	40–45	1912	77	22
1881	120	50			

Sources: AD Aude 13M61, "Vignoble départemental, cépages et produits, an XIII–
1878"; 13M281, "Statistique agricole et recensement général des produits végétaux et
animaux domestiques, 1851"; 13M282, "Statistique agricole annuelle, Tableaux récapitulatifs et tableaux synoptiques, 1856–1857"; 13M283, ibid., "1858–1859";
13M287, "Enquête sur la situation et les besoins de l'agriculture, 1866–1867"; 13M289,
ibid., "1868, 1871–1872"; 13M296, "Statistique agricole annuelle de l'arrondissement
de Narbonne, 1888"; 13M307, "Statistique agricole annuelle, commune de Coursan,
Renseignements divers sur la récolte de 1890"; 13M313, ibid., "1900"; 13M318, ibid.,
"1908"; 13M323, ibid., "1910"; Georges Barbut, Enquête sur la production du vin dans
l'Aude en 1899 (Carcassonne: Gabelle, 1900), 15; Georges Barbut, Etude sur le vignoble de
l'Aude et sa production (récolte de 1912) (Carcassonne: Pierre Polère, 1912), 6; France,
Statistique générale, Prix et salaires à diverses époques (Strasbourg: Berger-Levrault, 1864),
xxiii; Aude, Annuaire administratif, statistique et historique du département de l'Aude pour
l'année 1869–1870 (Carcassonne: P. Labau, 1869), 71.

[a]Year of oidium outbreak.

[b]One source reported that the yield of vines planted in the alluvial soils of the plain of
Coursan sometimes reached 200 hl/ha in the period 1869–1870; this was unusually high
for the period of vineyard expansion. See Aude, Annuaire administratif, statistique et
historique du département de l'Aude pour l'année 1869–1870 (Carcassonne: P. Labau, 1869),
71.

itable.[10] By 1830, the transformation of the Aude's economy was
under way; in the breadbasket region of the Narbonnais, vineyards began to replace grain fields (Table 2).

Under the Second Empire, three additional factors inter-
vened to complete the transformation. A fungal disease of vines,
oidium, seriously reduced harvests between 1851 and 1856 and
pushed wine prices up to 45 and 50 francs per hectoliter (Table
3). Farmers who accumulated capital during the crisis used it to
plant vines. Second, the expansion of railroads allowed south-

erners to buy wheat from the north and center of France more
cheaply than previously, thus ending the Aude's previous domination of the southern wheat market. The opening of the
Bordeaux-Cette rail line in April 1857, connecting the Paris-
Lyon-Mediterranean line to the Compagnie du Midi, which ran
through Carcassonne, Narbonne, and Béziers, also extended
the market for Audois wine. Now producers along the line in
towns like Lézignan brought their wine directly to the local
railway station for distribution to the rest of France, and profited
from the preferential rates accorded southern wine by the Compagnie du Midi. Finally, the commercial treaties of the 1860s also
encouraged the expansion of vineyards. Treaties with England
in 1860, Belgium in 1862, Prussia in 1864, and Switzerland, the
Netherlands, Sweden, and Norway in 1865 opened foreign markets that Audois growers had previously only marginally exploited because of high protective tariffs.[11] For the first time,
southern wines competed with the wines of Burgundy.[12] Not
surprisingly, during this period of vineyard expansion the vineyard bourgeoisie in the Aude, anxious to profit from new commercial opportunities, earnestly advocated free trade and protested against the high duties (*octrois*) levied on wines entering
towns and cities, especially in the east and north, which raised
the cost of southern wine in those regions.

Two points must be added to this picture of agricultural revolution. First, whereas the eastern Aude almost completely abandoned grain growing, farmers in the west (Castelnaudary) continued to produce grain almost exclusively, and those in both
Limoux and Carcassonne arrondissements grew both wheat and
wine. These agricultural differences gave rise to striking social
and political differences later in the nineteenth century.

Second, the importance of the agricultural revolution lay not
only in the increasing area devoted to vineyards but also in the
fact that viticulture began to dominate the local economy in virtually all respects. Wine became the very basis of wealth in the
south. Local investors rushed to put their money into vineyards,
as did investors from more distant regional cities like Bordeaux
and Toulouse. Narbonne and Montpellier (in the Hérault)
changed from exclusively commercial centers into cities dominated by *propriétaires-viticulteurs*—large vineyard entrepreneurs

who preferred to live in major centers where they could maintain their contacts with wine dealers, keep abreast of wine prices, and oversee the sale of their wines. By the end of the nineteenth century, virtually all regional investment was in the hands of the *grande bourgeoisie vinicole*.[13]

The agricultural revolution also changed local industry. By the late 1870s, the drapery and ceramics industries in Chalabre and Castelnaudary that had flourished in the first half of that century began to decline. Although several factors affected the demise of the drapery industry in the Aude—the 1860 free trade treaty with Britain, for example, which opened local drapers to British competition, and the cancellation of government orders of cloth for the military—an immediate cause was a serious labor shortage that developed as underpaid textile workers sought higher wages as vineyard workers (at 3.50–4 francs per day).[14]

Nonetheless, the development of viticulture did not bring about the "deindustrialization" of the Aude. In this respect there was more continuity than change in the wake of the region's agricultural transformation. By 1882 the Aude still boasted forty-two draperies and fourteen hat factories. More important, in large towns like Narbonne local industries connected with the vineyards, particularly caskmaking, harnessmaking, masonry, and ceramics, flourished with the growth of vineyards. In 1876 in Coursan, for example, ten household heads worked as coopers (as opposed to eight in 1866), and the number of household heads who worked as masons grew from twelve in 1836 to twenty-seven in 1876. With the corresponding growth of commercial activity in wine, the number of *commissionnaires de vin* (wine commission agents) in Coursan increased from two in 1866 to seven a decade later.[15] Thus, the "ruralization" of the countryside that Philippe Pinchemel observed in Picardie, in the north of France, did not occur throughout lower Languedoc, and certainly not in the vinegrowing Aude.[16]

The Vineyard Revolution, Landownership, and Social Structure

Patterns of landownership and social structure naturally bore the imprint of the vineyard revolution. Many of the vineyards

Table 4. Property Distribution by Size of Property in the Aude, 1862–1892

Property Size	1862	1882	1892
Very small (less than 1 hectare)[a]		36,019 (45.6%)	40,205 (49.3%)
	32,162 (73.9%)		
Small (1–5 hectares)		25,548 (32.4%)	25,465 (31.2%)
Medium (6–20 hectares)	7,124 (16.4%)	12,338 (15.6%)	11,417 (14.0%)
Large (over 20 hectares)	4,262 (9.7%)	5,049 (6.4%)	4,497 (5.5%)
Total	43,548 (100%)	78,954 (100%)	81,584 (100%)

Sources: France, Ministère de l'agriculture, Statistique de la France, Agriculture, *Résultats généraux de l'enquête décennale de 1862* (Strasbourg: Berger-Levrault, 1868), 198; ibid., *1882* (Nancy: Berger-Levrault, 1887), 171; ibid., *1892* (Paris: Imprimerie nationale, 1898), 218–219, 226–227.

Note: These figures cover all property in the Aude and include wheat farms in the west as well as vineyards in the east.

[a]These property divisions are those used by the *Enquêtes agricoles* (see source note). In 1862 the smallest category of property holding for which figures were recorded was less than five hectares.

that came to dominate the economy of the Aude in the second half of the nineteenth century were planted on land previously farmed in grain. Even though some large wheat farmers sold and divided their land during the agricultural transformation of 1850–1880, large estates continued to exist side by side with small properties of five hectares and less. The coexistence of these two forms of property was a fundamental feature of the prosperous expansion years.[17] Thus, the process of capital concentration that ultimately accompanied the development of the modern, "industrial" twentieth-century vineyard, and the parallel process of parceling of vineyard property, were both well under way by 1880 (Tables 4 and 5).

The agricultural revolution modified the existing patterns of capitalist agriculture in Coursan within the elite of large pro-

Table 5. Number of Proprietors by Size of Property in Coursan, Aude, 1851–1911

Proprietors	1851	1876	1896	1911
Very small				
(less than 1 hectare)	474	735	738	1,020
	(56.0%)	(63.4%)	(67.5%)	(70.6%)
Small				
(1–5 hectares)	259	327	277	340
	(30.6%)	(28.2%)	(25.3%)	(23.5%)
Medium				
(6–20 hectares)	88	75	61	67
	(10.4%)	(6.5%)	(5.6%)	(4.6%)
Large				
(over 20 hectares)[a]	25	23	18	18
	(3.0%)	(1.9%)	(1.6%)	(1.3%)
Total	846	1,160	1,094	1,445
	(100%)	(100%)	(100%)	(100%)
Total population				
of Coursan	2,172	2,709	3,767	3,793

Source: Service de cadastre de l'Aude, Narbonne, "Cadastre foncier de Coursan, 1851–1911."

[a] In this category are included both estate vineyard owners and the holders of *biens du village* whose holdings totaled over twenty hectares.

ducers. Four of the village's large wheat farms changed hands by 1880; all but one were broken up and sold, parcel by parcel.[18] The estate of Auriac remained intact and became one of the most important estate vineyards in the late nineteenth and early twentieth centuries.[19] Of the four estates still in the hands of the original owners (that is, from the 1830s and 1840s), all became large vineyards. The Salaman family, owners of the estate of La Vié, planted vines where once they had sown wheat, as did the Podénas family, owners of the 66-hectare Pontserme estate. The enormous 190-hectare estate of the Propriétaires de la Tour and the large estate owned by Pierre Joseph Fabre from Cuxac d'Aude, who purchased a 63-hectare farm from Honoré Laserre, a lawyer from Narbonne, each became huge vineyards, the latter being called La Coutelle. Of the ten largest vineyards in Coursan at the turn of the century, eight were built before

1880.[20] The importance of these estates lay not only in their
surface area, but also in their large-scale production of wine.[21]
These new vineyard barons built expensive homes that resem-
bled small châteaux, surrounded by luxurious gardens planted
in cypress and fruit trees. Their high roofs and towers stood out
incongruously above the vineyards, contrasting sharply with the
more humble dwellings of small peasants and workers in nearby
villages.

In some respects the estate vineyards did not differ significantly from the large grain farms that had preceded them. Lo-
cated outside of the village center, some large estates in the
vinegrowing Aude, such as Celeyran in Salles d'Aude or Grand
Caumon near Lézignan, included dormitories for housing unskilled farmhands, barns for storing equipment and housing
work animals, a distillery and cellar for winemaking, a chicken
coop, and a small vegetable garden. But in contrast to the wheat
farms with their relatively small number of workers, the large
vineyards employed anywhere from fifty to seventy skilled workers and another ten to twenty unskilled farmhands. Not only
were the estate vineyards the largest employers of wage labor,
but they also dominated the economic life of Audois villages as
consumers of local masonry, cooperage, and harnessmaking. As
concentrated property, the estate could operate much more effi-
ciently than large properties composed of fragmented parcels in
virtually all aspects of production, ranging from cultivation,
pruning, and fertilizing to winemaking.[22]

In addition to transforming large farms into large estate vineyards, the agricultural revolution in the Aude led to the increasing subdivision of property (Table 4).[23] As Table 5 shows, the
number of properties of less than one hectare grew significantly
in the expansion years, partly because vines could be grown
profitably in a relatively small area, whereas grains could not, but
also because the mad rush to acquire vines caused land prices to
skyrocket. Grain fields that had sold for 3,000 francs per hectare
before 1850 commanded prices of between 6,000 and 8,000
francs per hectare when planted in vines; particularly rich land
could fetch up to 20,000 francs a hectare.[24] Between 1851 and
1880, of the 873 individuals who entered the land records of
Coursan for the first time, 84.3 percent made purchases of

under one hectare; only 2.3 percent made purchases of over six hectares.[25] One wonders how modest workers and artisans managed to scrape together the money to buy. Some, like the brothers Louis and Hilaire Bertrand, pooled their funds; others obtained loans from wealthy estate owners who in turn earned a sizable portion of their income from interest on loans.[26] Considering the profits to be made, the "gold rush" mentality of these years is not hard to comprehend.

Families who owned less than a hectare could not expect to support themselves from working their vines alone, but income from what they did grow could contribute substantially to the household's total earnings (see also Chapter 4). In the early 1870s, the owner of a hectare of vines could hope to make between 1,460 and 1,685 francs a year. Owners of over a hectare could live on their vineyard income as independent petty producers, *cultivateurs*. Very large estate owners (over twenty hectares) typically referred to themselves as *propriétaires*. These individuals produced a commercial product designed to be marketed. Even those who initially bought only tiny plots of land, however, managed to accumulate more property over the years. Jean Bauderuc, a mason, for example, bought 71 ares in 1857; by 1870 he owned 2.38 hectares, and by 1899, just over 4 hectares.[27] His case was not exceptional.

Indeed, one of the most significant features of the agricultural revolution in the Aude was the continued spread of landownership among all social and occupational groups—vineyard workers, artisans, tradesmen, and professional men—a phenomenon that created a strong community of interests among rural dwellers of the winegrowing Aude. As Table 1 shows, vineyard workers in Coursan became the largest group of landowners in the expansion years (about 26 percent of all landowners in 1876); these men owned an average of 0.65 hectares, which they worked part-time. Artisans and tradesmen made up the next largest group.

As Harvey Smith has noted in his study of Cruzy, Hérault, men who acquired vines in the age of vineyard expansion differed from earlier vinegrowers in the more mixed economy.[28] These new *vignerons* paid more attention to the skills and profits of vine cultivation. Their social backgrounds also changed. In

Table 6. Occupations of Fathers of *Cultivateurs* Who Married in
Coursan, 1850–1880 (percent)

Occupation	1850–1860	1861–1870	1871–1880
Proprietor/professional	10.3	2.6	1.4
Cultivateur	62.1	65.8	82.9
Laborer	7.0	5.3	1.4
Artisan/tradesman	10.3	21.0	11.4
Other (farmhand/shepherd)	10.3	5.3	2.9
Total	100.0	100.0	100.0

Source: Bureau de greffier du Tribunal de grande instance, Narbonne, Aude, Etat-civil
du village de Coursan, "Actes de mariages, 1850–1880."

the peak years of vineyard expansion, men marrying in Coursan
who were the sons of artisans and tradesmen increasingly turned
their talents to vinedressing (Table 6). In addition, whereas in
the 1850s sons of small vineyard owners and *cultivateurs* marrying in Coursan had become farmhands or manual laborers, in
the 1860s and 1870s they increasingly followed their fathers in
the trade.

The double spread of vineyards and landownership meant
both upward mobility for these men and subtle shifts in the
occupational structure of vinegrowing villages. Most important,
the term used to identify agricultural workers changed, reflecting the recognition of vinedressers' new status as skilled workers.
Whereas unskilled agricultural workers known as *journaliers agricoles* constituted the majority of village workers prior to the
1870s, officials now referred to the new, skilled agricultural
workers as *cultivateurs*. Although the term signified the actual
landowning status of vinedressers, officials used it to describe
vineyard workers whether or not they owned land. Assuming
that the vineyard labor force in Coursan increased proportion-
ally to the overall increase in population between 1851 and
1881, the years of vineyard expansion (see Table 9), and that the
1876 census did not record all occupations in Coursan, the
village labor force appears to have grown dramatically by 40
percent between 1876 and 1886. A high demand for skilled
labor in the vineyards of the 1860s and 1870s likewise led to an

Table 7. Occupational Distribution of Men in Coursan, 1851, 1876, and 1911

Occupation	1851		1876		1911	
	No.	Percent	No.	Percent	No.	Percent
Day laborer	261	31.9	25	3.2	624	45.8
Cultivateur (small owner)	111	13.6	379	48.0	7	0.5
Estate worker (farmhand, manager, overseer)	66	8.1	51	6.5	111	8.2
Other agricultural worker	127	15.5	54	6.9	56	4.1
Artisan/tradesman	164	20.1	163	20.7	306	22.5
Proprietor	73	9.0	67	8.5	175	12.9
Professional/*rentier*	15	1.8	49	6.2	82	6.0
Total	817	100.0	788	100.0	1,361	100.0

Sources: AD Aude 11M78, 117, 157, "Dénombrements de la population. Etats nominatifs des habitants de Coursan, 1851, 1876, 1911."

increase in the proportion of men and women who worked as *cultivateurs* in Coursan during those decades (Table 7; see also Table 12). If landownership contributed to the relatively high status that vineyard workers enjoyed in these years, so did changes in work patterns that came with the spread of vineyards during the agricultural revolution.

The Transformation of Vinedressing

Vinegrowing has often been described as the aristocracy of agriculture, and the vinedresser as the peasant aristocrat. As one nineteenth-century scholar of vines and vineyards, Jules Guyot, noted, "The cultivation of vines is . . . the complement of all good agriculture; it is master by virtue of the money that it produces; it is the force and resource of agriculture by virtue of the . . . mouths that it feeds."[29] But the peasant aristocrat had to deal with a temperamental product. As Arthur Young remarked in 1789,

There is scarcely any product so variable as that of wine. Corn lands
and meadow have their good and bad years, but they always yield
something, and the average produce is rarely far removed from that
of any particular year. With vines, the difference is enormous; this
year yields nothing; in another, perhaps the casks . . . contain the
exuberant produce of the vintage; now the price is extravagantly
high, and again so low as to menace with poverty all who are concerned in it.[30]

In fact, Young was right. Vinegrowing involved considerable
risks. Too much rain in spring could prevent flowering; fungal
diseases, frost, or hail could easily destroy an entire crop. In
addition, unlike other crops that could be planted, cultivated,
and then forgotten until harvest or where the work rhythm involved alternate periods of intense activity and rest, vines had to
be cared for individually, regularly, and throughout the year, following a prescribed routine. These characteristics of vinegrowing shaped the work and mentality of the vinedresser. Thus, the
rise of vineyard monoculture not only changed patterns of landownership and capitalist production; it also meant the adapta-
tion of both owners and workers to different techniques, skills,
and work rhythms. Workers who tilled wheat fields and dressed
vines in the 1840s acquired new skills and developed new expertise in vinedressing just as did the sons of skilled artisans who
acquired vines for the first time in the 1860s.

The vinegrower's year commonly ran from one harvest to
another. The work year in the Aude began in late October or
early November, immediately following the grape harvest, with
the first pruning, or *l'époudassage*, designed primarily to permit
access to the vines for cultivating and cleaning.[31] At this time,
southern vinedressers aggressively pruned their vines in the
"goblet" shape of three or four main branches typical of vines in
lower Languedoc, cultivated the soil, and began winemaking
once the crushed grapes were placed in large cisterns to ferment.
In December they pruned and cultivated again and performed
the first drawing off of the wine (*premier soutirage*). In winter they
planted new vines and fertilized; winter prunings continued into
February and March, and in March came the final drawing off of
wine in the cellar. Throughout pruning, workers cleared fallen

branches from the vines, gathered them into bundles, and sold them as kindling, if the vineyard owner did not keep them.

In April, vinedressers cultivated again and began the "green pruning," cutting back unproductive shoots from unproductive wood and pruning woody stems from the base of the vine to encourage more prolific growth on top where leaves and fruit could more easily receive the hot southern sun. The vinedresser spread sulphur in the vines in May and June as a preventive measure against oidium; a third sulphuring would follow in July, and additional cultivation. Finally, in August, if the season had been unusually damp, the vinedresser might give the vines a fourth sulphuring, prepare material for the harvest, and ready the winemaking vessels and equipment in the *cave*. Then at the end of September came the harvest, the busiest time of the year, lasting about twenty days. And once it was over, the cycle began again.[32]

The cultivation of vines thus required continuous, regular work throughout the year. Before the 1880s, pruning was the most important of all vinedressing skills; the primary means by which the vinedresser controlled both quality and yield, it required specialized knowledge of the plant and some training.[33] In the late 1850s, agricultural societies (*comices agricoles*) in Carcassonne and Narbonne gave courses in pruning to agricultural workers and vinedressers. Yet the increasingly complex work of the vinedresser in the "golden age of the vine" did not immediately transform tools and equipment, and until the 1870s vinedressers used traditional methods and ancient tools, performing all operations by hand. In the 1860s vinedressers still used wooden swing plows and cultivated by hand, with spades.[34] Gradually the agricultural revolution brought changes in this domain as well.

As wine prices rose in the 1870s and vineyard owners became more concerned to turn a profit, vinedressers improved techniques. They began to use new equipment, such as the *sécateur*, a special curved knife for pruning, and the iron plow, and they cared for their vines still more intensively. Now they fertilized their vines regularly and frequently, pruned aggressively, and planted prolific varieties such as the Aramon and Carignan grapes, to replace older, less productive Terret and Grenache grapes. In order to cultivate with plows, vineyard owners began to plant their vines farther apart in the 1860s and 1870s. Vine-dressers in general took a greater interest in increasing yields, and, as Table 3 shows, wine production steadily increased. Partly as a result of more intensive cultivation and the expansion of vineyards between 1860 and 1880, owners of large properties relied on growing numbers of skilled workers. This factor, plus the tremendous profitability of vines in this period, pushed wages up and, as contemporaries themselves observed, ac-counted for an increased willingness to improve techniques and equipment.[35] The agricultural revolution and the gradual trans-formation of vinedressing also affected the labor structure of the estate vineyard.

Division of Labor and the New Vineyard Laborer

The division of labor on large estate vineyards reflected nuances of skill in vinedressing. In fact, the estate vineyard in the period of expansion came to resemble a small industrial establishment, with its sophisticated division of labor and work discipline. In the last two decades of the century, as workers became ever more dependent on the large estates for work, the industrial analogy would become even more appropriate. The potential for conflict between groups of workers, as well as for the formation of class solidarity, was built into the productive relations of the estate vineyard.

Increasingly over the nineteenth century, absentee propri-etors of estates in the Aude who lived in large towns like Car-cassonne, Narbonne, Béziers, or Montpellier delegated the di-rection of the vineyard to a manager, the *régisseur*.[36] These estate managers, themselves former small landowners or older work-ers, generally came from the Aude, and even though they had no formal training for their job, they occupied a position of high status and some privilege as the representatives of the *patron*.

The manager's responsibilities included directing work in the vines, distributing tools, paying wages, and keeping the vine-yard's account books. In addition, he supervised the upkeep of the *cave* and the delivery of wine to the wholesaler (the proprietor carried out the sale of wine himself). As the representative of the owner's authority on the estate, he had to be able to deal firmly with workers and suppress arguments among personnel, a role that brought him into conflict with striking workers on more than one occasion between 1903 and 1914. Hired on a yearly contract, the manager and his family lived on the estate, received unlimited wine for their own use, and were permitted use of the work animals on the estate to cultivate their own land. By 1880, an estate manager could earn a yearly salary of between 1,000 and 1,500 francs, to which might be added a bonus of 500 francs in a good harvest year.[37] A well-paid manager could accumulate substantial savings. Jean-Pierre Aribaud, for example, *régisseur* on the estate of Lastours in Coursan, left 8,000 francs to his heirs in 1911.[38] Materially, the manager was quite comfortable in comparison with other estate workers.

On those Audois vineyards where owners lived directly on the estate or in the village, the tasks of looking after work animals and resident workers were delegated to an overseer or foreman, the *ramonet*. These men usually came from the surrounding mountain areas of the Tarn or the Ariège, although later, after the turn of the century, Spanish immigrants often came on as overseers. If the overseer was married, his wife (the *ramonette*) prepared meals for the resident personnel on the *domaine* and served as the head of a team of women workers.[39] Although the *ramonet* was of a slightly higher status than the other resident workers, he did not have the same privileged position as the *régisseur*, and in the labor conflicts that filled the prewar years overseers usually sided with workers.

The social construction of authority relations between husbands and wives dictated that even though the *ramonet* and *ramonette* performed distinct tasks, only the man received the wage, from 480 to 600 francs a year.[40] He also received the wheat, oil, salt, and wine allocation from the estate owner, which he then passed on to his wife. Besides not receiving a separate wage, the *ramonette* was allocated only half the amount of food accorded to the male workers whom she had to feed, a condition that lasted into the twentieth century and that was indicative of contemporary beliefs about gender differences in food requirements.[41] Perhaps she had her revenge on this unjust system after all, however, for "she took her pay from the economies she was able to make in the food allocations of others. One understands how this system was defective. . . . Even on vineyards where the well-intentioned proprietor gave out sufficient quantities [for the upkeep of workers] . . . the food was often terrible!"[42] Still, in the final analysis the *ramonette*'s situation was better than that of the unskilled farmhands for whom she cooked.

Most unskilled labor of digging and cultivation on large estates fell to the migrant farmhand, or *domestique*. Some in this reserve army of labor, *gagés*, worked on yearly contracts (their name came from the *gages*—yearly wages—that they were paid); others, *mésadiers*, were hired and paid by the month. Most of these workers were men; generally, vineyard owners preferred to hire women on an even less permanent basis, by the day.[43] In addition to performing unskilled hand labor, *domestiques* drove the wagons used for carrying tools and grapes at harvest and spread chemicals in the vines. Despite the importance of their jobs in the vineyard, these workers occupied the lowest status of all. One contemporary claimed, "A woman's work is worth more than the work of one of these men"; another emphasized that farmhands were "not as capable when it comes to the proper cultivation of the vine, which demands care and attention. These [folks] are laborers and not *vignerons*."[44] Skilled workers also looked down on the migrant farmhands as *gavaches*, a pejorative term meaning careless and crude. As Abel Chatelain has noted, apart from the economic threat to the local laboring population that these "foreigners" posed, as migrants they were inherently less respectable and socially inferior.[45]

Estate owners, though, saw advantages to hiring such workers. Employers paid them less than the local skilled workers, viewing them as a submissive or passive work force that would do their bidding and then obediently return to their mountain homes in the Tarn, the Ariège, or the Aveyron. Sometimes estate owners and managers attempted to use farmhands to influence the outcome of elections. One manager from Narbonne boasted that he hired his *mésadiers* in October so that when elections occurred in April or May they would have the six months of residence necessary to vote, obviously for the candidate of the manager's preference.[46]

The working conditions and pay of these workers were deplorable. They typically worked a twelve-hour day (as opposed to six or eight hours for the day laborers), and the annual wage of the *gagés*, which could reach 650 francs per year (plus wheat, wine, and beans) in the expansion years, was about 300 francs less than skilled laborers' earnings. *Mésadiers* made even less, some 380 francs per year, and often tried to supplement these wages with piecework.[47] Housed in dormitories or haylofts, they slept on straw, without even the barest sanitary amenities. Although their conditions improved somewhat around the turn of the century, overall the *domestique* remained the lumpenproletarian of the vineyards into the early twentieth century.

The condition of skilled day laborers (vinedressers), who made up the majority of workers on large estate vineyards, could not have contrasted more sharply with that of the farmhands. In Coursan, skilled *journaliers* were the largest occupational group in the village in 1866, 37 percent of the working population, and ten years later they stood at just under 45 percent. In the vineyard expansion years these men were mainly local dwellers who had been born and raised in the villages in which they worked. They enjoyed a comfortable and stable position thanks not only to the prosperity of the growing vineyard economy, rising wages, and job security, but also to the special position many of them occupied as both wage workers and property owners.

As skilled workers, vinedressers performed all the delicate hand operations: pruning, certain types of cultivation and chemical treatments, planting, cellar work, and, after 1880, grafting. Not all *journaliers* were skilled, however, for a clear gender division of labor left unskilled work—such as gathering branches that fell to the ground during pruning, spreading fertilizer in the vines, sulphuring against oidium and mildew, and harvesting— to women. (Their work is discussed more fully in Chapter 4.) Contemporaries considered male vinedressers to be the real artisans of the vineyard and assumed skill in vineyard work to be exclusively masculine. The fact that many male vineyard workers were also landowners—in Coursan in 1876, at least 41 percent (and probably more) of vineyard workers owned a parcel of vines—only reinforced their status as artisans.[48] Indeed, in addition to defining skill in gendered terms, contemporaries consciously associated skill and landownership. As one turn-of-the-century observer remarked, "The day laborer doesn't complain about work that he will later perform for himself. . . . His pride is engaged; . . . how can he appear capable of working his own property if he works clumsily or badly the property of others?"[49]

In the golden age of vineyard expansion, landowning *journaliers* prospered. As wage earners they could earn 25 centimes more per day than propertyless day laborers, the wage bonus being a reward for the expertise that was presumed to come from ownership of vines. Moreover, income from their vines in the expansion years could be considerable. Assuming production costs of one hectare of vines to be 340 francs, a worker who owned one hectare of vines in 1872, harvested forty-five hectoliters of wine, and sold it at 45 francs per hectoliter could have made 1,685 francs, considerably more than a propertyless worker could have earned in a year.[50] These workers generally enjoyed a shorter workday than other estate workers (six as opposed to eight hours) so that they might cultivate their own vines; as Smith has noted for Cruzy, the shorter workday was an important feature of the status that these skilled workers enjoyed during the Second Empire.[51] In addition to the material security and status that landownership provided, it gave vinedressers an important measure of psychological independence from wage labor. Moreover, landowning skilled workers who did work for wages were not entirely dependent on the large estate vineyards for work, given the numerous large, nonestate enterprises that regularly hired workers. In fact, during the 1860s and 1870s the term *journalier* virtually disappeared from official records. Manuscript census and agricultural surveys henceforth used the term *cultivateur*, meaning small proprietor or small proprietor-vinedresser, whether or not the individual owned land.[52] The shift in terminology reflected both a blurring of class distinctions and the perception of the vinedresser as a skilled worker.

Vinedressers in the Aude in the golden age of the vine enjoyed a comfortable material situation. In this period of widespread landownership when labor was in relatively short supply, the high demand for skilled workers helped to keep wages high. Nominal wages rose almost consistently between 1850 and 1880 (see Table 11), comparing favorably with the national average wage of agricultural workers (1.63 francs a day in 1862, 3.11 francs a day in 1882) and with the wages of local artisans, which stagnated over the same period.[53] Pride in the craft of vinedressing distinguished these workers from the migrant *domestiques*, as did their permanent residence and social roots in local vinegrowing communities.

The status, flexibility, and freedom of the vinedresser also contrasted sharply with the situation of other skilled workers in France at this time, such as textile workers, metal workers, tailors, and printers, all of whom began to feel the effects of mechanization, devaluation of skill, and new methods of work organization and supervision.[54] Vinedressers had the advantage of creating a product for which demand continuously rose in these years but where the nature of production precluded mechanization. Ironically, these comfortable rural workers profited from the misery of their urban counterparts, who, by calling on the fruits of the vine to escape the troubles of the workplace, raised the demand for southern wine.[55]

During the years when vineyard capitalism came to dominate the Mediterranean economy, the Aude experienced a growth and prosperity almost unparalleled in its history. By the 1860s, inspectors from the Banque de France enthusiastically reported that whatever the cost of a piece of land, a *cultivateur* could easily pay for it with two harvests. Vinegrowers made fortunes right and left, creating "un luxe insensé." In 1875 the government inspector A. Ditandy reported, "Land of great wealth and hard work, land of wine and of gold, the Narbonnais appears to neighboring populations as a sort of El Dorado or Promised Land, where the poor man becomes rich and the rich man becomes a millionaire."[56] Indeed, the agricultural revolution with its accompanying changes in the forms of capitalist production, property distribution, and social structure benefited a broad spectrum of peasants, artisans, and workers in the Aude. Most important, it brought forth a new group of agricultural workers:

skilled vinedressers. These changes had profound consequences for the politics of vinegrowing communities as vinedressers joined forces with other small landowners and the artisans of prosperous wine-producing villages to defend their common interests as producers. Thus, the development of vineyard capitalism created the conditions in which left-wing—*démoc soc* and republican—political movements would thrive.

2

PROTOURBANIZATION OF THE COUNTRYSIDE, CULTURE, AND POLITICS IN THE GOLDEN AGE OF THE VINE

If one could have looked at an eastern Audois vinegrowing village like Coursan from the air in about 1850, it would have appeared as a dark center of red-roofed houses, shops, and workshops, with a few houses and shops radiating out along the main road, the whole surrounded by a vast, flat plain of vines and pasture. In the center of town cafés, shops, and the church ringed the village square, where the broad, thick leaves of plane trees provided shade from the hot meridional sun. Old men gathered to play *boules*, and ambulatory merchants sold their produce, just as they do today. Unlike the dispersed villages of the mountainous regions of the Massif Central or the Pyrénées, the hamlets of the Dordogne or the Nivernais, Mediterranean villages formed densely populated agglomerated settlements. Dwellers in these nucleated, protourban villages enjoyed regular contact and communication, both with each other and with neighboring villages. The midcentury agricultural revolution not only brought wealth and upward mobility, allowing vine-dressing to emerge as a skilled profession; it also brought rural dwellers into closer touch with market towns and urban culture. By midcentury, some vineyard villages had acquired the status of *gros bourgs*. As Ted Margadant has pointed out, "Just as proto-industrial workers participated in an urbanizing society without, themselves, working in factories, so 'proto-urban' craftsmen and *cultivateurs* participated in an urbanizing society without residing in cities."[1] In the crucible of the protourban village, itself a product of the agricultural revolution, artisans, vinedressers, and petty bourgeois vineyard owners forged a republican political tradition.

Culture and Society in the Protourban Village

Density of habitation in agglomerated settlements shaped community culture and sociability in protourban villages in the golden age of the vine. Around the center of town, artisans and vinedressers lived side by side in two- or three-story dwellings often containing as many as three households. Most owners of the large vineyards lived either on their estates or in large centers like Narbonne and Carcassonne; a few lived in the village center, as did professional men—lawyers, doctors—and small landowners. *Cultivateurs*, artisans, and independent proprietors lived in split-level dwellings that earlier, in the mixed agricultural economy, had housed animals and agricultural tools as well as the farm family. Now these men converted the ground floor or storerooms into wine cellars to house winemaking equipment and large vessels for storing wine.[2]

In these dense villages, artisans, small proprietors, and vinedressers lived in close proximity to one another and shared the life of the community just as they shared the fortunes of the vines. On hot summer nights, neighbors gathered in the street or in cafés; popular *cercles* and *chambrées* flourished year-round for reading and discussing newspapers and politics. By the 1840s and 1850s village cafés had become not merely venues of village sociability; they also served as centers of political organization. By 1878 Coursan, already a large *bourg* and *chef-lieu de canton*, had five cafés, which had begun to acquire their own political colors and class associations.[3] Rural dwellers in the vinegrowing Aude shared an associational life comparable to that of town and city dwellers.

The rhythm of the vineyard year also engendered a culture of community sociability. The harvest constituted an occasion for celebration in which virtually the entire working population of the village took part (even as it increasingly involved immigrant labor over the century). Here the fast-paced, strenuous collective effort of three to four weeks' duration was interspersed with equally vigorous drinking, eating, pranks, and rituals such as the *fardage*, in which young harvesters, especially women, could be given an involuntary bath in crushed grapes. During the harvest future spouses met and couples formed. More than one estate manager deplored the debilitating effects of nocturnal festivities on the following day's work. Overall, the harvest confirmed and reinforced the community's collective interest in the vineyards.[4]

In addition to the harvest, the village *fête* provided another occasion for individuals to reaffirm collective ties to village and region. Although July 14 did not become a national holiday until 1880, for centuries rural dwellers celebrated village festivals in summer before the harvest with street dancing, feasts, and parades. After 1870, as the working-class population of the Aude's vineyards grew, in some villages the *fête* involved singing the "Internationale" and other songs describing workers' struggles. Saints' days, carnival, Ash Wednesday, and the first of May all served as occasions of popular festivity in the Aude, as in the rest of Languedoc, and brought protourban rural dwellers into contact with one another. As we shall see, these celebrations sometimes took on political significance as well.[5]

Nonetheless, the unity of the village community in popular celebration should not be overemphasized. Village territory was divided into male and female space. The wine cellar, the barn, and blacksmith's forge were all traditionally meeting places for men, as were the café and the *cercle*. Custom and tradition in principle excluded women from these areas (although women could and did enter cafés, it was not common for them to meet there to socialize). Women's sociability was specific to the home, the laundry area at riverbank or in the washhouse, and the market. In addition to the gendering of social space, by midcentury class divisions could be seen in villages like Coursan as well, in the kinds of cafés villagers frequented and the kinds of social clubs they joined. In the golden age of the vine, however, prosperity, the high status of vinedressers, and widespread property ownership masked or at least blurred class differences.[6] Sociability and sense of community, then, characterized southern protourban villages. Markets linked them to nearby urban centers.

The flourishing of regional markets under the expanding vineyard economy, together with the building of new railway lines linking Narbonne, Carcassonne, and Castelnaudary with Toulouse to the north and Béziers and Cette in the Hérault to the east, facilitated the protourbanization of the Aude. With the exception of Castelnaudary and Toulouse, these towns were important centers of the wine trade, with weekly markets that attracted local producers, wine merchants, artisans, and villagers, as consumers.

By 1913 Narbonne had the largest number of wine dealers in the south (117, as opposed to 80 in Béziers).[7] In this bustling market center the commercial rituals of the wine trade developed. Large proprietors regularly frequented the markets and in establishments with names like Café des Négociants and Café des 87 Départements they made their business deals over a glass of *gros rouge* that might well have come from their own vines.[8] In many cases, business and friendship overlapped: large proprietors were often related to dealers. Moreover, as Rémy Pech has pointed out, important subtleties in social status distinguished various levels of viticultural capitalists. Medium and small proprietors or worker-proprietors appeared less frequently in Carcassonne or Narbonne than large owners; they simply did not produce enough wine to warrant a regular presence at markets. Late in the century, however, after economic crisis struck southern viticulture, worker-proprietors could ill afford to lose a day's work to "faire le marché." As Pech has noted, "aller faire le jeudi [ou] faire le mardi" became a mark of social status.[9]

Not surprisingly, wine dealers became increasingly familiar figures in village communities in the period of vineyard expansion. Not only did they become conspicuous in the economic life of towns (they often owned large vineyards themselves), but they also organized carnival celebrations and lent money for village *fêtes*; after the turn of the century they organized the first rugby clubs in Narbonne. Until the late 1840s they dominated political life in the Aude, along with large proprietors, sitting on municipal councils and on the departmental general council. At the end of the century, some, such as Bartissol of Narbonne, made successful political careers.[10]

Apart from the sale of wine, local markets also served as the

Table 8. Population of the Aude, 1866–1911

Arrondissement	1866	1872	1876	1881	1886	1911
Carcassonne	93,916	93,574	99,119	105,911	106,525	99,174
Castelnaudary	48,953	48,136	44,424	46,491	46,349	41,069
Limoux	67,191	65,555	65,127	63,380	64,544	58,206
Narbonne	78,566	78,662	89,395	112,160	114,662	102,088
Total	288,626	285,927	300,065	327,942	332,080	300,537

Sources: *La grande encyclopédie*, vol. 4 (Paris: H. Lamirault, 1887), 600; AD Aude 11M7–10, 15–17, "Dénombrements de la population, Tableaux récapitulatifs"; France, Ministère du travail, Statistique générale, *Résultats statistiques du recensement général de la population* (Paris: Imprimerie nationale, 1913), 49.

point of exchange for products not found in village commerce, such as textiles, clothing, and manufactured items, as artisanal production geared exclusively to viticulture replaced the more diversified industrial and protoindustrial activity of the previne-yard days. Centers like Narbonne, Carcassonne, and Béziers thus drew villagers from the surrounding area and provided a setting in which rural dwellers' consciousness broadened through regular contact with townspeople and the larger commercial world.

The agricultural revolution not only favored the growth of markets and urban influence; it also led to tremendous population growth, migration, and subtle changes in the occupational structure of vinegrowing villages. A shift of population in the Aude from west to east (Table 8) coincided with the expansion of vineyards: with the decline of rural industry in the arrondissements of Castelnaudary and Limoux, and as farmers and agricultural workers sought profits and higher wages in the vineyards, population in the west of the department stagnated while the wine-producing Carcassonnais and Narbonnais grew (the latter at a rate three times that of the department as a whole between 1872 and 1881). Between 1861 and 1881 the population of Coursan grew 60.5 percent, from 2,154 to 3,458 (Table 9), largely as a result of immigration. Relatively few foreigners could be counted among migrants to the Aude in the 1870s, however. In 1876, for example, only 2.5 percent of the popula-

Table 9. Population of Coursan, 1836–1911

	1836	1846	1851	1861	1866	1872	1876	1881	1886	1891	1896	1901	1906	1911
Village center (*population agglomérée*)	—	2,040	2,002	1,941	2,250	2,285	2,507	—	3,589	3,695	3,641	3,556	3,553	3,527
Outlying area (*population éparse*)	—	10	170	213	227	253	202	—	197	152	126	273	249	266
Total	1,850	2,050	2,172	2,154	2,477	2,538	2,709	3,458	3,786	3,847	3,767	3,829	3,802	3,793
Foreign population (Spanish and Italian)	—	—	2 (0.1%)	—	—	—	26 (1.0%)	—	143 (3.8%)	267 (6.9%)	150 (4.0%)	277 (7.2%)	210 (5.5%)	251 (6.6%)
No. households	474	574	579	632	731	730	783	—	902	—	—	—	—	1,106
Mean household size	3.9	3.6	3.8	3.4	3.4	3.5	3.5	—	4.2	—	—	—	—	3.4

Sources: AD Aude 11M58, 67, 78, 93, 101, 108, 117, 157, "Dénombrements de la population. Etats nominatifs des habitants de Coursan, 1836, 1846, 1851, 1861, 1866, 1872, 1876, 1911"; 11M28, 35, 37, 43, 48, 49, "Tableaux récapitulatifs des dénombrements de 1886, 1891, 1896, 1901, 1906."

tion of Narbonne was non-French, only 1 percent of the population of Coursan, and only 1.4 percent of the population of nearby Cuxac d'Aude (this situation changed in the 1880s, as we shall see).[11] The majority of newcomers came from surrounding departments.

Wine producers had always relied on temporary migrants for planting and harvesting—mountain dwellers from the Tarn and the Ariège who made a *tour de France*, traveling to the vineyards in spring to cultivate, then to the Camargue and Provence for summer fruit harvests and back to the vineyards in the fall to pick grapes.[12] Yet as vineyard owners pruned and cultivated their vines more intensively in the 1860s and 1870s, they came to rely on a more permanent labor force. Workers who formerly came to the vineyard plains of the Aude on a temporary basis as *mésadiers* now stayed on for longer periods of time, and many settled there permanently.[13] Other migrants to the Aude were *cultivateurs* and workers from the Gard and the Hérault escaping the phylloxera that attacked their vines in the 1860s and 1870s.

In fact, the rural population of the Mediterranean region was highly mobile in this period. As Table 10 shows, growing numbers of vinedressers and *cultivateurs* who married in Coursan came from outside the arrondissement of Narbonne or from other villages in the immediate region. By 1871–1880 about one-third of those marrying in the village had been born outside Coursan. In 1876, 40 percent of the population of Narbonne was not originally Audois, whereas in Carcassonne arrondissement, where vines did not take over the local economy, only 20 percent of the population had been born outside of the department.[14]

Vines drew people. Moreover, the social composition of temporary migrants changed as unemployed urban workers made their way into the vineyards to pick grapes and eventually settled in vineyard villages in the Aude.[15] These newcomers also enhanced the contacts between rural dwellers and urban culture, as did the spread of education in the age of vineyard expansion.

Education, Religion, and Standard of Living

The expansion of vineyards in the eastern Aude brought with it an eagerness for education. In the Narbonnais, young boys

Table 10. Geographic Origins of Vinedressers and *Cultivateurs* Marrying in Coursan, 1850–1910

Place of Origin	1850–1860		1861–1870		1871–1880		1881–1890		1891–1900		1901–1910	
	No.	Percent	No.	Percent	No.	Percent	No.	Percent	No.	Percent	No.	Percent
Coursan or neighboring village in Narbonne arrondissement	71	72.5	66	75.0	78	62.9	42	35.9	73	39.2	88	49.5
Other village in Aude or in Midi	26	26.5	22	25.0	44	33.1	58	49.6	85	45.7	78	43.8
Outside of region/outside of France	1	1.0	0	0.0	5	4.0	17	14.5	28	15.1	12	6.7
Total	98	100.0	88	100.0	124	100.0	117	100.0	186	100.0	178	100.0

Source: Bureau de greffier du Tribunal de grande instance, Narbonne, Aude, Etat civil du village de Coursan, "Actes de mariages, 1850–1910."

Note: These figures represent only those individuals whose place of birth and occupation were given in the marriage records. The 1911 manuscript census (the only census to list place of birth) was used to check the accuracy of the marriage records in reflecting geographic origins. Of the vinedressers listed in the census, 45 percent were born in Coursan or in a neighboring village, and 45 percent came from another village in the department or region. Only 1 percent came from outside the region or outside France, and of these, all but a few Italian farmhands came from Spain.

attended school in greater numbers and more regularly than in nonvineyard areas. School inspectors in the west of the department shook their heads in dismay at parents who kept their children out of school to watch the sheep or work in the fields. One village schoolteacher in the isolated mountain town of Axat went so far as to practice his trade of shoemaking during class hours while his thirteen-year-old brother-in-law "taught" the poorly attended class.[16] But in the prosperous eastern vineyard plain school inspectors applauded the high level of school attendance and quality of education from the 1850s on, linking the desire for education to the booming economy.[17] In fact, by the late 1870s and early 1880s the literacy of young conscripts from the Aude proved higher than the national average (over 88 percent literate, and over 96 percent literate in the Narbonnais, compared to the national average of 84 percent). By 1885–1886, 96 percent of the boys in the Aude between the ages of six and thirteen attended school (in the Narbonnais that figure was 98 percent; the national average was 82 percent).[18] This sterling record did not apply to girls in the early years of vineyard expansion under the Third Republic; inspectors complained in the 1870s that parents attached no importance to the education of their daughters, and if their observations for Coursan are to be believed, in 1878–1879 no village girls attended school. This situation changed after primary school attendance was made compulsory in the early 1880s, when girls' school attendance in vinegrowing villages shot up.[19]

If some local officials attributed the desire for education to the prosperity of viticulture, others blamed the golden age of the vine for religious indifference. Under the Second Empire, religious officials continuously deplored low church attendance (five times lower for men than for women) and the spread of civil marriage. "A large proportion of the population displays a spiritual lethargy close to death," wrote one priest. This situation, he averred, resulted from "unrestrained luxury, a passion for dancing, and an exceptional attachment to land." Such vices afflicted not only the "lower social orders," but "a notable portion of men belonging to the *classe dirigeante*" as well. There was some truth to these observations. Attendance at Easter service, generally taken as a reliable indicator of religious practice, declined by 50

percent in vinegrowing cantons between the early 1870s and the
early 1880s.[20] The urban café culture of wine-producing towns
nourished religious officials' views of moral degeneracy. "In the
Narbonnais, prosperity contributes to the proliferation of *cafés
concerts* and dance halls that we have vehemently denounced;
the Alcazar, for example, a public place, is the scene of every
conceivable pleasure, a veritable brothel, where men drown in
their own wealth."[21]

It is not clear, however, that vineyards fostered religious indifference. Gérard Cholvy's work has shown that in the Hérault
patterns of economic and social change similar to those in the
Narbonnais did not necessarily cause villagers to withdraw from
religion. Parishes around the vineyard plains of Montpellier, for
example, remained strongly Protestant. Raymond Huard's recent study of the republican movement in the Gard has likewise
found that Catholicism persisted in the plains of the eastern
Gard, where vineyards prospered during the Second Empire.[22]
Nor were the radical politics of the vinegrowing Aude decisive in
the region's de-Christianization. In other vineyard areas of the
south that experienced the development of radical politics and
parties religious practice remained strong. In fact, in the Aude
weak religious observance predated the vineyard expansion.
During the revolution of 1789 there, parish priests and villagers
alike accepted the civil constitution of the clergy, and in 1794 the
municipality of Narbonne authorized the dedication of the Ca-
thedral of St-Just to the celebration of Reason. Unlike some
rural areas such as the Vivarais and Guévaudan, the Aude's
contributions to the church were among the lowest in France
under the Restoration.[23]

During the golden age of the vine, moreover, villagers in the
Aude indulged in their own forms of popular religion, occasionally mixed with superstition. Processions to honor Saint Vincent,
patron saint of the vines, took place in times of economic depression, and sailors and fishermen in the coastal town of Gruissan
regularly prayed to the Virgin for protection from the dangers
of the sea. In Gruissan, young women devotees of Saint Salvaire
threw stones onto a rock intoning, "Saint Salvaire, donnez-moi
un amoureux, ou je vous fiche un coup sur le nez!" ("Saint

Salvaire, give me a lover or I'll give you a punch in the nose!"). When the inhabitants of Mailhac wanted rain in 1874, they asked the local priest to lead a procession to St-Jean-de-Caps, the ruins of an old sanctuary; and during droughts, villagers in Puzols carried a statue of the Virgin two miles to a natural spring.[24] Finally, during the disastrous phylloxera crisis that struck the Aude in the 1880s, Narbonnais villagers claimed to have had visions of the Virgin in their vines. These forms of popular religion suggest that neither rural protourbanization nor vineyard expansion had eliminated religious belief from the lives of local inhabitants, low church attendance notwithstanding.[25]

Perhaps what bothered local officials most were the new forms of sociability and urban temptations that made their way into the countryside. Republican officials echoed local priests in their association of immorality and prosperity as they, too, deplored the expansion of music halls and the apparent growth of prostitution in wine towns. One local observer, writing just after the turn of the twentieth century, looked back with a critical eye at the golden age of the vine. It was, he wrote, "l'âge de la folie d'or"—a period of decadence and debauchery:

> In Coursan there were two music halls with private boxes and closed curtains. *Cultivateurs* in their work clothes, boots covered with mud, drank and talked loudly in *patois* without paying any attention to what was going on on the stage. After the show, they would unleash their entire repertoire of *patois* abuses on the women performers and spit on the dresses of those who protested. There was gambling everywhere and even a baccarat table in the attic.[26]

Others expressed different concerns about the consequences of prosperity and noted that although workers enjoyed a relatively high standard of living, their relations with their employers showed signs of strain in the tightening labor market. "More sought after, more necessary than ever before, vinedressers have become more demanding. The taste for material pleasures, the result of rising wages and spreading wealth, dominates them more and more."[27] Vinedressers and *cultivateurs* who bought pianos for their wives and daughters and frequented *cafés con-*

certs and music halls had adopted urban forms of entertainment. These protourban villagers also developed a political culture that paralleled national political movements of the age.

In these densely populated villages of the winegrowing Aude, a community of interests in support of vineyard capitalism fostered the growth of republicanism and eventually of radicalism as the dominant political forces. This development was especially significant in that the revolution of 1789 had revealed much of lower Languedoc to be strongly royalist. Purged of Jacobinism by the White Terror, the local Audois welcomed the Restoration and ultimately seesawed from Legitimism to Orleanism and back again under the influence of local notables and large landowners. Well before the agricultural revolution was complete, however, peasants and farmers in the Aude shifted away from royalism. Under the July Monarchy several Saint-Simonian groups appeared briefly around Narbonne, and by the late 1840s Orleanist officials worried less about legitimist opponents in the department than about "socialists" and democratic republicans, also known as *démoc socs*.[28]

Republican Politics in the Rural Community

Republicanism in the rural Aude during the golden age of the vine developed in three stages: first, with the beginnings of a republican opposition in rural communities under the July Monarchy and in 1848; second, with underground political associations during the repressive phase of the Second Republic; and third, with the Narbonne Commune, which clearly divided republicans in the Aude, much as the Paris Commune divided republicans nationally.

Underground republican opposition to the July Monarchy had acquired enough of a following that in the Aude, as elsewhere in France, the February revolution of 1848 immediately catapulted republicans into key administrative offices, and democratic socialist clubs burst into activity.[29] These "rouges" (also called *démoc socs* or "montagnards") supported universal male suffrage under a democratic republic, the right to work, and social and economic reforms for the laboring poor. Their leaders included the socialist Armand Barbès, known as an alleged conspirator in the Fieschi plot and as a member of the Société des droits de l'homme, and elected deputy in April 1848; Emile Digeon, also a *démoc soc* active in the leftist Club de l'union in Narbonne; and Théodore Raynal, who took over as subprefect of the Aude in February 1848 and became republican deputy for the Aude the following April.[30] In the *démoc soc* clubs that appeared in market towns and rural *bourgs* in 1848, peasants and artisans discussed republican and socialist ideas and mobilized support for republican candidates.[31] They ended their meetings with torchlight processions, sometimes parading a small statue of the Marianne—revolutionary symbol of the republic—singing the "Marseillaise," or shouting, "A bas les blancs!" "A bas les chouans!" "Vive Barbès!" "Vive Ledru-Rollin!" Women joined these processions from time to time dressed as goddesses of liberty. Their presence symbolized the ambiguity of female representation within early republican political culture: they symbolized the republic but were excluded from it. Women did not join these political clubs, nor did Audois *démoc soc* clubs address the issues of work, civil liberties, and political rights for women that political groups elsewhere raised in 1848.[32]

Groups analogous to the Club de l'union sprang up in villages throughout the Aude. In Coursan, Cuxac d'Aude, Ornaisons, Ouveillan, and Salles d'Aude *démoc soc* clubs drew small landowners and artisans, vinedressers, schoolteachers, café owners and wine wholesalers.[33] These groups showed that the petty bourgeoisie, workers, and artisans had begun to challenge the "official" structures of political authority and were able to act independently of powerful conservative notables.[34] In addition to clubs, a left republican political press, notably Théophile Marcou's *La Fraternité* in Carcassonne, spread republican ideas. Drawing on the symbols and images of the revolution of 1789, Audois republicans addressed each other as "citoyen commissaire" and used the term *montagnard* to describe the left-wing republican deputies in the Constituent Assembly. Republican electoral propaganda proclaimed the reign of "Liberty, Equality, and Fraternity."

Despite their agreement on certain fundamental issues, republicans in the Aude, like republicans in the Haute Garonne and elsewhere, represented a mixture of class interests. These differences are important because they typified two divergent views of the Republic.[35] On one side were Armand Barbès and Théophile Marcou, who represented the radical democratic socialist wing of republicanism; Marcou's *La Fraternité* supported universal suffrage, the right to work, the equal distribution of property, the abolition of usury, and the establishment of a progressive income tax.[36] In their propaganda for the elections of April 1848 addressed to peasants and vinegrowers, *démoc socs* pledged to reorganize taxation, establish cheap credit and free education, and abolish the hated wine tax, a sentiment immortalized in Claude Durand's popular "Chant des vignerons," sung in many areas of France. A year later they added to their platform nationalization of transportation, banks, and mines, foreshadowing the radical republicans' electoral promises of the 1880s.[37] The depression of 1846–1847, which brought falling wheat and wine prices, made peasants and farmers especially receptive to republicans' promises to abolish the wine tax and reform taxation. The fact that in the south the agricultural depression hurt not only farmers and vinegrowers but also urban artisans and workers (unlike in the north, where lower agricultural prices benefited urban workers) helped to create political alliances between these groups in the late 1840s and early 1850s; both formed the base of a *démoc soc* constituency.[38] On the other side, Théodore Raynal represented the more moderate republicanism of property owners and professionals—those who disdained political privilege but at the same time were concerned to protect their property and status. Writing in his short-lived newspaper *Le Populus* (begun in August 1849), Raynal rejected "the distribution of wealth that the Communists dream of" and pledged to oppose any improvement for the laboring classes that threatened the right to property.[39] These two strains of republicanism in the Aude followed national patterns and formed the foundations of radicalism and moderate republicanism later in the Third Republic.

After the moderate republicans triumphed in the Aude in April 1848 (except that Barbès, too, was elected), the Aude became a political battleground in the struggles between republicans and conservatives. In formerly tranquil villages, disgruntled conservatives, encouraged by the slaughter of Paris workers in June, demonstrated against republicans during the August municipal elections. In Ginestas, a mob attacked the republican national guards stationed at the ballot box; in Lézignan, conservatives tried to tear down a red flag that had been draped in the public square; and in Narbonne, where republican Théodore Raynal was elected, a crowd stormed the town hall demanding a ballot recount.[40] The continued effects of the nationwide agricultural depression of the late 1840s, combined with the shock of revolution, resulted in a political shift to the right: the "peasant insurrection" of December 10. Whether as the defender of order in the wake of revolution or as the beneficiary of the Bonapartist legend, Louis-Napoléon garnered strong support in the Aude (over 75 percent of the vote, somewhat higher than the national average) from peasants hostile to the wine tax and the 45 percent surtax on land (he opposed both).[41]

In the Narbonnais, however, leftist republicans did not hesitate to express their hostility to the new president. The Club de l'union in Narbonne openly proclaimed its opposition by transforming a carnival masquerade on Ash Wednesday, February 21, 1849, into a political demonstration. The procession included the Garbage Cart of the Reactionary Press; the Cattle Car of the Moderate Party; the Chariot of Justice, carrying a scale with balances of unequal lengths; a masked man carrying an empty chest inscribed with the words "Treasury-Savings Bank"; and finally, the pièce de résistance, another masked man riding backward on a donkey (a traditional symbolic form of humiliation in charivaris and English rough music), representing the president of the Republic.[42] The transformation of traditional popular cultural forms such as carnival into vehicles of political protest constituted an important stage in rural dwellers' assimilation of national politics. But demonstrations like these also touched off a wave of repression that included the dismissal of both the subprefect of the Aude, Théophile Vallière, suspected of collaborating with the *démoc socs* who staged the demonstration, and the National Guard of Narbonne. The resurgence of the right persisted through the May 1849 elections, which dealt a blow to the *démoc socs* and strengthened Bonapartists in the department.[43]

In some areas, employers threatened to dismiss workers if they refused to vote for conservative candidates.[44] Although repression of left-wing organizations made it more difficult for *démoc socs* to organize, they continued to receive support from woodcutters and small farmers in the Corbières hills, who had been hurt by the alienation of public forests; from similar groups in the Montagne noire north of Carcassonne; and from small farmers and agricultural workers in the Narbonnais. Likewise, textile artisans in Chalabre backed the left, and *démoc socs* won all four major towns in the Aude, Narbonne, Carcassonne, Limoux, and Castelnaudary, where the combination of markets and industrial depression made their program appealing and facilitated the establishment of a base among urban artisans.[45] These economic conditions permitted a left constituency to survive despite the authoritarian and repressive policies of the Napoleonic Republic and early Second Empire. Thus the politics of peasants and rural artisans began to acquire a certain autonomy, apart from the influence of local notables.

Repression and Persistence of Leftist Opposition in the Countryside

The "agony of the republic"—the progressive destruction of left republican and *démoc soc* opposition groups that accompanied the decline of the Second Republic—touched the Aude just as it touched the rest of provincial France in 1849–1852.[46] Between November 1849 and the summer of 1851, thirty-five republican mayors lost their posts, and in 1851 both Raynal and Marcou fled to Barcelona.[47] Nonetheless, in the countryside, continued economic depression created a climate in which popular democratic socialism survived. When police arrested agricultural workers for singing revolutionary songs such as the "Marseillaise" and shouting "seditious slogans," workers adopted new symbols of opposition. They wore red sashes while working, and when the police seized their sashes, they made new ones. Dress functioned to articulate political solidarity in the fields or at the worksite. In the fields just outside Narbonne, a group of fifty workers bearing a red flag marched to tend the vines of a comrade imprisoned for his left-wing political activities; others used funerals as occasions for political demonstrations. Even after the coup d'état of December 2, 1851, *démoc soc* activities continued underground.[48]

The same kinds of secret societies that John Merriman and Ted Margadant have described in other areas of rural France proliferated in the Audois countryside in the early 1850s, and survived by means of common symbols, rituals, and rhetoric.[49] Republican secret societies comprised rural artisans (shoemakers and tailors), agricultural workers, and small landowners; men who read Marcou's *La Fraternité*, Proudhon's *Le Peuple*, and tracts by Armand Barbès. Their political discourse reflected a general concern for the well-being of the worker, including increased wages and lower taxes. They also served as mutual aid societies and provided benefits such as sickness insurance. Members underwent an initiation ceremony in which they knelt blindfolded and, touching the blade of a knife, pledged to defend "la république démocratique et sociale" and to keep the secrets of the society. Special greetings involved a question and response: "République?" "Universelle." "Bientôt?" "Arrivera."[50]

These rituals and the language of ritual, reproduced in secret societies all over France, were part of a forging of national left republicanism as yet unmediated by institutional structures.[51] The societies showed that rural dwellers had begun to develop modern forms of political organization as they used meetings, newspapers, and political pamphlets to disseminate their ideas. They also signaled the decline of older forms of personal influence that had determined the politics of the countryside for generations.

The growth of republican opposition politics was also aided as the Aude was opened more fully to the national market by the Second Empire's railway-building program of the 1850s. *Vignerons* and farmers could now have closer contact with the larger world of national politics. The amnesty of 1859 allowed exiled republican leaders Marcou and Raynal to reenter the political arena, and the restoration of press freedoms under the liberal Empire enabled republicans to reconstitute the left in the Aude—as the legislative elections of 1869 proved.[52] Just weeks after the plebiscite of 1869 on the emperor's reform program, in which vinedressers and rural artisans in the winegrowing Narbonnais returned a majority of "no" votes (the only district in the Aude where this was so), republicans won the municipality of Narbonne.[53] The collapse of the Empire, the Prussian invasion, and the Paris Commune, however, accentuated already existing divisions between left republicans (heirs of the *démoc socs* of 1848) and moderates, further changing the political map of the Aude.

The Narbonne Commune and
Sharpening Divisions in Republican Ranks

Villagers in the Aude greeted the Third Republic with celebrations and dancing in the streets; in some parts of the Narbonnais they brought out red flags and displayed statues of the Marianne in public squares.[54] But the proclamation of the Commune in Paris had still more dramatic repercussions. The Club de l'union in Narbonne changed its name to the Club de la révolution and declared Narbonne to be an independent commune under the leadership of Emile Digeon.[55] On March 24, 1871, Digeon took the town hall and replaced the tricolor with the red flag, "symbol of the people's rights." Just a year earlier masons and glass workers had struck in Narbonne, and in the south the Ligue du Midi had supported a regional defense against the Prussians. Digeon was convinced that a local insurrection could succeed given that urban workers had already begun to defend their rights against employers.[56] He also appealed to the rural workers, artisans, and vinegrowers who formed the base of the left republican movement in the countryside. Speaking at the Club de la révolution, Digeon linked the Paris Commune to the defense of the nation and the Republic, and to the struggle of the poor against the rich.[57]

> If we must . . . take up arms, let it be for the work of democratic propaganda, for the way of the oppressed against the oppressors, the exploited against the exploiters. . . . Let us unite around [the red flag] to prevent the resurrection of the scaffold, to prevent the cemeteries of Africa, already filled with republicans by Cavaignac and Bonaparte, from receiving newcomers from the reaction of 1871. . . .
>
> Workers, laborers of Narbonne, go to the countryside, tell the peasants that their interests are the same as yours, that the Revolu-

tion . . . means the emancipation of those whom misery oppresses under the yoke of the rich. . . . Tell them that the Revolution means peace by the abolition of permanent armies, by the abolition of taxes for the small proprietor, and for the day laborer.[58]

The Narbonne commune did not become a mass movement, however. The sudden prosperity of the vineyards hardly created a favorable climate for insurrection. Audois vinegrowers gathered full harvests and enormous profits even as the phylloxera ravaged the vineyards of the Gard and the Hérault. Vinedressers and other rural workers likewise enjoyed the highest wages they had ever seen. The relatively small group of three hundred men and women who occupied the town hall, supported by two hundred fifty soldiers, did not hold out for long. After less than a week, on March 30, President Thiers sent a regiment of Algerian sharpshooters to Narbonne to force the insurrectionists out of the town hall, and police arrested thirty-two activists, including Digeon.[59]

Both nationally and locally the repression of the communes allowed some French citizens to accept the Republic as the guardian of order; for others the Communards became martyrs who died defending workers' and artisans' rights and the rights of local communities against arbitrary state authority. These differences corresponded to the divisions between radical republicans and moderates. Radicals continued to organize in the Aude, building on the political organizing techniques of their *démoc soc* predecessors: they held nighttime meetings in barns or fields in an attempt to attract peasants and rural workers, and occasionally they used village cafés as meeting halls.[60] Radicals helped to found urban artisans' political associations such as the Cercle de l'union des travailleurs in Limoux, and the Fédération radicale tried to organize urban and rural artisans elsewhere in the department. Their organizing efforts bore some fruit as landowners, vinedressers, and urban workers sent radical republicans to the Chamber of Deputies in 1871 and 1873.[61] Moderate republican officials linked the growth of radicalism (as left republicanism came to be known) to the passionate Latin temperament of local voters and to the prosperity of vineyard workers and bourgeois alike, deploring the fact that men of property and standing eagerly took part "in this worker and agricultural radicalism."[62] In truth, however, the success of radicalism in the Aude owed more to the crises of viticultural capitalism than to its fortunes.

The nearly total domination of vineyards made the local economy especially vulnerable. By the mid 1870s the phylloxera, a tiny aphid that kills vines by living off their roots, had already ravaged vineyards elsewhere in the south, but it had not yet touched the Aude. Vinegrowers, desperate for government assistance to prevent phylloxera from spreading, warmed to the interventionist position of southern radicalism. Although the radicals' national program, following the ideas of Louis Blanc and Georges Clemenceau, did not address the concerns of vineyard owners specifically, many of its features, recalling the social program of 1848, would have directly or indirectly benefited *vignerons*: the defense of individual rights, and especially the rights of small producers; the nationalization of railroads and the Canal du Midi; the lowering of taxes and transport rates for both industrial and agricultural goods; the creation of credit facilities; and the regulation of working hours and working conditions.[63] In July 1878, just after phylloxera first appeared in the Audois villages of Ouveillan and Argelliers, the radical majority in the Chamber of Deputies passed legislation that gave significant financial support for treatment of vines attacked by the insect.[64]

By the late 1870s, then, the growth of the viticultural bourgeoisie and the prosperity of vinedressers and urban artisans had helped to transform the politics of the Aude in three ways. First, densely populated, agglomerated rural villages in the Aude provided a welcome setting for *démoc socs* and republicans to organize and establish a base among rural workers, artisans, and small landowners, who shared an interest in the fate of the vines. The viticultural petty bourgeoisie's economic security during this golden age enabled it to escape the influence of the local notables who had shaped rural politics for generations. Second, the expansion of markets, the protourbanization of the countryside, the spread of education, and the unparalleled prosperity of the growing vineyard economy brought vinedressers and workers into contact with urban political leaders and new organizing techniques and facilitated political alliances between rural dwellers and town folk. Third, new political ideologies and movements began to take root in protourban villages, with republicanism prospering where vineyards grew. Ultimately the defense of the vine drew *cultivateurs* and the viticultural petty bourgeoisie to radicalism. Once the vineyard economy crumbled under the impact of the phylloxera crisis, however, the underlying class divisions of peasant society came into sharper focus. This process in turn paved the way for the development of socialism in the Aude.

3
ECONOMIC CRISIS AND CLASS FORMATION

Commenting on life in the vineyards of the Aude at the beginning of the 1880s, the head of the Société nationale des agriculteurs de France, J. A. Barral, painted a depressing picture of decline and decay:

> In villages where everyone was comfortable, where the population was dense, today, trouble is everywhere; inhabitants emigrate; there is no longer any work; people are leaving to seek their fortune in the new world or in Algeria, so as not to die of hunger in France. And now, when I consider the families of vineyard owners, . . . how many rich men—millionaires—have I seen who no longer have a centime?[1]

This portrait, which clashed so dramatically with the prosperity of the golden age of the vine, described the beginning of a series of economic crises from which southern viticulture has barely recovered over a hundred years later. The first, the phylloxera crisis, resulted in the destruction of over half of the Aude's vines between 1879 and 1886. Just as the vineyards began to recover in the 1890s, an exceptionally abundant harvest in 1893 caused wine prices to plummet, not to rise again until three years later. Finally, the great wine glut of 1900–1901 again drove vineyard owners and vinedressers alike to despair; its repercussions continued right up to World War I. The long-range political and social effects of these crises are explored in some detail in the chapters that follow. Of the three, however, the phylloxera crisis brought about the most far-reaching changes. It transformed the economy and work rhythms of vinegrowing, thus accelerating the concentration of large vineyard capital and the development of the large "industrial" vineyard (though not expro-

priating the viticultural petty bourgeoisie). It also led to significant changes in the wine market. Most important, it irrevocably
changed the work and class relations of the vineyards and of
vineyard communities. These changes led to the forging of a
class identity among vineyard workers and help to explain both
the emergence of socialist politics and the explosion of labor
protest in the Aude between 1888 and 1914.

The Phylloxera and the
Changing Economy of Vinedressing

During the 1860s and 1870s, while Audois vinedressers and proprietors alike reaped the profits of expanding vineyards, winegrowers in the rest of France suffered the worst agricultural
disaster in the history of French viticulture. Vineyards that formerly flourished under the Mediterranean sun now turned
brown and bare as vine leaves yellowed and withered in the space
of a few months. Winegrowers wrung their hands as harvests
dwindled to nothing and debts mounted. The phylloxera, intro-
duced into France on American vine cuttings, spread with alarm-
ing rapidity through the southeast and more slowly through the
southwest. By 1871 it had destroyed nearly all of the vines in
the Vaucluse and the Gard, and by 1875 much of those in the
Hérault as well. Small growers and large, artisans and local
merchants, railway men and bankers—all suffered. The ruinous
insect recognized no class boundaries. Winegrowers in the Aude,
temporarily spared, profited both from the rising wine prices
that resulted from short supplies (as high as 50 francs per hectoliter in some areas) and from a virtual monopoly of the southern
wine market. From 1878 to 1884 the Aude's income from wine
was three times what it had been in the period of prosperity
before the phylloxera.[2] In the summer of 1878, however, traces
of damage appeared in the Audois villages of Ouveillan, Argelliers, Ginestas, and Mirepeisset. By 1882 one thousand hectares
had been attacked; four years later over one hundred thousand
hectares, 54 percent of the Audois vineyard, had been totally
destroyed.[3] Wine production in the Aude dropped drastically,
from almost five million hectoliters in 1882 to just short of two
million in 1887.[4] Although the nationwide economic depression

closed down workshops in the west of the department, the bulk of the Aude's industrial depression in these years resulted from the phylloxera, which affected the building trades and cooperage.[5] Entire families, financially ruined by the disaster, departed for Algeria or for industrial centers. The somber streets of vine-growing villages, houses dotted with "For Sale" signs, could not have contrasted more sharply with the gaiety and abandon of just a few years earlier.

In some ways winegrowers in the Aude fared better than their counterparts in other Mediterranean departments. They could use profits accumulated in the 1870s to replant and treat their vines, and they were able to take advantage of methods of prevention and treatment proven effective elsewhere by the early 1880s.[6] Moreover, the government had by now begun to grant vineyard owners subsidies for treatment and to free them from land taxes.[7] But Audois *vignerons* could not entirely escape the ruinous cost of treating damaged vines. The least expensive remedy, spraying with carbon sulfide, cost 180 to 200 francs per hectare. Submersion of vines in water from irrigation canals that drew on the Aude River was more reliable but also more expensive, costing up to 1,800 francs per hectare. And replanting a vineyard entirely in sandy soil, where the phylloxera could not survive, required between 2,500 and 3,500 francs per hectare.[8] Despite government subsidies to local associations formed to fight the phylloxera, the amounts landowners received amounted to only a fraction of the total cost required.[9] Still, southern wine producers became increasingly dependent on government assistance, a fact that made Audois winegrowers sympathetic to state economic intervention and powerfully influenced their politics.

The high costs of replanting and treatment of phylloxera-stricken vines, however, were only part of the problem. Vineyard owners who replanted had to wait four years for new vines to become fully productive. Moreover, annual production costs were rising, partly because of a change in the entrepreneurial mentality of southern winegrowers.

Vignerons' desperate efforts to rebuild the vineyards of the golden age led to more intensive cultivation and an attempt to raise yields by adding new procedures to the traditional tech-

niques of vinedressing. Unlike industries such as glassmaking
and textiles, in which the introduction of more sophisticated
technologies toward the end of the nineteenth century standardized and simplified production methods, vinedressing became
increasingly complex.[10] Vinedressers now fertilized their vines
more aggressively and began to graft French grape stalks to
phylloxera-resistant American vine roots, with instructional assistance from local agricultural associations.[11] Vineyard owners
uniformly planted high-yield varieties and cut their alcoholically
weak wines (7–9°) with more alcoholic Algerian wines (13–14°).
They also practiced *chaptalisation* more aggressively, adding
sugar and hot water to the residue left in the vats after the wine
had been drawn off to produce a second fermentation.[12] Normally it was illegal to market these second wines, or *piquettes*, but
in the 1880s and 1890s the government overlooked those who
did so, even sanctioning the practice by lowering the sugar tax
and by legalising the use of sugar to make third and sometimes
fourth or fifth wines. The state thus supported the new entrepreneurial mentality of the post-phylloxera winegrower, which
favored quantity over quality.[13]

Despite these innovations, however, no mechanical revolution
played a part in the reconstitution of the southern vineyards.
Workers continued to perform virtually all tasks by hand, simply incorporating new chemical treatments and skills such as
grafting into their repertoire. Rising costs now made vineyards
capital-intensive as well as labor-intensive operations. Whereas
contemporaries estimated that in the 1860s and 1870s annual
costs of production would amount to 340 francs per hectare of
mature vines for pruning, cultivation, sulphuring, harvesting,
and winemaking, by 1892 that figure had risen to around 1,000
francs per hectare, taking into account additional chemical treatment, fertilizer, grafting, and more aggressive pruning.[14] Needless to say, large vineyard owners, especially estate owners, could
more easily handle these changes than small ones. *Les grands*
could purchase chemicals and equipment in bulk, and hence
more cheaply, and could also benefit from preferential rail transport rates. Most had sufficient reserve capital to meet higher
production costs as well.

These changes irrevocably transformed the nature of southern vinegrowing in three ways. First, they accentuated the cleavages between large growers and small—between *grande* and *petite bourgeoisie*. Second, they paved the way for the "industrialization" of southern viticulture. As one contemporary observer commented, "This [is] no longer the gardening of laborious peasants; it [is] industrial agriculture, demanding continual care, scrupulous vigilance, broad knowledge, and considerable capital."[15] Third, they dramatically changed the southern wine market.

Transformation of the Wine Market in an Era of Crises

During the phylloxera crisis, rising demand for domestic table wine had led to massive imports of Spanish and Italian wine—an astonishing twelvefold increase in the 1880s over the previous decade.[16] These imports did not stop once French wine production returned to normal and now that foreign wine directly competed with southern wine. To make matters worse, countries that had been clients of southern French winegrowers began to produce wines of their own; the French now had to compete with them on the European market.[17] Small growers, who lacked the advantages of economies of scale, low transportation rates for bulk shipments, and reserve capital, suffered most from these changes. Wine dealers used the competition to pressure small growers into accepting inferior prices for their wine. Small producers often sold their meager harvests right from the vine, for fear that any delay would oblige them to accept a price lower than the one originally offered.[18]

The combination of more aggressive entrepreneurship in winegrowing and a more competitive market made southern viticulture ever more susceptible to economic crises, with disastrous effects for vinedressers and small vineyard owners. By 1893 replanted Audois vineyards were in full production, yielding a monumental harvest of over four million hectoliters, and wine prices plummeted from 23 to 12 francs per hectoliter, dropping again in 1896.[19] Falling prices translated into layoffs on the large estate vineyards, and numerous vinedressers found themselves unemployed overnight. In a spirit of contestation by now familiar to urban villages and rural *bourgs*, vinedressers and landowners assembled in demonstrations of up to thirty thousand in November and December 1893 to pressure the government for assistance. Deputies, mayors, and representatives of local agricultural organizations all pleaded with the state to intervene, proposing such measures as nationalization of the Canal du Midi, lowering of railroad rates, restoration of the distiller's privilege (*privilège des bouilleurs de cru*, which allowed individuals to distill wine for private consumption), and an increase in tariffs on foreign wines. This radical departure from the free-trade liberalism characteristic of winegrowers a generation earlier even included the demand that local municipalities resign and that winegrowers refuse to pay the tax on alcoholic beverages.[20]

In fact, wine prices did not improve for another three years. When harvests and prices finally did return to normal in 1897, winegrowers breathed a sigh of relief—but not for long. An exceptionally abundant harvest throughout lower Languedoc in 1900 resulted in a major, long-term, regionwide depression that lasted until World War I. Wine prices in the Aude fell as low as 5 francs per hectoliter the next year, and in 1902 as low as 1.25 francs. Although a small harvest in 1903 caused prices to rise somewhat, not until 1909–1910 did they return to respectable levels of 22, 24, and even 36 francs per hectoliter.[21]

The political economy of the more or less constantly depressed wine market between 1900 and 1914 generated a great debate among contemporaries, who looked for monocausal explanations for the depression. Some, such as the economists Charles Gide and Pierre Genieys, charged that the wine glut of 1900–1901 was due to overproduction.[22] Others blamed declining wine consumption. Still others pointed the finger at inadequate tariffs that failed to keep foreign wines off the French market. All, however, agreed that "fraud" bore a large measure of responsibility—that is, the production of artificial wines with sugar, water, or raisins.[23] Some of these explanations were off the mark; others were more accurate. A recent study of the wine market in this period has shown that although fraud occupied a central place in the collective mentality of vinedressers and small peasant proprietors in the 1907 revolt (see Chapter 7), "artificial

wines" represented no more than 5 percent of regional production. Moreover, wine consumption actually rose faster than
southern production in the last seven or eight years of the nineteenth century.[24] Still, contemporaries were correct to point out
that the practice of cutting southern wine with more alcoholic
wine, along with growing imports, increased the quantity of
wine on the market and drove down prices. In fact, it was a
combination of factors—fraud, cutting wine, and imports—
rather than one single factor that produced the most enormous
glut of southern wine that France had ever seen.

We will examine the full effects of this turn-of-century crisis
on the labor and politics of Audois peasants and workers in
Chapter 6. Suffice it here to say that the disaster once again
plunged southern winegrowers into massive debt and outright
poverty. The writer Ardouin Dumazet, traveling through lower
Languedoc, sadly observed regarding the passionate devotion of
southerners to their vines: "If this region were to be separated
from the rest of France by some sort of disaster, the population
would die of hunger in the midst of its vines."[25] This statement
was no exaggeration. Beggars roamed the countryside, often
masked so as not to be identified. Between 1900 and 1906 loans
made by the Caisse régionale de crédit agricole du Midi in Narbonne rose from 540,000 francs to just over 9 million francs; and
by the height of the crisis the Crédit foncier had taken over two-
thirds of the vineyards in the south.[26] Not surprisingly, the
nearly continuous economic depression lasting from the 1880s
to World War I produced subtle changes in the configurations of
property ownership in Audois vineyards.

The Shifting Property Structure of the Post-Phylloxera Vineyard and the Emergence of the "Industrial Vineyard"

Surprisingly, neither the short-term devastation of vines by the
phylloxera nor the more or less permanently depressed market
that followed radically transformed the property structure and
landholding patterns of villages in the Aude. Rather, the pattern
evident before the phylloxera crisis persisted: the coexistence of
a large number of very small landowners at one end of the scale

with a small number of very large landowners at the other. Two parallel changes did occur, however, between the late 1870s and the years before World War I, and these were visible in Coursan. On the one hand, the proportion of medium and large proprietors declined in the period 1876 to 1911, and on the other, both the number and proportion of small and very small proprietors increased, and the parceling of vines continued (see Table 5).

This pattern in Coursan reflects a departmentwide trend. By the 1890s, just under half the property owners in the Aude owned less than one hectare (an increase over 1882), whereas the number of large property owners had declined, as had that of medium owners (see Table 4). At the same time, owners of over ten hectares in the department now controlled 59 percent of the land; those owning under one hectare, 8.4 percent.[27] It is true that some large vineyard owners in the Aude sold undesirable parcels to offset the enormous costs of reconstitution, and again sold land during the great turn-of-century wine glut.[28] By and large, however, owners of estate vineyards in Coursan (Pontserme, La Française, and La Ricardelle) profited from the 60–70 percent decline in the price of land by acquiring new land. The estate of Lastours grew spectacularly from 36 hectares in 1879 to 114 hectares in 1884, and the Laforgue family built its holdings from 28 to 107 hectares during the phylloxera years.[29] Still more important, large estates continued to dominate the local economy not only in terms of size but also in terms of the vast quantities of wine they produced. The village of Vinassan near Coursan provides a striking example, for here the four largest vineyards accounted for almost 70 percent of the total wine produced in the village.[30]

A few enterprising large vineyard capitalists managed to build estates from scratch in this period, among whom many were absentee proprietors. A case in point is Léopold Roudier, a wealthy banker from Béziers, who purchased 300 hectares of completely ruined vines for 700,000 francs in June 1892 to build the estate of Jouarres in the Minervois. By 1897, after an enormous capital outlay that included building an ultramodern winery and acquisition of an additional 218 hectares, Roudier's vineyard employed some 120 to 140 workers.[31] As an absentee owner, Roudier typified a new type of entrepreneur who lived far from his estate and relied on a manager (*régisseur*) for daily vineyard administration. These men included Cyprien Crozals, a wine merchant from Béziers and owner of La Française in Coursan, and the owner of Lastours, Louis Cazals, an engineer from Bordeaux. By the turn of the century 340 absentee proprietors held land in Coursan, as opposed to 133 at midcentury.

Another new type of entrepreneur became increasingly common in the late nineteenth century as well: the multiproprietor, who owned two and sometimes three estate vineyards, not all necessarily in the Aude. Between 1897 and 1900, sixty-five such men in the arrondissements of Narbonne and Carcassonne owned a total of 139 estates.[32] Adolphe Turrel, opportunist deputy from Narbonne, accumulated five large vineyards in the vicinity of Narbonne; the comte de Beauxhostes, president of the Comice agricole de Narbonne, owned five even more widely dispersed estates that together produced a mammoth sixty-six thousand hectoliters of wine annually. In the Narbonnais, the enormous output of these multiproperties accounted for one-third of production in the area. As Rémy Pech has observed, the combination of size, production capacity, and management style (by *régisseur*) were all suggestive of "viticultural capitalism and a viticultural industry."[33]

This, then, was how large *vignerons* experienced the subtle changes in landownership of the post-phylloxera vineyard. But what of the small petty bourgeois vintners who continued to dominate production in the hilly Corbières region south of Carcassonne and who still figured prominently in the Narbonnais? If capital emerged from the end-of-century crises reinforced, how did labor fare?

Amazingly, small vineyard owners managed to survive the era of crises that to all appearances should have wiped them out. These individuals, mainly vinedressers and artisans, held on to their precious if capricious vines. In the Aude overall, vinedresser landowners declined in number during the phylloxera crisis and after (from 26 percent in 1882 to 19 percent ten years later).[34] By 1896, vinedressers in the land records of Coursan amounted to only some 12 percent of total landowners (see Table 1), and they also owned less land than previously (0.53 versus 0.65 hectares). Nonetheless, these records identify only two-thirds of the landowners in that year, and it is possible that they underestimate the true number of vinedressers who possessed land in the village. It is also possible that even within the Aude conditions varied. In the arrondissement of Narbonne, for instance, almost 50 percent of the vinedressers owned vines, and in the Minervois as many as 65 percent of the workers may have owned land around the turn of the century. In the village of Arzens, some 90 percent of the vinedressers owned their own vines before World War I.[35] Some artisans also benefited from falling prices and land sales during the phylloxera and were able to acquire new land. Antoine Jacques Pagès, a cooper who had purchased a minuscule five ares of vines in Coursan in 1873, increased his holdings to twenty-six hectares by 1911.

Overall, though, continued landownership no longer automatically meant material comfort. Just as Harvey Smith has found for Cruzy, Hérault, the continued parceling of land resulted in lower status for small landowners in the Aude, who could now barely eke out an existence from their vines. How did these courageous men and women cope—and why did the *grande bourgeoisie vinicole* allow them to survive?

Small owners, like large, benefited from local and national financial assistance, as well as from the suspension of land taxes. Ultimately, however, they survived by eliminating labor costs, performing the work themselves, and by working from dawn to dusk. In the Minervois, friends and neighbors exchanged labor services and formed "bourrades" to help one another cultivate their vines on Sunday mornings.[36] Some of the agricultural associations (*syndicats agricoles*) that appeared in the Aude and elsewhere after 1884 also assisted small vineyard owners by enabling them to purchase equipment, fertilizer, and vines cheaply. Large owners lent equipment and the use of their wineries to small vintners in return for labor services on their estates. And, as we have already noted, they lent money. In fact, more than a few small landowners financed the reconstitution of their vines after the phylloxera by becoming indebted to *les grands*.

Large vineyard owners, it seems, were convinced that small property ownership combined with entrepreneurial paternalism would ultimately guarantee social stability. Moreover, it was in their interest to encourage the survival of small vineyard property: the little income that workers could now eke out of their tiny properties would justify keeping their wages low. The continued existence of small owners would also provide a reserve army of labor that would not burden employers with a permanent wage bill. Finally, some large owners saw vinedresser-owners as potential allies in the battle to defend their interests before the state.[37] Whether these visions of a community of *vignerons* were borne out is another matter, as we shall see later.

Repeated economic crises, even as they reinforced the dominant position of large vineyards, created a new entrepreneurial mentality, and brought about important changes in the wine market, did not destroy small peasant producers at the bottom of the social ladder. The gradual and visible impoverishment of small *vignerons* led them to form alliances not with *les grands*, but with landless workers, to whom they grew increasingly close in both economic status and shared interests.

Proletarianization of the Vinedresser

The creation and re-creation of the European working class at different stages in the development of capitalism and in different milieux across the nineteenth century occurred as the result of changing material conditions, changing ideology, and changing social life. Because class consists in the relationships of human beings to one another and to the productive forces that govern their lives, class composition itself changed. Individuals' "membership" in a class shifted as their relationship to productive forces changed and as their perceptions of relatedness and shared interests altered. This was no less true in the sunny villages of the winegrowing Aude than in the dark industrial centers of Lille or St-Chamond. Here we examine the changing material conditions of vinedressers; we will look at ideology and political culture in Chapters 5 and 6.

Vinedressers in the Aude acutely felt the impact of the economic crises of the early Third Republic on both wages and the structure of the labor market. When the phylloxera finally appeared in the department in the early 1880s, vineyard workers still enjoyed the same high incomes and comfortable conditions that had characterized the 1870s. As soon as the insect began to

Table 11. Wages, Hours, and Annual Income of Male Vineyard Workers in Coursan, 1857–1911

Year	Wage (fr.)	Workday (hrs.)	Workdays per Year	Annual Income (fr.)
1857	2	8	226	452
1862	2.25/3.50	8	280	667.50
1868	3/5	7½–8	280	900
1882	4/5	7½–8	280	1,140
1892	2.50/2.75	6–7	250	762.50
1900	2/2.25	7½–8	200	407.50
1903–1904	3.50	7	250	875
1910	3	7	280	840
1911	3.50 plus 2 liters wine	7	280	980

Sources: AD Aude 13M282, "Statistique agricole annuelle, Tableaux récapitulatifs et tableaux synoptiques, 1856–1857"; 13M300, "Statistique décennale des communes, 1882"; 15M125, 133, "Grèves agricoles"; 5M11, Monthly prefect reports; AN F[11]2698, "Enquête agricole de 1862"; France, Ministère de l'agriculture, Statistique agricole de la France, *Résultats généraux de l'enquête décennale de 1882* (Nancy: Berger-Levrault, 1887), pt. 1, 382–396; pt. 2, 183; Michel Augé-Laribé, *Le Problème agraire du socialisme. La viticulture industrielle du Midi de la France* (Paris: Giard & Brière, 1907), 76–77, 282–288, 290.

Note: Wages and hours are given for male workers who received no meals (men generally earned at least twice as much as women). Where two wages are given, the first is the normal wage throughout the year, the second is the harvest wage. In some areas, wages for summer and winter work were also slightly different, but as the data vary in detail, I have used the average yearly wages given by most sources. After the turn of the century, workers fought for and won hourly rates. Here, annual income is computed taking into account harvest wages; the harvest is assumed to have lasted twenty days. For purposes of comparison, in 1882 the national average daily wage for a male agricultural worker was just over 3 francs.

decimate vines locally, however, employers cut wages by as much as one-third (Table 11) and reduced the number of work hours and days. Many workers were simply laid off.

Far from improving once harvests returned to normal, the vinedressers' situation worsened in the 1890s because of structural changes in the labor market. One result of the economic crises was the appearance of a new labor force.[38] Immigration to the Aude from surrounding departments had begun in the late 1860s, swelling the vinegrowing population of areas such as the

Narbonnais; this immigration continued through the 1880s. Although the population of Coursan peaked in 1891 and stagnated thereafter, by the turn of the century well over half of all male vinedressers who married in Coursan came from outside the Narbonnais (see Table 10). Most had traveled to Coursan from other departments in the region—the Hérault, the Gard, the Tarn, the Ariège, the Aveyron, and the Lozère. Yet increasingly, new immigrants now came from beyond the borders of France—from Spain, and a few from Italy. Between 1876 and 1891, foreigners living in Coursan jumped in number from 26 to 267.[39] These immigrants, who rarely succeeded in obtaining land of their own, were especially tied to the estate vineyards. The majority performed unskilled work as *terrassiers* or as farmhands, planting and digging new vineyards (such as Roudier's estate, Jouarres) for piece rates that undercut the wages of skilled French vinedressers. When an estate owner in Narbonne, for example, offered thirty-five centimes a square meter for a job leveling land in part of his vineyard, the French workers whom he approached asked sixty centimes; an Italian agreed to do the job for thirty.[40] Competition also came from small vineyard owners who could no longer live from their land and turned to the estates for work. Vinedressers later accused these men of competing with them for jobs.

Two additional factors contributed to a more competitive labor market, as well as to the sharpening of class distinctions in vineyard villages. First, the enormous expense of reconstituting vineyards after the phylloxera, vastly increased annual costs of production, and the inability of many small vineyard owners to sustain themselves through prolonged periods of depression all meant that many vinedresser-owners of microproperties now experienced landownership more as a liability than a benefit. Because of growing indebtedness, if not impoverishment, microproprietors, like the landless immigrants who now competed with them, relied more than ever on wage work. One contemporary observer bemoaned the fact that "today, whoever has a bit of vines also has debts. The small property of the day laborer has no other effect than that of taking away their independence." Under changed conditions, this writer noted prophetically, landownership could no longer be expected to confer stability and political conservatism: "[These worker-owners] cannot be counted on to resist the progress of socialism."[41] Second, in a village like Coursan, where medium and large proprietors declined in number over this period, workers now had a more limited choice of employers and became more dependent on the large estate vineyards for income.

By far the most important factor in the making of a vineyard working class in the Aude, however, was the change in work rhythms and routines.[42] Male vinedressers in the region, unlike many skilled industrial artisans in France at this time, did not experience a downgrading of their skills as the technology of vinedressing grew more sophisticated. On the contrary, these "artisans of the vineyard" added new tasks to their repertoire: grafting, preparation of vines for submersion, plus the more aggressive use of insecticides and fertilizer. Yet even as their work became more complex and demanding of dexterity and technical expertise (as in grafting especially), their position deteriorated—both materially, in relation to other workers on the estates, and practically, with the introduction of new forms of labor control and work discipline.

Within the hierarchy of the estate vineyard, the distinction between day laborers and other personnel sharpened in the postphylloxera period. For managers, overseers, and farmhands, material life improved between 1881 and 1900. The manager who earned a yearly salary of 1,000 to 1,500 francs in 1880 saw his income rise to between 1,400 and 1,800 francs in the 1890s.[43] More managers acquired land after the crisis as well. In addition, the position of the estate manager became more important over the years, both because of the growing complexity of viticulture, which required more careful administration and prudent engineering, and because absentee and multiple estate ownership made management by proxy increasingly common. The position of overseers also improved in the 1880s and 1890s. Their salaries increased, and, like the managers, more became landowners. Finally, unskilled farmhands benefited from employers' efforts to reconstitute their vineyards. These men, mostly immigrants, who undertook the strenuous digging of canals and replanting, now increasingly worked on yearly contracts rather than by the month. Given the relative stability of prices during this period (see Chapter 4), increased wages meant that the purchasing power of most estate employees increased. The situation of skilled vinedressers, however, was another story. Their position became less, not more, secure.

Not only did vinedressers face dwindling returns from their own vines and competition from unskilled immigrant workers in the 1880s and 1890s, but they also faced declining wages and a shorter work year. As we have seen, employers almost immediately cut wages and the number of workdays during the phylloxera crisis, and wages did not improve thereafter (see Table 11). Vinedressers in the Aude earned some 500 francs less, annually, in the 1890s than they had during the golden age of the vine. Moreover, although the vinedresser was normally hired on at the end of October for the year, custom rather than contract fixed the terms of employment. Because employers calculated wages on a daily basis and sometimes paid workers a piece rate, in slow seasons they might dismiss workers for weeks at a time. In wet weather workers had to dress the vines in mud and rain. Such conditions were not new, but workers could tolerate them more easily in a period of high wages. The quality of relations between employers and workers changed as well. More rational-minded estate owners in the 1890s suppressed such traditional practices as granting workers the right to glean after harvest or to gather wood and vine trimmings (an important source of cooking fuel in the forest-poor Aude) for their own use. Employers' increasing reliance on estate managers, too, led to a breakdown in the personal relations between employers and workers that had earlier allowed these age-old customs.[44]

The gradual and complex process of class formation, however, resulted from much more than the deterioration of material conditions; it was also the product of changing work relations. In the post-phylloxera period, new forms of labor discipline reflected employers' efforts to rationalize production. Employers now expected day laborers to work fixed hours and to follow a work routine set forth by the employer or his estate manager. The establishment of a seven- or eight-hour day meant that workers who owned vines had less time for private cultivation. Likewise, in the 1890s estate owners used piece rates more frequently to extract maximum output. In the age of vineyard

expansion, workers tolerated piece rates insofar as they permitted worker-proprietors to dress vines on an estate at their own
pace, without the constraint of a fixed workday, so that they could
later work their own vines. In the 1890s, however, employers
used piecework to replant their vines as cheaply as possible,
playing on the willingness of immigrants to work under this
system. Not surprisingly, in many of the strikes that occurred in
the Aude after the turn of the century vinedressers demanded
the abolition of piece rates.

Team labor was another way for employers to acquire skilled
labor and impose work discipline in the post-phylloxera years.
In addition to facilitating labor recruitment, team work is a
classic form of labor discipline, where task organization and
payment are simplified by keeping workers dependent on one
another for the completion of tasks and for "self-supervision." In
the Aude, teams (called *colles*) of ten or fifteen skilled vinedressers circulated from estate to estate to perform operations such as
pruning and grafting. Employers paid the entire team a fixed
wage, which the team members divided among themselves. The
leader not only hired the workers and supervised the job, but he
also set the price of the job with the employer.[45]

Although the team served as a form of labor discipline, it also
held the potential for subversion. The experience of team labor
and the collective wage constituted an early element of worker
control that promoted workplace solidarity. Moreover, since
team workers rotated from estate to estate, they enjoyed more
independence than workers who were obliged to work for a
single employer. Finally, team work provided an opportunity for
workers to communicate with one another at the work site.
These vinedressers, then, played an important role in the later
development of revolutionary syndicalism among agricultural
workers in the Aude.[46]

All of these changes in work relations contributed to the proletarianization of vinedressers in the Aude, who, whether they
owned land or not, now depended primarily on wages for their
livelihood. The "golden age of the vine" was long gone.

By 1905, the agricultural economist Michel Augé-Laribé
could write, "the high-yield . . . viticulture of the south is clear-

ly . . . industrial . . . , both because of the quantity of capital that
it requires and because of the production methods that it uses:
territorial specialization pushed to the point of monoculture, . . .
piecework and the formation of a wage-earning proletariat."[47]
In a sense he was right. Vinedressing and wine production,
already specialized and organized according to a clear-cut division of labor, grew technically more complex, if not more mech-
anized. Concentration of ownership and control of the market
by large vineyard capital became increasingly apparent in the
domination of production by a relatively small number of large
growers, including some powerful multiproprietors. The transforming agents of agricultural capitalism in this era of crises,
then, were not machines, but profiteering entrepreneurs ready
to cash in on a booming market in *vin ordinaire*. Unlike some
types of capitalist agriculture in industrial societies, the technical
modification of southern viticulture did not require a diminished work force, but rather the reverse.[48] Labor cutbacks came
only during depressions that forced owners to keep production
costs to a bare minimum—a goal they could also attain by reduc-
ing wages.

Nonetheless, even if most students of turn-of-the-century
southern French viticulture agree on its "industrial" character,
the analogy between agricultural capitalism and industrial capitalism cannot be pushed too far for the Aude. The evolution of
vineyards did not eliminate small producers. Far from it: in the
department overall, small property owners counted for 85 percent of all landowners, and in some areas, such as the Corbières,
these individuals together actually produced more wine than
some large growers. Furthermore, because agriculture is subject
to natural diseases and climatic variations, winegrowers, who
have never been able to standardize their product, faced much
greater market instability than did industrial producers. Finally,
although the large estate vineyards increasingly came to resemble factories in their labor discipline, large numbers of workers,
and market orientation, vinedressers remained very different
from industrial workers. Vinedressers did not experience proletarianization in the same way their industrial artisan counterparts did. Their status as skilled workers endowed them with a
certain spirit of independence and pride in their work. More-

over, the vineyard worker shared much with the small owner, in both material condition and interests. The complexity of the agricultural working class, which included that hybrid, the worker-proprietor, who occasionally performed wage labor in the vineyards, also distinguished the two groups of workers.

At the same time, vinedressers undeniably experienced a serious degradation in their position over the years. The crises of vineyard capitalism all allowed employers to intensify their control over production and to attempt to extract as much labor as possible at the lowest possible price. Concurrently, the new entrepreneurial mentality of the post-phylloxera years destroyed the customary bonds between employers and working people, creating new relations in the workplace and in vineyard communities. We can get a clearer picture of the human scale of these changes, and particularly of the complexity of proletarianization, by looking at the gender relations of the workplace, the evolving work roles of women, and the way families coped with the depressed vineyard economy.

4

GENDER, WORK, AND THE HOUSEHOLD ECONOMY OF VINEYARD WORKERS

On connaît la femme au pied et à la tête.
(You can tell a woman by her head and her feet.)

Brave femme dans une maison vaut plus que
métairie avec cheval.
(A strong woman in the house is worth more than a
horse in the stable.)

Une femme et un baril, plus qu'ils travaillent, mieux
ils valent.
(A woman and a barrel: the more they work, the
more they're worth.)[1]

Proverbs from Languedoc such as these attest to the real value placed on women's work in rural France, even if it was ironically expressed. In the nineteenth century as earlier, the labor of a farm wife could make or break the family economy. Likewise, contemporaries praised the moral and physical benefits of agricultural work for women over the perils of industrial labor. Thus Jules Rivals, an Audois economist, wrote that the real advantage of farming for women lay in the fact that it allowed "women and children to work without moral or physical danger. Care of the home, a fixed and regular workday, care of farm animals, raising chickens, are, for women and children, the sort of work whose main advantage is that they take place under the invigorating influence of fresh air and daylight."[2]

Most of Rivals's contemporaries probably shared this idealistic picture of women's agricultural work, with its underlying assumptions about a gender-based division of labor. But for most of the 43–48 percent of women in the French labor force who worked in agriculture in the second half of the nineteenth century, labor on farms and vineyards from sunrise to sunset differed little from factory work.[3] Moreover, whereas contemporaries certainly valued women's economic contribution, they operated from masculine definitions of work as activity performed outside the household for a wage. They often did not view women's productive activities in the home as work, because no wage was generated. And women themselves often did not distinguish between domestic tasks (performed in the household) and agricultural labor (performed in field or barn).[4] The overlap between women's domestic and nondomestic work meant that even when rural women did perform wage labor, contemporaries viewed their work as worth less than men's. Contemporaries' gendered definitions of work and skill meant that despite their praise for women's hard work and the benefits of fresh air and exercise, they had no doubt about women's secondary place in both the labor hierarchy and the wage structure of the vineyards.

Women effectively assisted the expansion of vineyard capitalism by providing cheap labor. As the vineyard economy of the Aude developed, a more formal gender-based division of labor appeared. But the crises of vineyard capitalism—all of which ultimately became crises of the family economy—changed the labor demands of men and women in important ways. Living standards for vineyard workers, which had dramatically improved during the age of expansion, fell sharply, and workers now mobilized the resources of their household economy to limit the effects of depression. An examination of gender relations in the vineyards is essential to understanding not only how workers dealt with the long period of economic difficulty that followed the golden age of the vines, but also how definitions of gender difference in the workplace contributed to proletarianization, and in ways different for women than for men.

Gender and the Making of Vineyard Capitalism

Prior to the great agricultural revolution in the Aude, women engaged in a diverse array of economic activities, growing, preparing, and selling food.[5] Most women worked as wage earners along with other family members or on small family farms. Some combined work as day laborers with their activities on household plots: in the 1851 census in Coursan, ninety-five women were listed as *journalières-propriétaires*. The domestic activities of small vineyard owners' wives spilled into the public arena when they sold their chickens, rabbits, and eggs in weekly markets in Carcassonne or Narbonne or rented stalls in villages like Cuxac d'Aude, Lézignan, or Coursan. Thus domestic production and associated entrepreneurial activity drew women into the larger world of market relations. Some migrated long distances to harvest so as to bring in cash.[6] Others worked as seamstresses, laundresses, grocers, dressmakers, and midwives. As *revendeuses* they purchased fruit and vegetables in bulk and hawked them in local markets, and some sold secondhand goods. The expansion of vineyards also brought women onto estate vineyards as overseers (*ramonettes*). Finally, as property owners some (mostly widows) sustained themselves on income from their land as rentiers.[7]

Around midcentury this kaleidoscope of activity changed. The combination of vineyard expansion and large wheat harvests in the 1850s created a demand for women's labor. In addition, the industrial depression of 1847–1852 and declining employment for women in the rural textile industry brought about a shift from industrial to agricultural work. The vast majority of women in Coursan now worked primarily as day laborers or estate workers (Table 12), sowing grain and harvesting, tending vines and cutting grapes, picking olives, and working vegetable gardens on small family plots, thus combining domestic, productive, and wage-earning activity. As vineyards came to dominate the economy of the Aude, women's position in that economy changed. The separation between public and private, between farm/vineyard and domestic space, became more acute, as did definitions of gender roles.

We have already seen how the agricultural revolution in the Aude brought about a more complex differentiation of vineyard tasks. Although women undoubtedly performed numerous procedures in the vines prior to the development of viticultural capitalism, vineyard "industrialization" led to a more formal

Table 12. Occupational Distribution and Marital Status of Women, Coursan, 1851, 1876, and 1911

	1851		1876		1911	
	No.	Percent	No.	Percent	No.	Percent
Occupation						
Day laborer	295	44.5	2	1.5	242	52.0
Cultivateur (small owner)	43	6.5	33	25.0	0	
Estate worker (farm manager, overseer, farmhand)	63	9.5	43	32.6	48	10.3
Other agricultural worker (gardener, shepherd)	68	10.3	1	0.8	23	5.0
Artisan/tradesperson	108	16.3	10	7.6	85	18.3
Proprietor	5	0.8	8	6.0	8	1.7
Professional/*rentier* (includes midwives)	79	11.9	34	25.7	14	3.0
Housewife (*ménagère*)	1	0.2	1	0.8	45	9.7
Total	662	100.0	132	100.0	465	100.0
Marital Status						
Married	369	55.7	18	13.6	269	57.8
Unmarried	293	44.3	114	86.4	196	42.2
Widowed	104	15.7	74	64.9	unknown	

Sources: AD Aude 11M78, 117, 157, "Dénombrement de la population, Etats nominatifs des habitants de Coursan de 1851, 1876, 1911." The *dénombrement* of 1876 most likely underestimated women's employment; see Etienne Van de Walle, *The Female Population of France in the Nineteenth Century* (Princeton: Princeton University Press, 1974), 24.

division of labor based on gender. Employers increasingly allocated certain tasks exclusively to men, while reserving others for women. Thus, in the Audois vineyards skilled work was by definition male: men performed all skilled and semiskilled work, such as pruning, cultivating, and winemaking. Most unskilled work was defined as female.

In the twentieth century the idea that men and women have different capabilities for work has led to forms of occupational segregation. For example, the notion that women have "nimble fingers" has been used to justify the employment of women as typists and clerical workers. In the nineteenth century the same

concept justified the employment of women in certain types of
vineyard work, such as pinching buds in the spring to encourage
the formation of fewer but more resilient flowers or cutting
grapes during the harvest. Ironically, vineyard owners did not
invoke this idea to allow women to perform other jobs requiring
manual dexterity, such as pruning or grafting; these tasks were
considered "men's work," in that they required skill and some
technical training. As we shall see, this situation sustained men's
superior position in the vineyard labor hierarchy and wage
structure by allowing them to exercise control over definitions of
skill.[8]

Nonetheless, women performed a wide variety of tasks. Following pruning (performed by men), women gathered the stems
and branches that fell to the ground and tied them in five-
kilogram bundles to be sold as kindling. Vineyard owners often
paid women partly in kind for this work by allowing them to take
some portion of the kindling home for use as cooking and heat-
ing fuel. But this method of payment also corresponded to a
reduced monetary wage. Otherwise women earned a piece rate
for gathering wood, which forced them to work fast in order to
earn a minimum wage. Women's work also included spreading
insecticides and fertilizer and sulphuring the vines to prevent
mildew. During sulphuring they carried an eight-liter tank and
sprayer on their backs, scarcely an enviable task, since the tank
weighed twenty-five kilos when full, and the smell of sulphur
lingered in the hair and clothing for hours afterward. At har-
vesttime women cut the grapes; men then carried the heavy
baskets filled with freshly picked fruit to wagons, which they
drove to the wine cellar.[9]

Consistent with their definitions of work and skill as gender-
based, contemporaries supported the division of labor in the
harvest, and more generally, on the grounds that women's work
permitted men to perform "more important" skilled jobs. One
vineyard owner gave women the responsibility for certain chemical treatments "so as not to distract the men from their ordinary
tasks."[10] Despite women's essential place in the labor structure of
the vineyard, they were seen as merely secondary actors in the
drama of production, their work but supplementary to that of
men. How ironic, then, that workers later used the gender-based

division of labor to promote solidarity in the labor conflicts that broke out after the turn of the century.

The tension between women's economic contribution and their subordinate role in the economy characterized the social relations of the sexes in other spheres of domestic and community life. Alphonse Daudet provides a telling description in his *Letters from My Windmill*, where he tells of a lunch with the Provençal poet and founder of the Félibrige,[11] Frédéric Mistral. Mistral's aged mother arrives from the market and immediately sets about preparing a sumptuous lunch. "In no time at all the table is laid; a beautiful white cloth and two place settings. I know the customs of the house; I know that when Mistral has visitors his mother does not sit at the table with them. . . . The dear old lady speaks only the Provençal tongue, and would not feel at ease talking to Frenchmen. . . . Besides, she is needed in the kitchen."[12] Similarly, when Léon Jouhaux, leader of the Confédération générale du travail, came to dine at the home of François Cheytion, leader of the vineyard workers' union in Coursan, and his sister, Anastasie Vergnes, who herself participated actively in strikes before and after the First World War, Anastasie and her mother, having served the meal, remained standing in the small kitchen cum living room–dining room while the men ate and discussed union affairs.[13]

In the rituals of harvest the ambiguity of gender relations again came into view. Apart from the "deplorable promiscuity" that one observer decried, there were practices such as the *fardage*. Male workers would chase a young female picker (*coupeuse*) unfortunate enough to have left a bunch of grapes on the vine and, when they caught her, would crush the grapes on her forehead or, more commonly, buttocks. In some cases a woman who experienced this indignity was able to get her revenge with the aid of friends, by grabbing a male harvester and stuffing his shirt with leaves. In such sexual horseplay men symbolically asserted their power over women in the rural community, and women simultaneously challenged them.[14]

As in industrial society, assumptions about gender-based differences in the workplace and social life governed women's material condition in the rural Aude. Women's wages in vineyard work (as in most other paid employment) were generally half

Table 13. Wages, Hours, and Annual Income of Female Vineyard Workers, Coursan, 1862–1912

	Average Wage (fr.) (Ordinary work/ Harvest)	Workday (hrs.)	Workdays per Year	Annual Income (fr.)
1862	.90/1.75	7–8	250	250.50
1882	2.00/2.50	6–7	250	515
1892	1.55/2.00	6–7	200	323.50
1900	1.25/1.50	7	200	257.50
1903–1904[a]	1.50/1.75	7	200	307.50
1911–1912	1.75 plus 1 liter wine/ 2.00 plus 2 liters wine	6–7	250	445

Sources: AN F[11]2698, "Enquête agricole de 1862"; France, Ministère de l'agriculture, Statistique agricole de France, *Résultats généraux de l'enquête décennale de 1882* (Nancy: Berger-Levrault, 1887), pt. 1, 382–396; ibid., *1892* (Paris: Imprimerie nationale, 1898), 243; AD Aude 13M300, "Statistique agricole décennale des communes, 1882, Canton de Coursan"; 15M125, 133, "Grèves agricoles"; 5M11, Monthly prefect reports; Michel Augé-Laribé, *Le problème agraire du socialisme. La viticulture industrielle du Midi de la France* (Paris: Giard & Brière, 1907), 76–77, 283–288, 290.

Note: The wages and the number of workdays for 1862 in Coursan were higher than departmental averages given in France, Ministère de l'agriculture, *Résultats généraux de l'enquête décennale de 1862* (Nancy: Berger-Levrault, 1868). Wages for 1892 have been estimated from departmental averages, which were usually about 50 centimes lower than rates in Coursan.

[a]Figures given for 1903–1904 date from after strikes.

and sometimes less than half those of men. In 1862 *journalières* earned on average 90 centimes a day. (To put that sum into perspective, a kilo of bread cost from 32 to 36 centimes.)[15] Employers, in calculating wages, made no distinction between the various types of work women performed, except during the harvest, when they paid women more in order to attract harvesters (Table 13). Nor did they take physical effort into account, even though *journalières* spent much of the day bent over, if they were gathering branches or cutting grapes, or sweating under the weight of the sulphur tank.

In terms of wages, women workers, like men, profited from the expansion of viticulture, as Table 13 shows; by 1882, in the vineyards' golden age, their wages had doubled. Yet while women vineyard workers in the Aude made more than the average for women agricultural workers nationally, it would have been impossible for one to support a family on her own, or even to sustain herself on her own wages. It is therefore not surprising that few women in the protourban villages of the Narbonnais lived alone.[16] Nor did women have an opportunity to improve their skills; the gender-based division of labor flatly denied them access to skilled "men's work." In addition, estate vineyard owners saved money not only from the lower wages they paid women, but also by feeding women workers less than men. Whereas men had the right to meat at all meals, women had to make do with cooked beans and whatever meat was left over when the men were through. For the vineyard owner, this practice could mean a small but significant monthly savings, depending on the number of women employed.[17] Mme. Marie Garrigues, for instance, *ramonette* on the estate of Canague-Neuve in Capestang, not far from Coursan, received one franc a day per man to feed the male *domestiques* on the estate, and only fifty centimes a day per woman. A typical "women's meal" consisted of a bowl of vegetable stew, to which a small piece of meat might be parsimoniously added.[18] In the wage settlements just before World War I, where workers won the right to some wine as part of their daily wage, women generally were allotted half as much wine as men (see below, especially Chapter 7). Of course, the assumption that men and women had different food requirements was not unique to the vineyards; it has been true of peasant and working-class families not just in France but all over the world.[19] Here as elsewhere, it underscored women's secondary status in both the family and the workplace, and illustrates how the proletarianization of women differed from that of men.

Women, Work, and Family

The experience of women in rural working-class families of the Aude was influenced not only by the material forces of production, but also by a culture that assigned them specific capabilities and roles in the dual worlds of work and home. Women's decisions to work or not to work were thus determined by a delicate balance between economic survival and the demands of reproduction and child care. Over a period of nearly sixty-five years,

Table 14. Mean Ages at First Marriage, Coursan and France, 1850–1910

Marriages	1850–1860		1861–1870		1871–1880		1881–1890		1891–1900		1901–1910	
	M	F	M	F	M	F	M	F	M	F	M	F
Coursan, vineyard workers	27.4	20.7	24.7	19.1	24.3	20.2	25.6	21.9	25.5	21.6	25.5	21.3
Coursan, total population	24.3	21.2	24.8	21.8	25.0	20.9	26.2	21.9	26.1	21.2	25.9	21.8
Aude, total population	—	22.7	—	23.1	—	22.6	—	22.5	—	22.8	—	—
France, total population	28.5	24.1	28.3	23.8	28.3	23.8	27.9	23.3	27.9	23.5	27.9	23.8

Sources: Bureau du greffier du Tribunal de grande instance, Narbonne, Aude, Etat civil du village de Coursan, "Actes de mariages, 1850–1910"; Wesley D. Camp, *Marriage and the Family in France Since the Revolution* (New York: Bookman Associates, 1961), 53; Etienne Van de Walle, *The Female Population of France in the Nineteenth Century* (Princeton: Princeton University Press, 1974), 255. Figures for marriage ages in the Aude are taken from Van de Walle for 1856, 1866, 1876, 1886, and 1896.

the timing and patterning of important life events such as marriage, childbearing, and work closely followed the boom-and-bust rhythm of the vineyards. Both women and men who worked in the vineyards in Coursan married earlier than men and women in France overall (see Table 14).[20] Even so, male agricultural workers in 1850s Coursan had to acquire some savings to begin a new household, and often did not marry until they were as old as twenty-seven. Even after they formed their own households, life was not easy. Poor harvests in the early 1860s and rising prices caused local officials to wonder how workers could survive the increasing cost of living.[21] A family of three in 1862 in which only the husband worked could just about make ends meet, and would benefit considerably from a small plot of vines or a soup garden (Figure 1). Even when a wife worked and a child was young, the family could barely meet basic expenses. Later, the consumption needs of a growing adolescent could impose additional burdens on the family economy.

Working-class families in 1882, at the height of the prosperous years of vineyard expansion, lived vastly more comfortably than twenty years earlier. As workers' wages rose and as more vineyard workers acquired land, they married earlier—the men about four years earlier than men in France generally—which also meant higher birth rates in this booming protourban village than in the population at large (Table 15). In this period, workers most often lived in single-family households. In Coursan, for example, less than 5 percent of the households consisted of a married couple living with the parents of one spouse. Even though rents and the prices of meat, wine, and bread increased steadily between 1860 and 1880,[22] contemporaries noted the great improvement in the standard of living of vineyard workers in the Narbonnais and pointed out that now these rural workers lived much better than urban artisans, whose incomes barely met expenses.[23] As Table 16 shows, income from landownership around 1881 meant real prosperity. A family that aggressively worked one hectare of vines could realize over 5,000 francs from sale of their wine, and even families who owned no land could be well off. At all stages of a family's development, as Figure 1 shows, working-class families could easily meet expenses.

The pattern of women's wage earning closely followed both

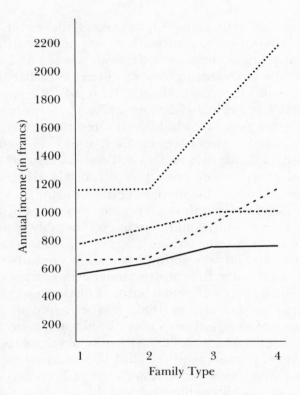

Figure 1. Changes in Expenses and Incomes of Vineyard Workers'
Families According to Family Types, 1862–1882. Sources: AN F¹¹2698,
"Enquête agricole de 1862"; AD Aude 13M300, "Statistique agricole
décennale des communes, 1882"; France, Ministère de l'agriculture,
Statistique agricole de la France, *Résultats généraux de l'enquête décennale
de 1882* (Nancy: Berger-Levrault, 1887), pt. 1, 382–396; pt. 2, 183.

Table 15. Crude Birth Rates, Coursan, 1850–1914

Years	Crude Birth Rate	Years	Crude Birth Rate
1850–1854	24.7	1885–1889	31.5
1855–1859	23.2	1890–1894	27.7
1860–1864	24.9	1895–1899	26.5
1865–1869	22.4	1900–1904	23.9
1870–1874	24.8	1905–1909	21.6
1875–1879	27.2	1910–1914	19.1
1880–1884	30.2		

Source: Bureau de greffier du Tribunal des grande instance, Narbonne, Aude, Etat civil du village de Coursan, "Actes de naissances, 1850–1914."

the overall economic conjuncture and the demands of child care at home. In the depression years of the 1840s and 1850s, many men did not earn enough to permit them to support a family on their own, and so their wives went to work as well: 56 percent of women wage earners during this period were married (see Table 12). This level of married women's labor force participation was much higher than the national aggregate level. In France as a whole, 40 percent of married women worked in 1851; in England, 25 percent.[24] A low crude birth rate in these years (see Table 15) also suggests that many married women, not having the responsibility of young children, were comparatively free to work for wages. Even the presence of a child under five at home did not prevent women from working, however. Many a young mother bundled her baby into a basket and took it to the vines or fields where she could nurse it; a child of three or four might be left to play.

Women's contribution to the working-class family economy was complemented and sometimes spelled by the labor of children. But if Coursan can be taken as a reliable example, child labor (that is, of children under fourteen), was relatively uncommon. Rural working-class families in the Aude relied more heavily on the wage contributions of adult children living at home than on the labor of youngsters. To be sure, before the Third Republic's compulsory education laws (beginning in 1881), chil-

Table 16. Estimated Costs and Net Income from One Hectare of Vines in Coursan, 1866–1910

	Yield (hl/ha)	Price (fr./hl)	Costs of Production (fr.)	Net Income (fr.)
1866	40	40	340	1,260
1872	45	40–45	340	1,460–1,685
1881	120	50	340	5,660
1890	175	15	1,130	1,495
1900	147	4	1,130	−582
1905	45	9	1,130	−595
1907	180ᵃ	10	1,130	670
1910	41	32	1,130	312

Sources: See Table 3, "Average Yields and Prices," above; France, Ministère de l'agriculture, *Enquête agricole de 1872. Deuxième série. Enquêtes départementales, 21ᵉ circonscription* (Paris: Imprimerie nationale, 1872), 147 (the 1872 figures for yields and prices are departmental averages). Comice agricole de Narbonne, *Questionnaire sur le revenu foncier des terres dans l'arrondissement de Narbonne* (Narbonne: F. Caillard, 1908), 6–12, 14–15.

ᵃHigh yields of 120–180 hl/ha were the result of intensive cultivation and pruning. Such high productivity was exceptional; in nearby Salles d'Aude vineyards yielded 60 hl/ha in 1907, and elsewhere yields averaged between 40 and 55 hl/ha, which would have produced considerably lower incomes.

dren joined their mothers in the vineyards from the age of seven or eight on, gathering branches and cutting grapes during harvest, for which they earned the same as or somewhat less than women's wages. In 1862, a child could contribute as much as 264 francs annually to the family purse. Twenty years later, that contribution might be 460 francs. These sums could add significantly to the total income of a vineyard worker's family. Even so, few children under fourteen (normal school-leaving age) actually left school to work full-time. In 1851 in Coursan, only sixty-two children under fourteen worked, and of these only three worked in the vines. More commonly, young unmarried adult sons and daughters (fourteen to thirty years old) continued to reside with parents and contributed to the family income—a situation similar to that of nineteenth-century working-class families in industrial centers like Roubaix.[25] In the period before the expansion of vineyard capitalism, the presence of multiple adult wage earners in rural working-class families could occasionally relieve married women from wage work. Thus Justine Canguilhem, fifty-six, wife of François Canguilhem, sixty-nine, a farmer, did not need to work for wages as long as her three older daughters, aged twenty, twenty-three, and thirty-five, brought in income as a day laborer, seamstress, and laundry worker, respectively.[26]

During the golden age of vineyard prosperity, women's work patterns changed. In 1876, many fewer women appeared in the census as wage earners and only 27 percent as day laborers or as *cultivateurs* (see Table 12). Moreover, considerably fewer married women were recorded as working. However, the census may not accurately reflect women's real occupational activity, for in this period of expanding landownership the wives of artisans and vinedressers most likely worked their families' vines rather than as wage workers.[27] While it is tempting to argue that increasing birth rates provided an incentive for women to remain at home, the need for women's labor on family vineyards probably had the stronger effect in determining their work patterns at this point. Once the phylloxera struck the Aude, however, the devastation to family property and the near destitution of small *vignerons* caused yet another redistribution of economic responsibility in the family.

Economic Crisis, the Family Economy, and Women's Work

The comparative comfort and security of Narbonnais working-class households in the early 1880s was short lived. The combined effects of the phylloxera crisis, the depression of the early 1890s, and the turn-of-the-century crisis accentuated the proletarianization of women workers and stressed working-class families to the breaking point. Unable to meet the high costs of treating and reconstituting their vineyards, small owners sold their vines. Working-class households in which men's wages plummeted now needed the income of wives and daughters. According to the crude *dénombrement* of 1886, some 733 women worked for wages, over half of them in the vineyards.[28] A combination of depressed wages, the absence of income from one's own vines, and young children to support (the birth rate remained high—see Table 15) obliged women to work for wages on the large estate vineyards, where reconstitution was in full force.

Although the vineyards gradually lost the dusty yellow and brown look of the 1880s and grew green and lush again, prolonged and repeated depressions continued to have an important impact on gender relations in the vineyards. In particular, the more aggressive "industrial" viticulture that developed in the post-phylloxera years affected women's work, in two ways. First, as we have seen, estate owners imposed team labor as a way of organizing not only labor recruitment but also work. Women were placed in groups of twelve to fifteen and given a group wage, much as occurred with men. Yet in the women's case too, the system functioned ambiguously as a form of discipline, for the work teams facilitated contact between the women and engendered a sense of group solidarity.

Second, the expansion of the industrial vineyard accentuated the gender-based division of labor—another important respect in which women's proletarianization differed from men's. When employers added new skilled and semiskilled procedures to the vinedresser's work routine (especially special methods of planting and grafting), women were not permitted to learn them. This denial of access to skill helped to keep women's wages low and reinforced their inferior position in the labor hierarchy. Occasionally, in an effort to rationalize production and cut costs, vineyard owners abandoned the rigid division of labor and asked women to perform jobs, such as pruning, that were normally considered "men's jobs"; yet still they did not pay them a man's wage.[29] Male workers ultimately fought against this form of exploitation, which they correctly viewed as a threat to their position. Thus the gender-based division of labor became an issue for workers of both sexes in the labor struggles that shook the Aude after the turn of the century (see Chapter 7).

The depression of the wine industry touched women in other ways as well. Women workers probably experienced less competition from foreign (primarily Spanish and Italian) labor than

Table 17. Cost of Living, Nominal Wage, and Real Wage Indices for the Narbonnais and France, 1860–1912

| | Cost of living | | Nominal wage[a] | | Real wage |
| | Narbonnais | France | Narbonnais | France | Narbonnais |
	(1900 = 100)		(1880 = 100)		(1880 = 100)
1860	88	96	58	79	72
1870	107	103	78	86	80
1880	109	110	100	100	100
1890	98	103	66	112	73
1895	101	101	—	—	71
1900	100	100	35	121	38
1905	108	94	76	106	76
1912	136	104[b]	85	134	68

Sources: On wages, see Table 11, "Wages, Hours, and Annual Income of Male Vineyard Workers," above; on wages and cost of living, see France, Statistique générale, *Salaires et coût de l'existence à diverses époques jusqu'en 1910* (Paris: Imprimerie nationale, 1911), 11.
[a] Figures represent values for 1862, 1868, 1882, 1892, 1900, 1905, and 1912.
[b] This figure represents the value for 1910.

did male workers in the phylloxera and post-phylloxera years; in Coursan in 1886, of 143 foreigners in the village, only 45 were women, and those who were in the labor force worked as *domestiques* on the large estates.[30] Nonetheless, as Table 13 shows, women's wages fell in the presence of a labor force swollen by impoverished workers and small proprietors. Moreover, although the replanted vineyards reached full productivity in the 1890s, employers, trying to keep down already skyrocketing production costs, did not increase the number of women's workdays.[31] During the turn-of-the-century market depression, women's wages fell again. Indeed, while the cost of living actually declined in the 1890s and rose only slightly around the turn of the century, both real and nominal wages declined steadily from the late 1880s to the first years of the twentieth century (Table 17). Families lucky enough not to have to send their children out to beg lived on potatoes.

The disastrous material situation of agricultural workers at the turn of the century did not result from some invisible play of market forces. If anything, the agricultural depression that spread across the wine-producing south meant that prices of food and other consumables remained relatively stable in the rural Aude. The poverty that working-class families experienced at this juncture resulted mainly from declining wages. In certain respects, living conditions at the beginning of the twentieth century differed little from those of the nineteenth. Small proprietors whose sudden wealth in the fabulous golden age of the vine had permitted them to purchase pianos (and singing lessons for their daughters) had by now sold them along with their diseased vines. Working-class families in the Narbonnais still relied on candles or kerosene lamps for light (electricity did not reach the Audois countryside until the 1920s); they cooked and heated their cramped dwellings with vine trimmings, in a region poor in forests and coal. Most dined simply on vegetable stews or potato soup with a bit of meat or salt pork. Bread counted for over one-third of the food consumed by a working-class family in the Narbonnais after 1900, and food counted for the vast majority of the vineyard worker's family budget.[32] In a family of three, only when all members of the family contributed wages could the family meet expenses (Figure 2).[33] It is also likely that women bore the brunt of the declining standard of living and smaller food budgets, by saving more nutritious items for men and skimping on themselves. When the Barnum and Bailey Circus came to Narbonne in April 1902, few agricultural families with only one working adult could afford the price of the cheapest ticket—1.50 franc, or a woman's entire day's wages.

Although living standards of French workers as a whole probably improved between 1900 and 1910, vineyard workers in the Aude did not share in this rise.[34] Indeed, the cost of living in the Narbonnais increased by 36 percent between 1900 and 1912 (see Table 17). Even though nominal wages more than doubled and real wages doubled between 1900 and 1905, vineyard workers' purchasing power had seriously declined since the golden age of the vine. Only the work of women and older children allowed working-class families to adapt to these deteriorating conditions. In fact, by 1911 married women's wages were essential to family

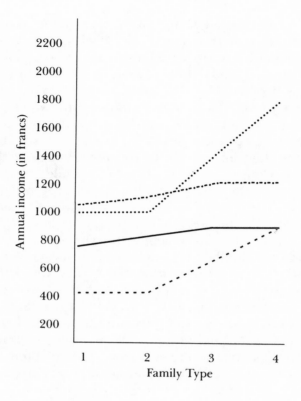

2200
2000
1800
1600
1400
1200
1000
800
600
400
200

Annual income (in francs)

1   2   3   4
Family Type

——— Expenses in 1900
- - - - Income in 1900
········ Expenses in 1912
·········· Income in 1912

Family types:
1. Husband working, wife nursing child
2. Husband working, wife and child under ten not working
3. Both adults working, child over fourteen not working
4. Both adults, child over fourteen working

Figure 2. Changes in Expenses and Incomes of Vineyard Workers' Families According to Family Types, 1900–1912. Sources: Michel Augé-Laribé, *Le problème agraire du socialisme. La viticulture industrielle du Midi de la France* (Paris: Giard & Brière, 1907), 76–77, 238–288, 290; Paul Passama, *La condition des ouvriers viticoles dans le Minervois* (Paris: Giard & Brière, 1906), 79–80, 100–115; AD Aude 9M78–79, 91, 106, "Mercuriales, Etats décadaires des denrées . . . Prix pratiqués sur les marchés, 1880–1905, 1912–1921"; "Tableaux généraux récapitulatifs."

survival; almost three-quarters of the women vineyard workers
in Coursan were married (see Table 12). Vineyard workers still
married somewhat younger than the total population, but the
crude birth rate had fallen steadily since the reconstitution
years; thus women may not have been constrained to stay at
home with young children and infants. Still, women who did
have young children could not afford not to work. As earlier,
unlike working-class families in industrial towns such as Roubaix, young children only rarely contributed wages to the family
economy in Coursan.[35] In 1911, only five children under fourteen worked in the vines, though a larger proportion of older
children between fourteen and thirty resided with their parents
and worked as day laborers than sixty years earlier (23 percent in
1911 as compared to 17 percent in 1851).[36]

Julien Coca's childhood typified that of working-class children
in Coursan just after the turn of the century. In 1979 assistant
mayor of Coursan, and head of the vineyard workers' union
since the early 1950s, Coca grew up on a large estate, where his
father worked as an overseer. His parents insisted that he finish
school before he began full-time work in the vines. Nevertheless,
he worked the harvest every year from the age of ten on to earn
extra money. As Coca said,"Child labor was a function of the
needs of the time. Economic crises were harder on families in the
past than they are today; children had to help out. But it was also
a question of duty to one's family. It was an honor for a child to
bring his wages into the house, to make a contribution."[37] This
view was echoed by Mme Cendrous, who worked as a day laborer in Coursan until her sixties. Families valued education,
and parents expected children at least to receive their secondary
school diploma; but after that, the assistance of older children in
bringing home income was vital. "You had to work if you wanted
to eat; the family was all we had. There was no social security,
you know."[38]

The case of Anastasie Vergnes illustrates another variation in
the pattern of children's and young adults' work experiences in
hard times. Born in 1890, Anastasie was the sixth child of Louis
Cheytion and Marie Bories, both vineyard workers in Coursan.
By 1911, Anastasie had left home.

After finishing school, I went to Paris with my sister Marie to work as a cook. When I returned to Coursan before the war, I continued to cook and also to work part-time in the vines. I worked for Madame X, preparing meals for baptisms and weddings. Since everything took place on Sunday, sometimes I didn't get home until four in the morning (by the time everything was cleaned up) and then I'd have to get up a few hours later to work in the vines the same day.[39]

In this family of seven children, the wage contributions of all family members were essential, especially in the years prior to World War I. As Figure 2 illustrates, only families with two working adults could meet the rising living costs of the prewar years. Those families whose budgets were strained to the breaking point even when wives and older children worked survived by relying on credit with the village grocer and baker. As Paul Passama observed in 1905, workers with no land could be in serious straits when there were illnesses or older family members who had to be cared for: "As soon as their credit with one shopkeeper has run out, they open a second account with another and so on until they find that no one will give them credit any longer."[40] Indeed, by the turn of the century many of these small shopkeepers were themselves reduced to bankruptcy by clients who had been living off their generosity.[41] These men and women, who likewise suffered from the turn-of-the-century depression, eventually supported workers' demands of vineyard owners and played a large part in the great winegrowers' revolt of 1907.

Gender differences in the workplace were part and parcel of the proletarianization of the vineyard workers of the Aude. Notions of such difference allocated the "lesser tasks" in the division of labor to women and maintained women's inferior position in labor and wage structures. This situation facilitated the growth of viticultural capitalism by allowing employers to profit from women's cheap labor. At the same time, women made an essential wage contribution to the economy of laboring families—a fact that contemporaries recognized, if only with the flippancy of folk sayings and proverbs. Women's work was key to the prosperity of small landowning and laboring families in good times and vital to their very survival in hard times. During the booming 1870s and early 1880s, women's labor on family vineyards helped to secure the healthy profits that even small owners could realize. In the depressed late 1880s and 1890s, vineyard workers' families coped with material difficulty by sending adult women and older children into the vines to work. Yet ironically, this situation enabled employers to keep men's wages low, since they knew that women and older children would pick up the slack in hard times.

Women's participation in the labor force as full-fledged workers but second-class citizens meant that they were doubly affected by the economic depression, which touched everyone as both consumers and producers. As we shall see in Chapter 7, this double exploitation, combined with their need to provide for their families, drew women into the labor conflicts and protests of the twentieth century, and ultimately led them to claim their rights in the workplace alongside men. Ironically, neither gender differences in proletarianization nor the process of proletarianization overall caught the attention of left-wing political movements in the Aude. Given the difficulties that Audois wage-earning families faced, it is all the more notable that radicals and socialists active in the department in the 1880s and 1890s made little effort to address the vineyard working class, even if their ideas ultimately influenced rural workers' class identity. The following chapter explores how radicals and then socialists developed a constituency, not among agricultural workers, but among rural artisans and small vinedressers in the Narbonnais.

5
RADICALS AND SOCIALISTS
IN THE VINEYARDS

The economic devastation that the working class and small vineyard owners experienced during the depression years of the 1880s and early 1890s profoundly influenced the development of left politics in the Aude. We have already seen how rural voters turned to radicalism in the prosperous 1870s before the phylloxera attacked their vines. Once the vineyards of the Aude entered a period of prolonged economic depression, however, indebted petty bourgeois vintners and vinedressers were even more attracted to the interventionist program of southern radicals and their promise of statist solutions. Economic depression simultaneously proved to be fertile soil for the growth of socialism as the ideas of Marx, Engels, Guesde, and Lafargue made their way into southern vineyards.

Yet socialism in the Aude was very different from the revolutionary socialism that developed elsewhere in France in this period (particularly in departments such as the Var or the Cher), mainly because it retained close ties to southern radicalism. Like the radicals, Audois socialists appealed primarily to unemployed rural artisans and impoverished small property owners in urban villages, and soft-pedaled the collectivism that characterized socialism elsewhere. Moreover, they did not attempt to carry the message of class struggle to the vineyard working class, a task that revolutionary syndicalists took up around the turn of the century (and which we will examine in Chapter 6).

Radicalism and Socialism in the Aude:
Political Culture, Organization, and Ideology

Radicalism in southern France developed as a seemingly paradoxical mixture of liberalism and statism. On the one hand, radicals defended small winegrowers' and artisans' independence, and on the other, they supported the nationalization of railroads and banks, lower rail rates for agriculture, the reduction of indirect wine taxes and land taxes, and the establishment of a progressive income tax.[1] In 1884, winegrowers in the Comice agricole de Narbonne who attacked the government's free trade policy on foreign wine supported radical programs for government intervention in the wine market and revision of tariffs.[2]

Radicals in lower Languedoc distinguished themselves as well by embracing the dual traditions of the Republic of 1792 and the *démoc soc* republicanism of 1848. As Leo Loubère has pointed out, these men supported improvements in workers' living and working conditions and, in the period before labor unions were legally sanctioned, championed workers' rights to organize and to strike. Clemenceau's left-leaning program of 1881 called for a shorter workday, employer responsibility for work safety, worker participation in the establishment and application of workshop regulations, and abolition of the law against the International Workingman's Association and the *livret*.[3] Camille Pelletan, who represented this strain of southern left radicalism, defended miners in the Gard against the government's attempts to break strikes in 1881 and 1893, and in 1901 proclaimed that the newly formed radical party united "all sons of the revolution, whatever their differences, against all men of the counterrevolution."[4]

The rich associational life of vineyard villages that favored the formation of *démoc soc* and republican organizations in the late 1840s also facilitated the formation of radical political groups in the Third Republic. By the late 1870s radicals who met in masonic lodges in Lézignan and Sigean and in "free thought" societies (*sociétés de libre pensée*) in the Narbonnais and in the villages around Carcassonne were drawing vinedressers and rural artisans into their fold.[5] Thus, aided by a sympathetic press—newspapers such as *La Fraternité*, *Le Bon Sens*, and *Le Républicain de Narbonne*—radicals established an organizational base in the countryside well before they were a formal political party.

With the Aude's vineyards withering under the ravages of phylloxera, the return of formerly exiled Communards to political life (thanks to the amnesty of 1880) allowed socialism to establish itself in southern soil. In 1880 one of these men, Paul

Narbonne, founded the newspaper that eventually became the voice of socialism in the Aude, *L'Emancipation sociale* (to be renamed *La République sociale* when Ernest Ferroul took it over in 1891).[6] Devoted to the "eternal principles of justice and freedom," Narbonne's paper dedicated itself to fighting "authoritarianism in all three of its forms: the altar, the throne, and 'bourgeoisisme.'"[7]

Agricultural workers and artisans devastated by the depression flocked to political discussion groups such as the Cercle de l'union des travailleurs in Limoux or the *groupes d'études sociales* in villages like Coursan, Argelliers, and Cuxac. Socialist *chambrées* and societies sprang up in viticultural towns; by 1882 a *groupe de libre pensée socialiste* had formed in Lézignan, and a *chambrée socialiste* existed in Narbonne. Ernest Ferroul represented these groups at the St-Etienne congress, where Jules Guesde founded the Parti ouvrier français (POF).[8] Interested in class issues, these groups aimed to "study all economic, social, and political questions of interest to workers" and to "seek . . . all measures and reforms of such a nature as to improve the condition of the proletariat."[9] Like the secret societies of the 1840s and 1850s, they allowed rural workers and urban workers to develop a shared political culture. By 1890–1891 socialist societies were active in ten villages in the Narbonnais: Armissan, Bagès, Coursan, Cuxac, Fabrézan, Fleury, Gruissan, Lézignan, Salles, and Vinassan. These and other villages—Bizanet, Marcorignan, Nevian, Moussan, Raissac, Montredon, Ouveillan, and St-Marcel—sent delegates to the eighth and ninth national congresses of the POF in Lille and Lyon. In 1891, the POF created a regional federation, based in Narbonne.[10] In addition to participating in national organizations, this impressive network of rural socialist groups organized election campaigns, distributed party propaganda, sponsored visits of socialist activists such as Guesde, Alexandre Millerand, and Paule Minck, and organized public celebrations commemorating the Paris and Narbonne communes and May Day.[11] Peasants and small winegrowers counted for almost 19 percent of POF membership in the Aude, and by 1896 socialists controlled thirteen municipalities in the department, including Narbonne.[12]

Socialism in the Aude before World War I was strongly influ-

enced by its most vocal activist, Ernest Ferroul. A physician and
freemason (he was a member of the Carcassonne lodge Egalité,
and in 1881 he headed the *libre pensée* society in Narbonne),
Ferroul joined the Narbonne municipal council in 1881, seven
years before he was elected deputy from the Aude and ten years
before becoming mayor of Narbonne. Although Ferroul sided
with the followers of Paul Brousse at the divided socialist congress at St-Etienne in 1882, he joined Guesde's Parti ouvrier
français in 1890, collaborated with Guesde on the paper *Egalité*,
and marched side by side with Guesde and Edouard Vaillant
during the Paris May Day celebration of 1890. Ferroul represented socialist groups from the Aude at POF national congresses at Roubaix (1884), Troyes (1888), Lille (1890), Lyon
(1891), Marseille (1892), Paris (1893), and Nantes (1894); in
1893 he was elected to the national council of the POF.[13]

Between 1891 and 1897, as socialist mayor of Narbonne,
Ferroul created the social republic in microcosm, by providing
urban workers with an alternative to competitive capitalism and
a disinterested state.[14] Thus he provided aid programs for the
poor, gave financial assistance to the Bourse du travail (labor exchange), and established public works projects and *soupes populaires* to provide relief for the unemployed.[15] In true Jacobin
fashion, the municipality organized huge public celebrations on
the anniversary of the First Republic and on May Day, and
replaced the "République française" inscribed on public build-
ings with "République sociale."[16]

During this period, Ferroul's political rhetoric evolved. Although he remained committed to the international alliance of
workers, socialization of the means of production, and the conquest of municipal governments, in the 1890s Ferroul down-
played the themes of class struggle and revolutionary seizure of
power.[17] Nor did the Audois socialists who followed Ferroul
promote the more revolutionary aspects of the Guesdist *programme du Havre* of 1880. Meeting in 1892 with agricultural
workers in Lézignan, for example, Ferroul and his socialist col-
league Félix Aldy supported a political solution to the social
question, maintaining that their efforts to end unemployment,
regulate working hours, and establish workers' retirement funds
could be realized only in the context of the legally constituted

republic.[18] Audois socialists abandoned the rhetoric of revolution and collectivism in addressing the economic issues dear to the hearts of small winegrowers in the Narbonnais. They supported vintners' demands for tariffs on foreign wine, unlike Paul Lafargue and socialists in the Var, who opposed protection on the grounds that it would starve out the urban working class.[19]

The Ferroulists, moreover, actively cultivated their ties with radicals, appearing regularly at banquets and public forums to honor radical luminaries such as Camille Pelletan, Gustave Rouanet, and Léon Bourgeois.[20] Radicals and socialists also rubbed elbows in *groupes d'études sociales* in Coursan and Argelliers, and closed ranks during the antirepublican reaction of the 1890s. As the century ended, the rhetoric of Audois socialism bore an uncanny resemblance to that of southern radicalism. By 1898 Ferroul, now sounding more like Jaurès than Guesde, insisted on the centrality of the republic to the socialist project and on the importance of constitutional revision and measures such as the income tax. That year the *congrès socialiste* in the Aude designated Ferroul as the socialist candidate; it then appealed to the broad spectrum of "radical, radical-socialist, and socialist voters" to prepare an electoral strategy.[21]

Ferroul's moderate, evolutionary stance at this point was not so different from Guesde's strategy of emphasizing legislative reform to recruit workers to the POF between 1893 and 1898.[22] But the two men parted company on other issues. In 1899 both Aldy and Ferroul left the POF in protest over Guesde's condemnation of Alexandre Millerand's entry into the ministry of Waldeck-Rousseau alongside Minister of Defense General Gallifet, known as the "butcher of the Commune." Ferroul argued that socialists should exclude no activity that would help them to "improve their effectiveness and influence; tactical differences between men who agree about fundamental doctrinal principles should not divide socialists from one another."[23]

Socialists, Small Vineyard Owners, and the Agrarian Question

Not only did socialists in the Aude increasingly divest themselves of rhetorical references to revolution, but they focused their attention mainly on urban and rural artisans and small vineyard owners, not the impoverished vineyard working class. In the Narbonnais, socialists energetically supported the interests of small *vignerons* devastated by the ravages of the phylloxera and the general depression of the 1880s and 1890s; one looks in vain in the pages of *La République sociale* or in socialist campaign speeches for references to the plight of agricultural workers, who suffered most from the phylloxera crisis. In the campaign for the 1893 elections Ferroul took the POF program to the countryside, promising nationalization of the Canal du Midi, railroads, and mines and establishment of agricultural credit, but he said virtually nothing about agricultural workers, whose situation had scarcely improved despite the modest recovery of the wine market in 1893.[24] For the small vineyard owners who supported Ferroul, however, socialism meant opposition to the anarchy of the free market and a demand for state regulation, not a *mise en question* of the capitalist system. This was the real meaning of the social republic in the Aude, and it differed little from the message of southern left radicalism.

Why did socialists, who claimed to represent the working class, support small vintners' demands for tax and tariff reform but fail to address the concerns of vineyard workers? It is unlikely that socialists were unaware of the plight of rural workers or blind to rural poverty. Ferroul's strategy of support for small vineyard owners may have been designed to assure him financial backing (from departmental officials); it was also undoubtedly related to the fact that many rural artisans and vineyard workers were also small property owners. In short, socialists may not have seen landless rural workers as a separate constituency at this stage.

In fact, the socialists were probably well aware of the complexities of class identity in the Aude. The vineyard working class was exceptionally heterogeneous at the end of the nineteenth century. Vinedressers and small proprietors shared similar conditions, and both faced proletarianization, if not destitution. Impoverished worker-owners and artisans sympathized with their nonlandowning confreres; these groups mingled and mixed in the local political clubs that flourished in the 1880s and 1890s, and formed a common political culture.

The socialists' decision to tone down their revolutionary rhetoric and back small winegrowers, then, was consistent with the general POF strategy of appealing to peasant farmers. France was still very much a nation of small-holding peasants. They had to be brought into the socialist fold.

At their 1880 congress in Le Havre, the Guesdists had adopted a radical agrarian program calling for the immediate collectivization of land, mines, and farm equipment. At their 1892 congress in Marseille, however, they cast aside their revolutionary rhetoric in favor of a more moderate platform calling for a minimum wage for agricultural workers; the creation of agricultural arbitration councils; the distribution of land to propertyless families; the establishment of a retirement fund from a tax on large estates; a reduction of sharecroppers' and tenants' rents; payment to sharecroppers and tenants of an indemnity from the surplus value they created on the property they farmed; the purchase of land and agricultural machinery by municipalities, which would then rent them to small farmers; the establishment of consumers' cooperatives; the suppression of sales tax on properties worth less than 5,000 francs; and the revision of land survey records (*cadastre*).[25] Nowhere did they mention class struggle in the countryside or the collectivization of peasant property.[26]

The relative lack of attention to the needs of landless laborers by a party that claimed to represent the working class was noteworthy. And in 1894 Guesde and Lafargue went still further, calling peasant property the "tool of the peasant, as the plane is of the cabinetmaker and the scalpel is of the surgeon. The peasant, the cabinetmaker, and the surgeon, who exploit no one with the tools of their trade, do not have to fear that they will be taken away by a socialist revolution."[27] In fact, some socialists believed that impoverished small property owners could be likened to workers. In the ensuing debate on this issue, for instance, Jean Jaurès (who helped draft the *considérants* to the 1894 revised program) drew an analogy between the small peasant proprietor and the worker: "Between large holdings and small, there is not only a quantitative difference, but . . . a qualitative one; the former is an expression of capital, the latter of labor."[28]

Ferroul and his supporters, however, did not translate these national debates and *prises de position* into a clear or consistent strategy. Their rhetorical attacks on private property and agricultural capitalism in *La République sociale* were not matched by concrete efforts to recruit agricultural workers.[29] Still worse, in some areas of France Guesdists failed to back rural workers' struggles, such as those of the lumbermen of the Allier, Nièvre, and the Cher who tried to form unions in the early 1890s—a serious omission for a major socialist political party claiming to represent the working class. Nonetheless, small vineyard owners and artisans continued to support socialists in the winegrowing Aude, even after Ferroul temporarily lost the municipality of Narbonne in 1897.[30]

Electoral Politics and Alliances: The Stormy Fortunes of Radicals and Socialists in the Aude

While the development of an organizational base in popular associations did not make socialist victories in national elections a foregone conclusion, the severity of the agricultural depression in the Aude in the 1880s helped to draw workers and petty bourgeois *vignerons* into socialist ranks. Socialist electoral successes were also linked to charismatic local personalities like Ferroul and Aldy and to socialists' alliances with left radicals.

Socialist politicians began to challenge (but not beat) radicals in the legislative elections of 1881 and in an 1883 by-election in Narbonne arrondissement (Table 18). In 1881, for example, Joseph Malric, left-radical mayor of Sigean, with strong personal political ties in the Narbonnais, won a deputy's seat in a close race against Emile Digeon, who captured Coursan and other winegrowing villages faithful to this local Communard.[31] A similar phenomenon occurred in 1883, when Clovis Papinaud, left-radical cooper and former mayor of Cuxac d'Aude, ran against two socialists: Digeon and Eugène Fournière, collaborator on *L'Emancipation sociale*, who had recently broken with Guesde and joined Brousse's possibilists.[32] Papinaud embodied the shifting ground between left radicals and Audois socialists of the 1880s and 1890s. He had been imprisoned with Narbonne and Digeon following the repression of the Paris Commune, and he had also collaborated on *L'Emancipation sociale*. Now, though, he ran as a left radical. Once again, winegrowing communities gave

Table 18. Legislative Elections of 1881, 1885, 1888, and 1889 in the Narbonnais (percent of votes cast)

	Socialist	Radical	Opportunist	Conservative (Boulangist)[a]	Abstentions
1881					
Narbonne	40.5	45.0	13.1	—	40.9
Coursan commune	80.4	4.3	12.3	—	55.8
1885					
Narbonne					
1st ballot	37.3		34.7	25.4	35.0
2d ballot	70.4		—	27.5	—
Coursan commune					
1st ballot	62.3		5.1	32.6	30.4
2d ballot	66.6		—	27.3	—
1888					
Narbonne					
1st ballot	48.2	—	38.7	12.0	43.4
2d ballot	79.7	—	—	14.4	—
Coursan commune					
1st ballot	86.1	—	3.3	10.1	43.6
2d ballot	89.9	—	—	9.9	—
1889					
Narbonne I					
1st ballot	33.3	37.1	—	16.9	33.8
2d ballot	52.1	46.3	—	—	—
Narbonne II					
1st ballot	25.5	31.0	43.2	—	24.4
2d ballot	52.7	46.7	—	—	—
Coursan commune					
1st ballot	40.4	42.8	15.7	2.4	27.8
2d ballot	52.7	46.7	—	—	—

Source: AD Aude 2M58, Recensement général des votes, 1876–1914.
[a] In the 1888 and 1889 elections only.

the strongest votes to socialist candidates, who promised relief to distressed winegrowers.[33] The real significance of the elections, however, was that they marked the beginning of a period of electoral cooperation between socialists and left radicals: Digeon and Fournière stood down on the second ballot to support Papinaud.

While the phylloxera silently ate away at the Aude's vineyards, socialists Ferroul and Digeon cooperated with radicals in the *scrutin de liste* elections of 1885.[34] They ran on the standard radical program calling for separation of church and state, amnesty for political prisoners, reform of land taxes, institution of an income tax, nationalization of railroads, canals, and mines, and social legislation.[35] Predictably, the radical-socialist list was strongest in the vinegrowing eastern half of the department, where workers and small *vignerons* gave it 37 percent of the vote (in Narbonne arrondissement), polling strong majorities in Coursan (62 percent; see Table 18), Fleury (58 percent), and Salles (44 percent).[36] Three years later, at the height of the vineyard depression, the sudden resignation of Papinaud from his seat as deputy from Narbonne opened the way for the first socialist victory in the Aude, when Ernest Ferroul was voted into the Chamber of Deputies (see Table 18).[37] Despite the division that Boulanger fostered between socialists (Ferroul briefly flirted with Boulangism) and radicals (who refused to make alliances with Boulangists), Ferroul held on to his deputy's seat in 1889.[38]

In the 1890s, however, socialist fortunes in the Aude did not follow those of socialists nationally. Whereas the 1893 elections brought Guesde, Vaillant, and Millerand to the Chamber of Deputies (Jaurès had been elected as a socialist in a by-election earlier that year), Ferroul lost to a radical, and Félix Aldy lost to the opportunist large vineyard owner Adolphe Turrel (Table 19).[39] Socialist supporters charged that the elections had been fixed. In Coursan women banged on pots and pans to protest the ballot count, an angry crowd threatened a radical member of the municipal council, and the mayor was struck on the head. Fights broke out, and a detachment of cavalry from Narbonne finally charged in to disperse the demonstrators. The incident vividly demonstrated the growing division between radicals and socialists at the base, among rural villagers, even if the programs of the groups' leaders were essentially similar.[40]

Again in 1898, while the POF sent twelve deputies to Paris (seven of whom came from the south), socialists in the Aude lost elections to Opportunists (see Table 19). This time, charges of electoral fraud precipitated a parliamentary inquiry, invalidation of the elections, and the withdrawal of the Opportunist

Table 19. Legislative Elections of 1893, 1898, and 1902 in the Narbonnais (percent of votes cast)

	Socialist	Radical	Opportunist	Conservative	Abstentions
1893					
Narbonne I	48.2	50.5	—	—	40.5
Narbonne II	36.1	—	62.4	—	29.1
Coursan commune	30.1	—	69.8	—	36.3
1898					
Narbonne I					
1st ballot	44.7	9.7	44.8	—	24.5
2d ballot	49.4	—	49.9	—	—
Narbonne II	27.4	—	51.0	19.8	20.8
Coursan commune					
1st ballot	38.3	5.9	51.9	—	37.1
2d ballot	47.8	—	51.8	—	—
1902					
Narbonne I					
1st ballot	48.2	—	29.6/21.3[a]	—	23.8
2d ballot	51.1	—	47.0	—	—
Narbonne II		50.4	27.3	—	21.0
Coursan commune					
1st ballot	35.0	—	32.4/31.3[a]	—	42.4
2d ballot	38.9	—	60.9	—	—

Source: AD Aude 2M58, "Recensement général des votes, 1876–1914."

[a] Two opportunists ran in Narbonne I in 1902: Adolphe Turrel and Félix Liouville; Turrel won on the second ballot in Coursan.

candidate.[41] As in 1893, abstentions in Coursan were much higher (36 percent in 1893, 37 percent in 1898) than the national average during the Third Republic (29 percent).[42]

The reversal of fortune for socialist politicians in the Narbonnais is curious, given an apparently well-organized popular base in villages throughout the area. To be sure, the existence of *groupes d'études sociales* and socialist free-thought societies did not guarantee electoral victories—particularly since socialism in the Aude was dominated by a small number of powerful personalities. Workers and former landowners who had become full- or part-time workers may have been alienated by Ferroul's lack of interest in the rural working class. In 1893 in Coursan, where

the voting population included over 500 vineyard workers, Ferroul received only 253 votes (and abstentions reached 41 percent); clearly, he did not have the full support of agricultural
workers.

In both 1893 and 1898, however, employer pressure on workers to vote for the Opportunist or abstain may have also played a
role. It was common knowledge that *régisseurs* used electoral
pressure to intimidate workers and score a few points with the
patron, and in this period of low wages and stiff competition for
jobs workers quite likely responded.[43] In addition, the suspi-
cious combination of socialist losses and high abstentions, which
reached 40 percent in winegrowing areas, may have resulted
because radicals and socialists represented similar interests in
the countryside.[44] Not only did both present themselves as defenders of petty bourgeois vineyard owners, but some radical
candidates even called themselves socialists. This is not entirely
surprising, for even after the formation of the Radical party
radical leaders in the Aude referred to the party as the Parti
républicain radical et radical socialiste.[45] Finally, at the same
time that local political movements became more integrated into
national politics, charismatic local political leaders and favorite
sons continued to pull considerable weight, even as they replaced the notables who had controlled local politics in an earlier
age.[46] Thus, in the 1890s climate of agricultural depression and
antirepublican reaction—when the Panama scandal and the
Dreyfus affair challenged the republic and divided the left—
Opportunist Adolphe Turrel, who defeated socialist Paul Narbonne in 1898, could benefit from his image as the paternalistic
notable and *grand propriétaire* to promote himself as the candidate
of *défense viticole*. Moreover, Turrel actually addressed some of
the problems of agricultural workers, which neither Ferroul nor
Aldy did. In fact, when wine prices fell drastically after the 1893
harvest it was Turrel, not Ferroul or Aldy, who spoke to the
plight of rural laborers.[47]

With the turn of the century, however, socialists suddenly
awakened to the potential of mobilizing agricultural workers. As
the wine market depression of 1900–1901 once again brought
the economy of the Aude to its knees, Ferroul and Aldy paid
somewhat more attention to vineyard workers, whose situation

had been steadily worsening. In an effort to address the growing unemployment in rural villages, Ferroul now proposed a law (which passed in the Chamber of Deputies on January 16, 1902) easing the rules that governed the financing of public works projects and authorizing communes to employ workers on these projects for the duration of the depression.[48] Likewise, Aldy proposed legislation to regulate work conditions; establish a minimum wage, retirement funds, unemployment insurance, and social insurance for all workers, agricultural and industrial alike; and extend laws on work-related accidents to agricultural workers.[49] With support from the Radical Federation of the Aude, Aldy now beat Turrel in the legislative contest of 1902. Still, it is not clear that Aldy captured the support of vineyard workers everywhere. In Coursan, for instance, 24 percent of the voters (though not necessarily only vineyard workers) abstained, and much of his support in the district came from railway workers, building workers, and artisans in Narbonne. One thing is clear, though: in 1902 the political constellation shifted as the revolutionary syndicalist unions began to organize vineyard workers throughout the Aude.

Ferroulist socialism in the Aude was very different from the socialism in the Var painted by Tony Judt, and somewhat more akin to that described by Harvey Smith and Jean Sagnes for the Hérault.[50] In contrast to the revolutionary collectivism of Varois Guesdists—notably Allard—Guesdists in the Aude (like their counterparts in the Hérault) followed the more moderate path of left radicals in supporting artisans and small winegrowers. One is thus inclined to accept Claude Willard's assessment of Guesdist socialism in Mediterranean France (which Judt rejects for the Var) as plausible for the Aude:

> On the shores of the Mediterranean, the POF took up where Jacobinism and radicalism left off. Voters and even party members didn't attach themselves to its specifically socialist or its revolutionary or Marxist character; rather, they came to the POF as the most advanced party, the most republican party . . . the most democratic party. . . . In this region, Guesdism . . . allowed itself to be reshaped, in part absorbed, by different political currents that were more or less colored by socialism.[51]

Rather than adopt cooperative solutions to rural depression, which Judt argues the peasants in the Var did, winegrowers in the Aude looked toward an interventionist and protectionist state. This was the basis of their attraction to socialism. Moreover, the ideal of state protection for southern wine producers—not the revolutionary expropriation of capital or political power—was what lay at the heart of the great winegrowers' revolt of 1907. And this ideal was, of course, shared by both radicals and socialists. In fact, the frequent blurring of distinction between radicalism and socialism in the Aude may help to explain why socialism had difficulty expanding beyond the Narbonnais, and why radical "favorite sons" remained more solidly entrenched there than in the rest of lower Languedoc.

Not only the character of Audois Guesdism differed from that of the Var, but rural constituents' responses to socialism differed as well. Judt argues that in the Var small producers' collective patterns of existence—their interdependence and cooperation—led them to "political movements which appealed to collective interests."[52] In the Aude, the agglomerated urban village facilitated the transmission of socialist ideas, and day-to-day relations between workers and small vineyard owners influenced these groups' perceptions of shared interests. As we shall see, the physical setting of the village itself furthered labor solidarity. But the idea of cooperation coexisted with a fierce independence on the part of small growers, workers, and artisans. This independence appeared in the revolutionary syndicalism of workers and small producers, and in the near absence of practical cooperative approaches to production and distribution in the Aude (in cooperative wineries, for example) before World War I.[53]

Although socialists in the Narbonnais did not appeal directly to rural vinedressers, these men could not help but be influenced by the activism of the 1880s and 1890s. Through their involvement in local socialist organizations—the *chambrées socialistes* and *libre pensée* societies—and in the Bourse du travail supported by the socialist municipality in Narbonne, agricultural workers came to associate and share a common political culture with artisans and small winegrowers. Socialist politics helped to create the rural working class by giving workers a language in which to express their grievances and new lenses through which to view their identity as workers. In the end, though, revolutionary syndicalism, its limitations notwithstanding, was far more successful than socialism in mobilizing agricultural workers and winning them tangible gains in the years before World War I.

6

REVOLUTIONARY SYNDICALISM
AND DIRECT ACTION

On an unseasonably cold May morning in 1903, in the sleepy village of Peyriac de Mer, ninety-five workers on one of the largest vineyards in the Narbonnais laid down their tools, walked out of the vines, and declared the formation of a labor union. Resisting their employer's efforts to increase their working hours—but not their wages—they pointed out that he had made 200,000 francs on his last harvest, and refused to return to work until he had granted them a wage increase.[1] This uneventful and short-lived strike was the first in a long series of occasionally violent confrontations between labor unions and vineyard owners that spread throughout the Midi before World War I. From 1903 to 1914, the peaceful vineyards of the south saw some of the most dramatic conflicts between labor and capital and between vinegrowers and the state of the prewar years, which culminated in the famous winegrowers' revolt of 1907.

This explosion of mass protest was created and coordinated by the revolutionary syndicalist labor unions that formed in the densely populated urban villages of the south. In the Aude, the labor movement drew on both the community solidarities and the class differences aroused by prolonged economic depression, and reflected the shifting class identity of vinedressers. Although workers' identity was undoubtedly shaped by their contact with socialism, labor leaders tried to present an alternative to political socialism, and between 1903 and 1914 they rejected collaboration with socialist politicians. Yet, just as Audois socialism developed along reformist rather than revolutionary lines, syndicalism in the Aude focused on bread-and-butter improvements for workers instead of social revolution. Syndicalism, like socialism, developed tactically, in response to local conditions, interests, and capacities for action. This was both its strength and, ultimately, its weakness in the Aude.

The Emergence of Agricultural Unions in the Aude

From the early 1880s, under the impact of the depression and following the legalization of labor unions, an organized labor movement began to take shape all over southern France. In the Aude in the 1880s, agricultural workers in the Minervois, northwest of Narbonne, formed insurance societies to assist in the expenses of illness, funerals, and unemployment.[2] When the wine depression of the 1890s threatened workers with unemployment and unskilled Spanish workers began to compete with local workers for scarce jobs, vineyard workers took the first steps toward unionizing. Rumors that estates in Narbonne had hired Spanish workers in exchange for a meal sparked a protest meeting in October 1896. Local workers drafted a letter to the prefect, asking that he protect the interests of French workers by discouraging the employment of Spaniards.[3] In 1897, vineyard workers in Narbonne, Cuxac, and Ouveillan formed the earliest agricultural workers' unions; four years later, workers in Bages, Coursan, Lézignan, and Ornaisons organized. By early 1905, sixty-seven agricultural workers' unions had emerged in the Aude, grouping close to seven thousand members (Table 20).[4] These unions developed under the influence of local Bourses du travail, all affiliated with the revolutionary syndicalist Confédération générale du travail (CGT). The Bourses in the Aude—in Carcassonne from 1892, and in Narbonne from 1893—functioned much as Bourses elsewhere: first and foremost as job placement bureaus, but also as social and educational centers for the working class. They maintained libraries; sponsored lectures; gave courses in grafting, pruning, and shoemaking; and, during the wine crisis, offered unemployed workers jobs on public works projects.[5] The Bourses played an important role in organizing vineyard workers in the Narbonnais. The Coursan union provides a good example of early-twentieth-century vineyard workers' organizations, their leadership, and their social base.

The wine market crisis of 1900–1901 brought major wage cutbacks for Audois workers, and large vineyard owners laid off

Table 20. Vineyard Workers' Union Membership in Coursan and in the Aude, 1900–1914

	No. Unions (Aude)	No. Members (Aude)	Average Union Size (Aude)	No. Members (Coursan)
1900	5	293	58.6	170
1902	6	393	65.5	
1903	—	—	—	166
1904	—	—	—	350
1905	67	6,346	103.7	—
1907	—	—	—	487
1909	67	3,900	58.2	76
1910	—	—	—	200
1911	60	2,742	45.7	—
1912	—	—	—	408
1914	51	3,606	70.7	470

Source: France, Ministère du Travail et de la prévoyance sociale, *Annuaire des syndicats professionnels, industriels, commerciaux et agricoles* (1900–1914) (Paris: Imprimerie nationale, 1900–1914). Data are missing for 1901, 1906, 1908, and 1913.

even more workers than usual during the slow months of January, February, and March. On a rainy April day in 1901, members of the Narbonne Bourse du travail gathered 170 workers from Coursan in the Café Pech (appropriately enough, on the rue de la Révolution) and formed the Syndicat des cultivateurs et travailleurs de la terre de Coursan.[6] The term *cultivateur* in the union's name reflected its diverse membership. For in addition to landless laborers, the union also included impoverished small property owners who now worked part-time on the large estate vineyards. Even for those who were no longer landowners, the term *cultivateur* reflected members' self-perception as independent craftsmen, as men who were masters of their own destiny— and therefore not thoroughly proletarianized. The conflation of the term *cultivateur* with the sense of day laborer also appeared in the regional agricultural workers' federation (see below), which appealed to "this poor martyr who is called *cultivateur* or *terrassier* because . . . for a long time our sweat has watered this earth that feeds the capitalists."[7]

Although no records for the union survive, other sources provide some insight into its membership. The twenty-six union members who were arrested during the strikes of December 1904, for example, had a mean age of thirty-eight. The fact that only four were actually born in Coursan, although all lived and worked there, reflected the great geographic mobility of vineyard workers in the post-phylloxera years.[8] The experience of François Cheytion, who headed the Coursan union from 1903 until his death in 1914, typified the mobility of young rural working-class men at the turn of the century. This vineyard laborer was born in Montpellier, Hérault, on January 14, 1875, the oldest son of Louis Cheytion and Marie Borie, both vineyard workers. Like many working-class families living in Coursan around 1900, the Cheytions had fled the Hérault during the phylloxera crisis sometime in the 1880s. In Coursan they found jobs working the vines and continued to raise their family, which by the turn of the century had grown by three more children.[9] After finishing school, François immediately went to work in the vineyards; military service took him briefly away from Coursan, but he returned, and in 1898 he joined the *cercle d'études sociales* there. This began a political education that eventually led him to run unsuccessfully for a deputy's seat from the Hérault in the 1902 legislative elections.[10] Perhaps this disappointing experience (he received only one vote!) fueled his syndicalist disdain for the legislative process. Later that year he joined the union in Coursan and rapidly became one of its most vocal and active members.

The Coursan vineyard workers' union represented the narrow, male-dominated craft unionism that developed throughout France in the nineteenth century. It did not initially invite women or unskilled workers (*domestiques* or *terrassiers*) into its ranks, and few foreign workers dared join at first for fear of being expelled from France. *Domestiques* and other foreign unskilled workers did, however, often support syndicalists' strikes.[11]

Most of the agricultural unions in the Aude were plainly hostile to women's wage work and took a frankly opportunistic position on women's union participation. Union members were fully aware that single women needed their wages, as did married women whose husbands' wages were inadequate. Although

they condemned the exploitation of women, citing their low
wages, the physical demands of their work, and employers' efforts to replace male with female workers, their real fear was
competition from women. In addition, they worried that women
were too easily manipulated by capital and would therefore
weaken the union's bargaining position. These views were by no
means peculiar to the Coursan union; they characterized unions
throughout the south, which, prior to about 1909, sought to
remove women from the workplace altogether.[12] Failing that,
they argued for admitting women into the unions and for pursu-
ing equal wages for equal work: "This . . . will . . . be profitable
from the moral as well as the material point of view; it will be one
more step toward the total suppression of wage work for women,
who will henceforth be returned to domestic work, the hearth,
and the family."[13]

Some in the labor movement disagreed, arguing that women
should be allowed to remain in the labor force but should be
excluded from men's work. In any case, the entire discussion of
women's work and union participation reflected an essentially
masculine concept of class, and reinforced the gender boundaries of rural society.[14]

The unions' negative attitude toward women's work by no
means prevented the male membership of the Syndicat des cultivateurs et travailleurs de la terre de Coursan from growing. As
Table 20 shows, the Coursan union almost tripled in size in six
years, with about half the skilled vineyard workers in the village
counting as members by 1907. (These workers were well unionized in relation to the rest of the French labor force as well: only
10–13 percent of French labor was unionized prior to World
War I, and of these about half were revolutionary syndicalists;
the average size of French unions was about 170.) But even
official membership figures do not measure the Coursan union's
real strength, for often during strikes twice as many workers
walked off the job as actually belonged to the union.[15]

Agricultural syndicalists in villages like Coursan followed the
ideas and aims of the CGT's 1906 Charter of Amiens: the primacy of class struggle, the self-emancipation of the working
class, the use of direct economic action (as opposed to legislation) to obtain bread-and-butter benefits (*la lutte quotidienne*), the

ultimate goal of expropriating the capitalists by means of a revolutionary general strike. But like workers everywhere that affiliated with the syndicalist-inspired CGT, the unionized agricultural workers in the Aude took these ideals on board and interpreted them to serve their own interests and needs, emphasizing some and leaving others aside. Thus in the Aude, the rejection of electoral politics became an important piece of the rhetorical repertoire of some syndicalist activists. Labor leaders wanted to avoid potential political divisions among the rank and file; they also wanted to prevent the unions from being controlled or manipulated by political parties—the way many, for example, felt that unions in the Nord were manipulated by the Guesdists.[16] For some this meant keeping union activities separate from political activities; for others it meant abstaining from voting in elections. In any case, the revolutionary rhetoric was vital to mobilizing workers: the ideology of the general strike gave workers an awareness of their own power independent of politicians.[17] Otherwise, the union regulations pledged to establish "solidarity and mutual defense between members," and to work toward a society in which workers would finally achieve "well-being and freedom" *(bien-être et liberté)*.[18]

On a more practical level, many agricultural unions in the Aude set up placement offices for workers, sickness insurance and unemployment funds, and assistance for traveling workers. Not all rank-and-file members looked toward long-term revolutionary goals such as expropriation of the vineyards; many joined unions for immediate reasons: increased wages, improved working conditions, and job security.[19] After all, while waiting for the revolution workers had to eat. Moreover, from 1900 on the CGT encouraged workers to obtain contracts, which, apart from regulating basic material conditions, forced employers to recognize the union as *the* bargaining agent of the worker. By 1904, four unions in the Aude had succeeded in this goal: those of Montlaur, Rieux-Minervois, Salles d'Aude, and Vinassan.[20] The signing of contracts, which from one standpoint might be considered "trade unionist" rather than revolutionary syndicalist, was in fact a tremendous victory for vineyard workers whose working conditions and wages had hitherto been determined by custom and by verbal agreements.

Three factors influenced the spread of syndicalism among vineyard workers: skill, collective workplace solidarity, and the southern French village community. First, as we have seen, the majority of local male vineyard workers were skilled (in contrast to the Spanish and Italian farmhands who began to compete with local workers toward the end of the nineteenth century). Planting, grafting, pruning, cultivation, and the application of chemicals all required manual dexterity and training. As Michael Hanagan has pointed out, artisans' determination to exercise control over working conditions and to assert their independence on the shop floor went hand in hand with both skill and their feeling that they were more knowledgeable about their work than the *patron*.[21] Although vineyard workers were not threatened by mechanization, they did suffer a loss of autonomy and declining wages. Syndicalism's attraction lay in its promise of a direct defense against proletarianization, as opposed to the more distant legislative protection promised by politicians.

Second, the skilled teams of ten to fifteen *ouvriers volants* or *colles* in which vineyard workers were organized allowed them to communicate at the work site, and their collective control over wages (they were paid as a group and divided the wage among themselves) was another element promoting "shop floor" solidarity. Team workers had a reputation for independence; they thus brought their own self-emancipatory style to Audois syndicalism.[22]

Third, the unions emerged from the same traditions of associational life that inspired the secret *démoc soc* societies of the 1850s and the *cercles d'études sociales* and *libre pensée* societies of the early Third Republic. The urban village community and local sociability facilitated the development of worker solidarity. Vineyard workers, artisans, and small vineyard owners who lived close to one another in protourban villages shared a social life in cafés and clubs that easily became transformed into centers of syndicalist activity.[23]

Skill, the work setting, and community life all reinforced people's consciousness of collective interests and were conducive to the development of syndicalist unions. But as Ronald Aminzade has noted, "Class entails more than a rational awareness and identification by workers of their own class interests. It also involves a recognition that those interests are in conflict with the class interests of the owners of capital and employers of their labor power."[24] The importance of syndicalism was precisely that: it provided workers with a discourse of conflict and resistance and ultimately brought them into the streets.

Workers Take Action

Between 1903 and 1905, thousands of agricultural workers in the Aude struck for higher wages and better working conditions. These strikes, beginning with the walkout at Peyriac de Mer, shared two characteristics. First, they were preeminently expressions of the moral economy of vineyard villages; second, they relied on the solidarity of whole winegrowing communities.

The notion of a moral economy, as historians E. P. Thompson, Louise, Charles, and Richard Tilly and the anthropologist James C. Scott have observed, was a fundamental component of precapitalist peasant societies. In early modern Europe, this concept obliged landlords and seigneurs to guarantee peasants, in the absence of civil and political rights, minimum social and economic rights, including gleaning after harvests and access to provisions in time of economic shortfall.[25] Custom dictated that landlords and political authorities use their influence in the market to insure a "just price" for daily necessities in the peasant budget: what this amounted to was the social right to subsistence.[26]

The growth of capitalist market relations, laissez-faire liberal political economy, and popular representation led to the temporary disappearance of the paternalistic idea that employers and landlords should insure these basic rights. Later the welfare state took over the function of providing for basic subsistence in the absence of personal resources. But this did not mean that for peasants and workers the ideal of a moral economy disappeared; rather, the concept now applied to a larger, more complex relationship, involving the employer, the market, the worker, and the wage. During the prosperous golden age of the vineyards, when custom and informal agreements regulated the price of labor (and labor was in a relatively strong bargaining position), the moral economy of the wage insured workers a just return. In a period of crisis, however, when the new entrepreneurial mentality sought to extract a maximum effort from workers at the lowest possible price, those customary relations broke down: employers no longer adhered to the moral economy. Awareness of this violation marked many of the seventy-two vineyard workers' strikes that occurred in the Aude in 1903 and 1904. The strike of January 12–21, 1904, in Coursan illustrates how vineyard workers sought to reassert this primitive balance of local justice.

Interestingly, workers in Coursan first struck not at the height of the turn-of-the-century *crise de mévente*, but during the brief recovery that followed in 1903. A meager harvest had allowed wine prices to rise to 20 francs per hectoliter, thus raising workers' hopes that wages might follow the logic of both the market and the moral economy. Not only were their expectations dashed, but their situation even worsened: employers did not increase wages, and from mid November on, owing to intense rains and flooding in the vineyards, workers were laid off. Some employers began paying workers on piece rates to cut costs.[27] Such practices had already led to strikes in the Hérault— strikes that resulted in the formation of unions and favorable settlements for workers.[28] The success of these actions encouraged workers elsewhere to call for change. Thus, when employers refused to accept a long list of demands in January 1904, the Coursan union met, resolved to show employers that "the worker has a right to live," and called a strike for the following day.[29]

On a brisk January morning villagers took to the streets. Someone hoisted a red flag in the bell tower of the church, and workers paraded with a red flag and a drum, singing the "Internationale" and shouting, "Vive la grève!" Some danced to the tune of the "Carmagnole" in front of the village hall. A journalist, astonished at the contrast between the almost carnival atmosphere of the strike in Coursan and the sobriety of the industrial strikes he had witnessed, observed, "Here strikers march with the flag of their demands and the rags and tatters of their poverty in a town humming with activity, where people are happy to live under . . . [blue] sky and the sun."[30] Workers appropriated public space en masse: the whole village became the union. The moderate republican mayor gave the strike committee a meeting room in the *mairie* and closed the village to all traffic. His support was not unusual: republican officials wanted to assure support from vineyard workers in an election year (municipal elections would occur later in 1904); moreover, many mayors and prefects were clearly hostile to politically conservative large proprietors.[31]

The Coursan union did not articulate the idea of the moral economy in its strike demands, which included a standard wage of 3.50 francs for a seven-hour day, suppression of piecework and of payment by the job (*travail à forfait*), the promise that no worker would be fired for striking, and the stipulation that women would be paid half what men earned, except for sulphuring, when they would earn exactly the same as men.[32] The assertion of a moral economy was present, however, in the action itself. Workers had seen the price of wine rise after the 1903 harvest and fully expected to benefit; they also knew that the highly competitive and now depressed market differed substantially from that of the golden age and so did not expect wages to return to pre-phylloxera levels. The demand for a just wage involved the recognition that their employers profited from the price increase "through violations of [their] own duties and other people's rights."[33] This was the same kind of argument used by the workers of Peyriac de Mer, who expected to benefit from the 200,000 franc profit their employer had made on his last harvest.

The notions of justice and the moral economy also surfaced later around issues other than the wage. In Fleury in November 1905, for instance, workers struck against an estate owner who they believed did not employ enough workers for the size of his vineyard.[34] But in the age of competitive market relations, the idea of the moral economy—or even of the right to work—meant little to employers.

Family and community solidarity was a second important component of strike activity in the Aude. The Coursannais who struck in January 1904 counted on the support of their families and of the entire village. Women marched and demonstrated with the men even though they were excluded from the union; women and children patrolled the vineyards to discourage strikebreakers from working. Shops closed, and local businesses shut down. Artisans took up collections for the strike fund, and workers as far away as Brest sent contributions to their comrades in Coursan.[35] Nearby supporters sent food. Community solidarity also appeared in the official strike statistics, which put the number of strikers at 1,000 (700 men, 250 women, and 50 children), even though the union counted only about 350 members at this time. The truly impressive support of small proprietors, artisans, and village merchants demonstrated their collective dependence on the vineyard economy—to which the union appealed in its "call to solidarity":

> Our exploiters refuse to recognize our right to live; those who produce nothing absorb everything, while the laboring class that produces all the social wealth has no bread for itself and its children. . . . Our wages do not permit us to live; in spite of our good intentions, we cannot pay the baker and the grocer who have done us favors in hard times.
>
> Comrades, with the spirit of solidarity, strike with us to prove to the bourgeoisie that the working class is united; do as we are doing; stop your work. Let women, small shopkeepers, and small proprietors . . . lend us their moral support.[36]

Higher wages for workers would, of course, enable village merchants to survive; yet interprofessional solidarity during strikes also emerged from artisans' own history of struggle over workplace issues, and from their experience of organizing with vineyard workers in political groups and clubs or in the Bourse du travail.[37]

Community support was one factor that accounted for the strike's success. In an agreement reached on January 21, nine days after the strike began, the union won all but two of its original demands. Employers refused to eliminate payment by the job but agreed to a modified version of an across-the-board wage increase, to 3.50 francs for a seven-hour day from February to October, but not during the slower winter months.[38] This settlement was significant: for the first time *journaliers* in Coursan succeeded in establishing a minimum wage for workers on all estate vineyards in the village.

Table 21. Strikes in the Aude, 1903–1907

	No. Strikes	No. Strikers	Outcome[a]			Mean Duration (days)	Mean Size
			S	F	C		
1903	1	95	0	0	1	8.0	95
1904[b]	50	4,434	30	2	18	6.9	125
	22	4,599	—	—	—	14.0	209
1905	7	546	4	2	1	16.0[c]	78
1906	3	393	3	0	0	2.0	131
1907	4	391	1	0	3	24.5[d]	130

Source: France, Ministère de commerce, Direction du travail, *Statistique des grèves et des recours à l'arbitrage* (1903–1907) (Paris: Imprimerie nationale, 1904–1908).

[a]S = success, F = failure, C = compromise

[b]Strikes prior to the general strike of Dec. 1904–Feb. 1905 are listed first; those involved in the general strike are second.

[c]Includes a long strike of eighty-three days; otherwise, mean duration was five days.

[d]Includes a long strike of eighty days; otherwise, mean duration was six days.

Successful strikes boosted the morale of unions throughout the Aude. By the end of March 1904 some nine thousand vineyard workers had struck in forty-five Audois villages (Table 21). Contemporaries estimated that 150 strikes had occurred in the Aude, the Hérault, the Pyrénées-Orientales, the Gard, and the Bouches-du-Rhône, involving approximately fifty thousand workers.[39] Almost everywhere in the Aude, workers succeeded in obtaining wage increases and improved working conditions, including the suppression of piecework and better wine allocations. These victories, however, were short-lived. Most workers still had no contracts, and employers were under no pressure to respect strike settlements.[40] When in the following months the price of wine again fell to turn-of-the-century levels, proprietors refused to honor the recent accords, and cut hours and wages. In March and April 1904, and at the end of October, strikes broke out anew in Coursan, Fleury, and Canet after employers laid off workers.[41] Employers' violation of earlier agreements, together with workers' continued willingness to resist, encouraged radical activists in the labor movement who argued for a general strike.

The FTAM and the General Strike

Led by an activist minority that included François Cheytion from Coursan and Paul Ader from Cuxac d'Aude, and inspired by the rush of unionization after the turn of the century, a regional agricultural workers' organization, the Fédération des travailleurs agricoles du Midi (FTAM), formed in Béziers in 1903. This new federation comprised close to fifteen thousand members at its peak in 1904 (Table 22) in the five departments of the Aude, the Hérault, the Pyrénées-Orientales, the Gard, and the Bouches-du-Rhône. Affiliated with the CGT, the FTAM attempted to coordinate strikes and create links between vineyard workers throughout the Mediterranean region through annual congresses and the union newspaper *Le Paysan* (replaced in 1907 by *Le Travailleur de la terre*, edited by Paul Ader). An initially diverse membership included vineyard workers, revolutionary syndicalists, anarchists, and small proprietors, and early congresses reflected a mixture of interests ranging from millenarian appeals for revolution by means of a general strike to wage issues and the creation of legislation (on work accidents, retirement, and agricultural *conseils de prud'hommes*) to benefit agricultural workers.[42] Increasingly, however, radicals like Cheytion dominated the federation; these men condemned the idea of working for social legislation, arguing instead for direct action and a general strike of agricultural workers across lower Languedoc.[43] The attempted general strike of 1904–1905 shows the limits of syndicalist action on a regional basis; in the evolution of the FTAM we see how a militant revolutionary syndicalist minority tried to push the labor movement in the Aude forward.

From the very founding of the FTAM, agricultural workers had debated the idea of a general strike to standardize wages and hours across the region. In fact, the 1904 settlements differed markedly from locality to locality and from department to department. In Lézignan, Aude, for instance, workers won a six-hour day in winter and a nine-hour day in summer, whereas in Carcassonne winter hours were seven and summer, eight. Likewise, hourly wages varied from 35 centimes in Carcassonne to 50 centimes in Coursan and in villages around Montpellier, Hérault.[44] Although rank-and-file union members such as small

Table 22. FTAM Membership in the Aude, the Hérault, the Gard, and the Pyrénées-Orientales, 1904–1912

	1904	1905[a]	1906	1907	1908	1911	1912
No. members	14,804	9,747	4,470	1,721	3,360	6,000	4,000
No. unions	145	157	143	108	71	64[b]	83

Sources: Fédération des travailleurs agricoles du Midi, *Compte rendu des travaux du 5e Congrès de la Fédération des travailleurs agricoles et partis similaires du Midi* (Bourges: Imprimerie ouvrière du Centre—ouvriers syndiqués et fédérés, 1907), 19–20; Philippe Gratton, *Les luttes de classes dans les campagnes* (Paris: Anthropos, 1971), 193, 195. Data are missing for 1909, 1910, 1913, and 1914.

Note: Only four unions in the Aude were not members of the FTAM in 1905. By 1908, however, only twenty-eight unions from the Aude were represented in the Federation congress in Narbonne, and in 1910 only ten. In the interim (after 1907), the FTAM had expelled many unions that continued to support the CGV. See Gratton, *Luttes de classes,* 166, 191–193.

[a] Figure for first trimester; by the last trimester membership had declined even further to 5,551.

[b] Figure for 1910.

proprietors were frankly unenthusiastic about an additional untimely and costly work stoppage, the FTAM called a strike for December 1, 1904,[45] appealing to "the exploited of the earth" to unite in striking for standardized wages and working conditions for vineyards throughout southern France.[46]

The strike call caused close to ten thousand workers to walk off the job in the Aude, the Hérault, and the Pyrénées-Orientales alone, with half of the strikes (twenty-two of forty-one) occurring in the Aude (see Table 21). Here the issue of the moral economy of the village community was somewhat less visible than earlier. In some villages, workers had already gained many of the conditions spelled out in the strike demands; elsewhere workers struck for as yet unachieved conditions: the 50 centime minimum wage and the suppression of piecework. These men and women did not see the general strike as leading to a transformation of capitalist viticulture; rather, they viewed a corporative mass strike as a means to win additional concessions from employers.

Moreover, syndicalists now used violence and sabotage to force employers' hands. In early December 1904 in Coursan and Fleury, strikers set fire to the doorways of houses and burned a

pile of vine trimmings at the château on the Salles d'Aude estate
of Celeyran. In Pouzols they raided a proprietor's wine cellar
and dumped out seven hundred hectoliters of wine, and in
Mirepeisset they pushed a railway car onto the main line, intend-
ing to provoke a derailment. In Fleury they cut telegraph lines.
In Ventenac d'Aude at the end of January strikers broke into a
régisseur's home and tried to force him to resign; in St-Nazaire
they broke into a château, cut the telephone lines, and threatened the owner, compelling him to sign their list of demands.[47]
The recourse to violence spoke volumes about the escalation of
class tension in the space of a few months.

Again community solidarity provided essential strike support.
Masons, wagon drivers, wine cellar workers, and carpenters all
walked out in support of vineyard workers, and in Narbonne the
Bourse du travail organized a general strike of all Bourse affili-
ates.[48] Sympathetic mayors in Coursan, Fleury, and Narbonne
(Ferroul) again supported the strikers, this time by refusing to
accept government troops sent to "protect the right to work" and
by protesting the use of troops to intimidate workers. These men
also protested against military and police obstruction of the right
to strike, as southern left-wing radicals had by now done on
several occasions.[49] In addition, the strike elicited remarkable
solidarity and support between villages. Workers from one village helped those of another; strong unions helped out weak.
Fifty men from Cuxac reinforced strikers in Sallèles; the Narbonne union sent men to Marcorignan; strikers in Coursan,
Armissan, and Vinassan helped their comrades in Fleury. Cy-
clists rode from village to village, carrying messages and relaying
news between union headquarters and workers.[50]

Buoyed by the spirit of intervillage support and emboldened
by strike leaders, unions became more aggressive in imposing
strike discipline and control than in earlier job actions. In Coursan, not only did the union try to prevent traffic from circulating
in the village, but union members now entered the distillers' and
wine merchants' shops to bring employees into the streets to join
the strike.[51] Police apprehended *cultivateurs* for appropriating
provisions from housewives and servants on their way home
from market. These efforts to secure "contributions" to the

strike fund in fact underscored the nearly desperate economic situation of many vineyard workers' families.[52]

Indeed, since the settlements of the previous winter workers' material situation had hardly improved at all. In the Hérault, placards emblazoned with "Du pain ou la mort!" (Bread or death!) appeared during demonstrations, along with flags bordered in black. In the village of Bessan, Hérault, strikers impaled a piece of bread atop the flagstaff, and in Florensac women stood before troops and police shouting, "Du pain!"[53] Women obtained provisions for the strike fund, forced nonstrikers to leave the vineyards, and collected money for strikers in neighboring villages. In Coursan, when the prefect sent mounted police to the village on December 6 to "protect the right to work," a crowd of some two hundred women and children lay down in the main road leading to the village to prevent them from entering. When a fight broke out between demonstrators and police, twenty-one were arrested for "obstructing the freedom to work," including the fifty-three-year-old mother of François Cheytion. Later, in March 1905 in nearby Salles d'Aude, women from Coursan threw themselves on the ground before mounted police who were attempting to disperse a crowd of strikers.[54] In this way women played on the social conventions that regarded them as the "weaker sex" to discourage violence. Their activities reveal much about the importance of community in southern French "urban villages" for forging strike solidarity.

Community support also helped workers win concessions from employers, even though no unions obtained the full list of FTAM conditions. In Vinassan workers demanded the firing of a *régisseur* who refused to respect their contract; this the employer did, and *journaliers* returned to work. In Montredon and Cuxac employers promised to abide by earlier accords, and workers won a shorter workday and an increased wine allocation. In Sallèles d'Aude workers and employers signed a renewable contract for the first time. In Coursan a compromise settlement resulted in proprietors agreeing to provide work for the unemployed on public works projects and to increase workers' wine allocation. Most important, employers agreed to recognize different degrees of skill among unionized workers by paying grafters more than other workers: 4 francs for seven hours of work and two liters of wine per day, throughout the year.[55] Despite these favorable settlements, however, as a mass movement the general strike failed.

Fewer than half of Audois unions affiliated with the FTAM (twenty-two of forty-five) followed the strike call. The same situation occurred in the Hérault and Pyrénées-Orientales, and no strikes at all occurred in the Bouches-du-Rhône. Among those unions that did strike, walkouts took place at different times and for different lengths of time. Settlements inevitably departed from the federation guidelines and from those of individual village unions. Workers in Cuxac, for example, settled on lower wages than did their neighbors in Coursan; workers in Sallèles d'Aude abolished piecework, whereas the Coursannais did not. Indeed, as the rank and file had argued earlier, wages, hours, and conditions varied too much from locality to locality and department to department to allow establishment of a regional standard.[56] Finally, the decision to call the strike for December was unquestionably a strategic error. December was one of the least active months in the vineyard calendar, a time when employers would be under little pressure to make concessions. Workers clearly appreciated this fact. It is not surprising, then, that some unions were reluctant to participate in the strike. In the end, both socialists and syndicalists criticized the action— socialists for its "localized, corporatist character" and the fact that workers had given in to the CGT's direct-action tactics, syndicalists for its poor timing.[57]

The general strike's failure had three important consequences for the regional agricultural workers' movement. For one thing—and most noticeably at first glance—union membership declined. As Table 22 suggests, between 1904 and the first trimester of 1905 FTAM membership fell drastically by over five thousand members, even though twelve more unions joined the federation during this period. By the end of 1905 another four thousand members had left. Although not all unions lost members (the Coursan union in fact grew between 1904 and 1907, from 359 to 487; see Table 20), membership fluctuated after 1907. As Paul Ader clearly saw, many workers' narrow vision of unionism meant that the attainment of higher wages and shorter workdays signified the end of the struggle. "Their eagerness declines, their cohesiveness is broken; the viticultural crisis only makes the situation worse; the worker looks no further than holding on to his job."[58] This pattern was not peculiar to agricultural workers; urban industrial workers' union membership also dropped off after periods of prolonged labor conflict.

Second, for those who stayed in the unions willingness to confront employers also appeared to wane in the aftermath of the general strike. Only seven strikes occurred in 1905 and 1906, and only three unions staged job actions (see Table 21). To be sure, the failure of the general strike did enervate the movement, but the continued decline of workers' living standards (see Chapter 6) also made it hard for workers to pay union dues, especially since workers had already sacrificed four or five weeks' wages in the recent strikes. Overall, events in the Aude bear out Charles Tilly and Edward Shorter's finding that before 1914 French workers held back from striking during inflationary periods, precisely because inflation mitigated against advantageous settlements for workers and made strikes doubly costly. This factor undoubtedly influenced the unions' weak participation in the general strike.[59]

Third, the FTAM became increasingly dominated by a radical leadership—Cheytion and Ader—committed to the revolutionary syndicalist idea of an "active minority." As Philippe Gratton has pointed out, whereas before 1905 moderates in the FTAM supported legislative reform such as accident legislation or arbitration councils, these men were soon drowned out by radical activists whose position was strongly antilegislative. In impassioned speeches at annual congresses, Cheytion appealed to workers to abandon politicians' empty promises: only direct action could bring immediate results to the working class; workers should forget about "so-called social legislation" and the meager measures of "les légiféreurs bourgeois."[60] In addition, the FTAM now more openly supported sabotage and boycotts as legitimate tactics in class war, tactics that were part of the arsenal of striking workers elsewhere in France. They also agreed to support the CGT-organized general strike planned for May 1, 1906, as part of a general May First celebration (recently revived at the confederation's 1904 Bourges congress). The CGT proposed to use this movement to demand the eight-hour day; vine-yard workers would use the opportunity to demand a six-hour day (to reduce unemployment), the 50 centime hourly wage, and a wine allocation for all workers throughout the year.[61]

Radical revolutionary syndicalist leaders also shifted their position on collaborating with small vineyard owners to combat fraudulent production of wine—that is, the production of second wines by *chaptalisation*, the dilution of wine with water, and the manufacture of wine from raisins—which most southerners believed to be responsible for the wine market depression. During the spring and early summer of 1905, a populist movement of small vineyard owners was launched in the face of the continued depression. Viticultural defense committees (*comités de défense viticole*) appeared throughout the Narbonnais and in the Bitterois in the Hérault, and the socialist municipality of Narbonne as well as several villages established public works projects for unemployed agricultural workers.[62] When legislation to control fraudulent wine production, sponsored by Audois deputies Félix Aldy, Albert Sarraut, and Gaston Doumergue, failed to pass, the defense committees appealed to the entire winegrowing population to unite behind a tax strike and the resignation of municipalities.[63] Although no mass movement occurred, several municipalities did resign briefly, and villagers prevented authorities from seizing property of those who refused to pay taxes.[64] At first the FTAM denounced fraudulent production of wine and encouraged workers not to participate in it. Later in 1905, however, the federation rejected cooperation with employers in combatting fraud, saying that workers should not waste their time worrying about the sale of a product that did not belong to them but should stick to defending their wages. The FTAM reminded its members that employers had been only too willing to use troops against them during the general strike: "Any economic entente with [them] . . . is contrary to the goal of syndicalism, which is the emancipation of the workers by the workers themselves."[65]

As Philippe Gratton has pointed out, this position threatened to split the FTAM rank and file from federation leaders by ignoring small vineyard owners' vested interest in the struggle against fraud.[66] Moreover, it illustrated the very heterogeneity of union membership and fluidity of class identity that later divided the labor movement. Ultimately, federation members did not follow the militant leadership, joining instead with vineyard owners of all kinds in the huge 1907 winegrowers' protest.

The FTAM's radicalization also appeared in the strong antimilitarism it nurtured prior to World War I, one area where the rank and file and the more radical leadership were in basic agreement. While peasant hostility to military conscription was well known, pre-1906 antimilitarism was largely a protest against use of the army to intimidate workers, protect capital, and break strikes—things that were by now familiar to workers in the Aude.[67] Indeed, the government's use of troops to "protect the right to work" in southern vineyards was well timed to coincide with the building antimilitarist feeling in the CGT. As early as 1900 the CGT launched an effort to organize soldiers and conscripts and called on them not to fire on strikers (the famous *sou au soldat*). Following the general strike, in the spring of 1905 the Narbonne section of the Association internationale antimilitariste appealed to "our friends, soldiers . . . who are merely proletarians torn away from [your] families and . . . work, [you] must not act as the guard dogs of capital!"[68] Soldiers in the Midi, for the most part local men, could not help but be influenced by such appeals. In March 1905, in the first of several incidents in which the military openly sympathized with strikers, the soldiers of the 100th infantry, brought to Salles d'Aude to "maintain order," marched through village streets at night singing the "Internationale" and fraternizing with striking workers.[69] In a similar vein, the arrest and sentencing of the signatories of the antimilitarist *affiche rouge* evoked an angry response. The *affiche*, which urged workers to resist conscription, had been sponsored and signed by a loose group of syndicalists, socialists, and anarchists. After these men were jailed in December 1905, the Syndicat des cultivateurs et travailleurs de la terre de Coursan issued a protest against the "unjust, criminal sentence inflicted on its comrades" and sent a "fraternal, revolutionary greeting to its comrades who are victims of these government atrocities." Union members marched out of their meeting shouting, "A bas les armées; à bas les patries!"[70]

Syndicalists' belief in the importance of the *minorité agissante* led the FTAM leadership onto a more radical path. The gap between an extremist leadership and a more moderate rank and file reflected the heterogeneity of the movement itself, which included not only landless workers—those constituting, in a sense, the beginnings of an agricultural proletariat—but also small vineyard owners. The latter were men whose near impoverishment and status as part-time workers allowed them to identify with the concerns of workers; they sought social legislation for agriculture, participated in the viticultural defense movement, and rejected the use of sabotage. Movement leaders François Cheytion, Paul Ader, and Justin Reynes, however, were not landowners; they had little to lose by rejecting the viticultural defense movement or by supporting sabotage as a weapon in the class war. The more radical stance of the FTAM leadership, then, although it was partly a reaction to the failure of the general strike, was also a reflection of differences between leaders' and rank-and-file workers' relationship to production. Syndicalist leaders' more radical position also extended to the sphere of electoral politics.

Syndicalists, Socialists, and Electoral Politics

Syndicalists had always manifested a certain rhetorical hostility to electoral politics and legislative solutions to workers' problems, but that hostility increased during this period of labor unrest in the Midi. Many syndicalists remained hesitant about if not hostile to collaboration with socialists. As one delegate to the founding congress of the FTAM (in 1903) pointed out, "When [a socialist employer pays] his workers . . . two francs a day and withdraws their wine allocation from the beginning of August, he deserves to be treated as a capitalist and as the enemy of the worker."[71] In the eyes of another syndicalist, socialists were no more trustworthy than radicals or Bonapartists: "If the Empire shot down workers at La Ricamarie, Constans did the same at Fourmies, and Millerand did the same at Chalons . . . were we to have our 'friends' in power, or those who call themselves our friends, it would be the same. . . . How can we be sure that even a socialist government would satisfy our demands?"[72]

Syndicalists' reservations about politics emerged from their practical efforts to establish their independence from political parties. The POF in particular made no secret of its disregard for syndicalist autonomy or syndicalist use of the strike. Ernest Ferroul, for instance, more than once defended the Guesdist position concerning strikes, arguing that the conquest of political power was far more important than the strike to the reconstruction of society; the strike was merely a secondary tool and could not, in and of itself, bring about the revolutionary expropriation of capital.[73] Southern syndicalists knew that Guesdists discouraged the use of strikes elsewhere in France, and it was in this context that their rhetorical distancing from political parties occurred—even after the SFIO supported syndicalist autonomy and in principle accepted the revolutionary value of the general strike. Some workers' hostility to electoral politics resulted also from their own experience of being pressured by employers or estate managers. Not everyone shared these views, however, as Paul Ader implied when he deplored workers' failure to disengage themselves from "democratic prejudices" and their continued attachment to "diverses manifestations éléctorales."[74] In fact Simon Castan, head of the Syndicat des travailleurs de la terre de Narbonne, argued that "it would be madness to think that the proletariat must detach itself from political struggles. Economic action cannot succeed without political action."[75]

Socialist unification in 1905, combined with awareness of the government's willingness to use force against workers, compelled syndicalists throughout France to debate cooperation with Socialists prior to the CGT's 1906 congress at Amiens. Meeting in Arles that summer, the FTAM defeated the proposal of the Fédération du textile for establishing ties between the CGT and the newly unified Socialist party (Section française de l'Internationale ouvrière, or SFIO)—"so that when circumstances warrant it, our exploiters and our governments will find themselves face to face with a united working class."[76] In a heated debate, Paul Ader argued that the Socialist party was a political party like any other, neither more nor less immune to political opportunism. While acknowledging the work of socialist leaders Jaurès, Vaillant, and Sembat, Ader (who had by now left the POF) also attacked Guesde's opposition to the CGT's campaign for the eight-hour day and the reformism of others like Basly, Socialist leader of the miner's union. Were the syndicalists to ally with the Socialists, Ader argued, they would quickly become dominated by the SFIO. The unions would do better to remain autonomous; that way the Socialists would be forced to take them seriously.[77] Thus the FTAM adopted a position that foreshadowed the CGT's rejection of cooperation with the SFIO several months later.

How did the strike movement of 1903–1905 affect election outcomes, and how did syndicalist anti-electoral discourse influence voting behavior in the Aude?[78] The turn-of-the-century economic depression helped Socialists to maintain a base in winegrowing villages of the Aude, and associations like the *groupes d'études sociales*, *cercles de jeunesse socialiste*, and *cercles républicains socialistes-révolutionnaires* continued to function.[79] Socialists captured municipalities in winegrowing towns like Couiza, Salles, and Narbonne, and Socialist municipal councillors sat in Coursan, Sigean, Carcassonne, and Cuxac. Radicalism similarly retained its populist appeal and continued to court small vintners still suffering from the *crise de mévente*. Thus, although Socialists competed with Radicals in municipal politics, regional economic depression and similar positions on both labor issues and solutions to the wine crisis meant that the two groups continued to cooperate in national elections.

Even though Radicalism as a national political force had degenerated "into a party of the 'satisfied' political center, its leading deputies increasingly more hostile to Socialism than to the right," in the Aude (unlike southern departments such as the Hérault, where the formation of the Radical party meant the end of electoral alliances between Radicals and Socialists and presaged the collapse of the governmental Bloc des gauches), the two groups had not yet parted company.[80] In 1906 the SFIO agreed not to run candidates against Radicals in districts where Radicals had strong chances of winning (such as Narbonne II). Radicals likewise cooperated with Socialists in the face of rightist reaction to the 1905 law on separation of church and state.[81]

Although the 1906 elections resulted in a Socialist victory (Aldy) in the district around Narbonne (Narbonne I), in the Aude results overall paralleled those of the elections nationwide: a solid victory for Radicals (Table 23).[82] In the Aude, however,

Table 23. Legislative Elections of 1906 in the Narbonnais (percent of votes cast)

	Socialist	Radical	Opportunist	Conservative	Abstentions
Narbonne I	56.3	—	25.1	17.3	29.1
Narbonne II	4.3	60.7	33.6	—	25.7
Coursan commune	55.1	—	24.5	18.9	45.8

Source: AD Aude 2M58, "Recensement général des votes, 1876–1914."

Radicalism's continued strength emerged not from approval of the use of force by the Combes government to enforce the "right to work." Rather, it stood both as a vote of confidence for local men who took the interests of bankrupt *vignerons* to heart and as a vote against right-wing extremism, which offered little promise for extricating the local economy from its present malaise.

The influence of the strikes of 1903–1905 on the 1906 elections in the Aude is difficult to assess. Socialist Félix Aldy gained votes both in villages in Narbonne I that had experienced strikes (ten out of eleven) and in six villages that had not. But Radicals did the same. As for the working-class vote, workers clearly did not follow the anti-electoral injunctions of syndicalist leaders nationwide; nonetheless, abstentions were especially high in the two villages where syndicalist leaders lived (in Coursan, 46 percent of the voters abstained, and in Cuxac d'Aude, 39 percent)—perhaps as a response to the syndicalists' anti-electoral rhetoric, but also surely as a manifestation of loyalty to local union leaders.[83] As we have seen, however, that loyalty was neither widespread nor enduring.

Revolutionary syndicalism in the Aude developed as both a social movement and a form of activism and protest. As a social movement, it grew out of a political culture indigenous to wine-growing communities and the work culture of skilled vinedressers. As a form of activism and protest, it proved to be a powerful manifestation of working-class solidarity in the vineyards. The rural unions succeeded in mobilizing workers to improve wages, hours, and working conditions and to win contracts as no political movement had yet managed to do. Perhaps their attention to bread-and-butter reforms made them appear more "trade unionist" than revolutionary. Yet wage demands are not as rudimentary as they may at first glance seem; for "by incessantly raising the issue of the value of labor, the working class expresses its fundamental condition in opposition to capital."[84] This happened in the Aude—although, in recognition of the many small vintners who marched arm in arm with landless workers in these early labor conflicts, it was, we must add, in opposition to *le grand capital*. In this respect syndicalism succeeded as an alternative to socialism, as a movement that could extract concessions from employers—but only very briefly.

Once workers' demands were met they withdrew from the unions, and the ranks of rural syndicalism shrank, leaving behind a radical activist rump. The next chapter examines how the winegrowers' revolt of 1907 and its aftermath further weakened and divided the labor movement. For it called into question the collaboration of workers and small vineyard owners and, indeed, the whole nature of class solidarity, and led union leaders to attempt to barricade the unions in an uncompromisingly workerist vision of class struggle that distanced vineyard workers even more from the Socialist movement in the Aude.

Plate 1.   Coursan: the main street and town hall, ca. 1907

Plate 2.   Villagers in Fleury, Aude, before World War I (Private collection of Rémy Pech)

Plate 3.   Workers in the Narbonnais, ca. 1913 (Private collection of Rémy Pech)

Plate 4.   Women doing laundry in the Aude River, ca. 1900

Plate 5. Demonstrators in front of Town Hall, Narbonne, May 1907 (Photo Bouscarle-Sallis, Narbonne)

Plate 6. "The Last Crust": carried by demonstrators from Ginestas in 1907 (Photo Bouscarle-Sallis, Narbonne)

Plate 7.   Demonstrators from Canet, Aude, in 1907 (Photo Bouscarle-Sallis, Narbonne)

Plate 8. Women from the Aude demonstrate in 1907 (Photo Bouscarle-Sallis, Narbonne)

Plate 9. Women and children from the village of Bages demonstrating in 1907 (Photo Bouscarle-Sallis, Narbonne)

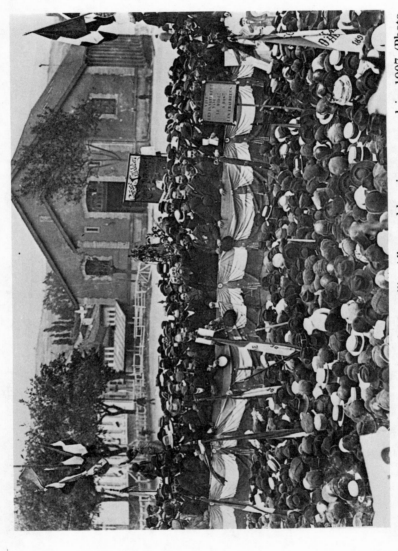

Plate 10. Ernest Ferroul and Marcellin Albert addressing a crowd in 1907 (Photo Bouscarle-Sallis, Narbonne)

7

WORKERS, SOCIALISTS, AND THE WINEGROWERS' REVOLT OF 1907

In early March in the tiny hill village of Argelliers in the Aude, a café owner and small vineyard owner, Marcellin Albert, called a meeting of the village viticultural defense committee and set in motion a protest movement that took the entire wine-producing south of France by storm. The committee's eighty-seven members, mostly small *vignerons* like Albert, had suffered year in and year out from the wine market depression, and they now blamed the government for failing to control the production of "fraudulent" wine. Marching to Narbonne on March 11 with drums and bugles and banners reading, "Death to *fraudeurs*," they brought their "cry of misery" to a parliamentary commission that had come to investigate the wine crisis. In Narbonne, they marched through the streets singing "La Vigneronne":

> War to the bandits who belittle our misery,
> War to the *fraudeurs* without mercy,
> Yes, war to the death to our exploiters . . .[1]

Meanwhile, the parliamentary committee sat safely inside its meeting hall, barely aware of the clamor outside. Committee members closed their dossiers, promised reforms, and left Narbonne for other towns. Little did they know that this demonstration would be the first of many to sweep the towns and villages of lower Languedoc throughout that spring and summer.

Indeed, in 1907, responding to a major crisis of regional economic development, winegrowers, vinedressers, and artisans in the Aude, Hérault, Gard, and Pyrénées-Orientales took to the streets to compel the government to impose controls on the production and marketing of wine.[2] As a form of regional pro-

139

test, the 1907 revolt was especially significant in that it drew together virtually all classes, all elements of southern viticultural society, in an interclass front against the government. This massive popular movement, sometimes called the largest peasant uprising since 1789, had a profoundly divisive effect on the agricultural labor movement in the Aude.[3]

As we have seen, the diverse membership of the vineyard workers' unions, which included both small vineyard owners–workers and propertyless skilled vinedressers, proved to be both a strength and a weakness. By 1914 there was no vineyard working class in the classic Marxist sense; agricultural workers had not been completely proletarianized. The 1907 revolt underlined the fundamental differences not only between small landholders and skilled workers, but also between the movement's moderate rank and file and its more militant leadership; it also led to the further decline of the labor movement before the war. These changes caused the unions to reevaluate their position on women in the labor movement as well. The revolt also drove Socialists and syndicalists further apart after 1907, as Socialists divided over how to organize peasants and agricultural workers, and as syndicalists struggled to define their position with respect to Socialists both nationally and locally.

1907 in the Aude

The regionwide wine market depression that led to the formation of viticultural defense committees in the Narbonnais in the spring and summer of 1905, causing municipal resignations and tax protests as well, persisted into 1906 and 1907. Despite a small harvest in 1906 and slightly higher prices, sales lagged, and some small vineyard owners, fearful of being able to make any sales at all, sold their grapes directly from the vine. In the fall of 1906, angry crowds attacked tax collectors in Narbonne arrondissement and disrupted attempts to auction off villagers' furniture, seized for nonpayment of taxes.[4] Local union officials renewed strikes: seven were called in 1905 and three in 1906, to protest wage reductions and layoffs. In some villages unemployed workers appealed to mayors or to the prefect for jobs on public works projects. The subprefect called attention to the activities of "revolutionary and anarchist elements."[5] Yet it was from neither revolutionaries nor anarchists that the most violent reaction came, but from communities of small vineyard owners.

Between March and June 1907, a series of mammoth meetings and demonstrations shook the entire wine-producing south. Mostly peaceful, these demonstrations snowballed under the leadership of Marcellin Albert and the Argelliers committee and of Narbonne's Socialist mayor, Ernest Ferroul. On March 31, 600 marched in Bize; 1,000 took to the streets of Ouveillan on April 7; and 5,000 gathered in Coursan on April 14. In the next weeks the numbers mounted: 80,000 protesters gathered in Narbonne on May 5; 120,000 in Béziers on May 12; 170,000 in Perpignan on May 19; 220,000 in Carcassonne on May 26; close to 300,000 in Nîmes on June 2; and over 500,000 in Montpellier on June 9. In demonstration after demonstration, the imagery of hunger and misery recurred on the banners and symbols that demonstrators displayed. Villagers from Bize carried empty purses on pikes; those from Ginestas carried an end of bread with a sign reading, "The last crust." A banner from La Redorte read, "Children of misery, freedom is coming, we are armed. Victory or death!" and marchers from Fitou carried placards reading, "Die standing up, yes. Die of hunger, no!" One from Bages punned, "La faim justifie les moyens." These symbols provided a dramatic reminder of the grinding poverty that winegrowers and workers faced.[6] Meeting in Nîmes, Narbonne, Montpellier, and Carcassonne under brilliant Mediterranean skies, Marcellin Albert and Ernest Ferroul urged all "sons and daughters of the Midi," regardless of political beliefs, to join the movement, and appealed to the government to take action against producers of "fraudulent" wines.[7]

The drama and excitement of the meetings electrified local populations. Entire villages mobilized to travel to distant towns by whatever means possible: some came on foot, others on bicycle, and still others by train.[8] Nor were the meetings exclusively men's affairs. Women marched in the forefront of long corteges that thronged the streets, bearing banners, flags, and placards; speakers recognized and addressed them in the mass meetings. Women engaged in the movement not only on the basis of their interests as producers and consumers; as the bearers and nur-

turers of life, too, they were concerned with the health issue of
the harmful additives that were used to manufacture wines.[9]

Indeed, the 1907 revolt galvanized the entire Midi. Despite
the class warfare that had so recently shaken the peaceful vineyards, despite the FTAM's declarations of war against employers, workers marched alongside small *vignerons* and large estate
owners who joined the movement once they realized they were
incapable of resolving the wine market depression. (Although,
as Harvey Smith has shown, large proprietors probably did not
assume control of the movement, they were definitely present in
viticultural defense committees in the Aude; indeed, some politically conservative estate owners did attempt to use the 1907
movement to discredit the Radical government by blaming the
Bloc des gauches for the wine depression.)[10]

Much to the dismay of revolutionary syndicalists, the viticultural defense movement made an energetic and largely successful attempt to enlist workers' support. Proprietors lent workers
wagons and horses to enable them to travel to the meetings; the
Compagnie des chemins de fer du Midi accorded a 50 percent
fare reduction and provided a special car for workers who could
not afford even a half-price ticket.[11] Throughout lower Languedoc, isolated groups of workers—such as the union in Cuxac
d'Aude—followed syndicalist discipline and refused to participate in the 1907 movement. In the inaugural issue of *Le Travailleur de la terre* (which replaced *Le Paysan* in June 1907), Ader
supported workers who did not "officially march in the demonstrations; . . . syndicalism requires a different strategy." Following the syndicalist model, Ader argued that the fight against
fraud demanded not class collaboration but class struggle. Although he acknowledged the "educative value" of the coordinated movement, he warned workers not to expect concessions
from employers just because they had marched side by side.[12]
The Bourse du travail in Montpellier characterized the meetings
as "bourgeois demonstrations"; one union activist went still further: "All our activities are directed against the capitalist class . . .
whose disappearance must be the basis of . . . the transformation of society. We do not really understand how, in this social
crisis, the working class can abdicate its ideals and get into bed
with its worst enemies."[13]

Despite FTAM leaders' appeals, however, most rank-and-file workers took part in the meetings and demonstrations of 1907. Their participation was scarcely surprising given the large proportion of small proprietor–workers in the unions. Moreover, concerns about basic material issues, including the effects of the crisis on wages, mingled with antigovernmental feeling (fueled by confrontations with troops and police in the recent strikes) to draw workers in. In the words of one worker who attended the mass meetings, "We went to the demonstrations because . . . they were a sort of Fronde against the government." In some villages employers even promised to hire the unemployed in return for workers' support in the mass demonstrations.[14] The manifesto of the impoverished, *Qui Nous Sommes* (Who we are), brilliantly illustrates the interclass character of the 1907 movement as well as its self-consciously apolitical thrust.

WHO WE ARE

We are those who work and don't have a cent;
We are landowners who are broke or ruined, workers without
   work or almost none;
We are merchants who are hard up or who are up against
   the wall;
We are the ones who are dying of hunger.

We are the ones who have wine to sell and can't find a buyer;
We are those who have our labor to sell and can scarcely find
   a job;
We are those who have goods that no one can afford to buy;
We are the ones who are dying of hunger.

We are the wretched, and what's in the air won't fill the
   stomachs of our women and children;
We are those who have vines in the sun and tools in our hands;
We are those who want to work in order to eat and who have
   the right to live;
We are the ones who are dying of hunger.

We are those who love the Republic, those who detest it, and
   those who could care less;
We are its ardent defenders and its open adversaries;
Radicals or conservatives, moderates or syndicalists, socialists
   or reactionaries,

We are those who have our intelligence and also our opinions;
But we also need to eat, and
We are the ones who are dying of hunger.[15]

In addition to the widespread economic depression, Ferroul's
and Albert's regionalism and attacks on the government also
facilitated a temporary cross-class alliance. The image of southern vineyards colonized by northern sugar interests; the rhetoric
of south against north; the implicit protest against a government that supported the interests of certain economic and social
groups against others'—all appeared prominently in speeches
and the press.[16] The regional and antigovernmental aspects of
the movement also surfaced in a series of dramatic actions that
galvanized local populations: a massive tax strike, the resignation of village municipalities on June 10, and the rebellion of
military troops following the military occupation of lower Languedoc.

Just a year earlier, in a few scattered areas, villagers had
refused to pay taxes and attacked tax collectors who attempted
to seize property in the Aude. Now, however, municipalities in
all four Mediterranean departments agreed to suspend not only
collection and payment of taxes but all municipal operations as
well. Fifty-six percent of all municipalities in the Aude resigned,
including many towns and villages not in wine-producing
areas.[17] When Clemenceau responded by arresting Albert and
several other members of the Argelliers committee and sending
troops to occupy the south, tensions escalated. Villagers in Coursan, outraged at the government's failure to pass a sugar tax,
tore down telegraph poles in anger.[18] On June 10 and 16 two
minor military rebellions erupted as troops in Narbonne and
Perpignan refused to obey orders and marched off singing the
"Internationale." A few days later, on June 19, demonstrators in
Narbonne responded to the arrest of Ferroul by battling police;
troops charged, killing one person. Later, when an angry crowd
stormed the town hall, the 139th Infantry opened fire, wound-
ing ten and killing five, including a young woman from Coursan.[19]

These tragic events provoked a storm of reaction. In the
subprefecture shocked and angry Narbonnais turned their hos-

tility on the police, stoning and very nearly drowning a Parisian officer. In Paris, Albert Sarraut, Radical deputy and undersecretary in the Ministry of the Interior, resigned his ministerial post in protest against the shooting. A palpable tension reigned in surrounding villages as well. In one incident, a crowd attacked a beggar whom they suspected of being a police informer. Placards reading, "Clemenceau assassin" and "Gouvernement d'assassins," printed by the CGT, appeared overnight and served as a potent reminder that until Clemenceau's military occupation of southern towns the demonstrations had been peaceful. But the rebellion of the 17th Infantry received even greater public attention. These men—the vast majority local recruits—were outraged that the military had fired on, killed, and maimed their own countrymen. During the night of June 20–21 they mutinied and marched from their temporary garrison in Agde to Béziers, where they were normally stationed.[20]

The Narbonne shootings and subsequent riots in Montpellier marked a sober turning point in the 1907 revolt. Demonstrations died down and the government finally took action, passing legislation requiring that all winegrowers declare the size of their vineyards and harvests each year. From July on a series of legislative initiatives outlawed the addition of water to wine, raised the surtax on sugar, required a special permit for sales and shipments of sugar weighing over twenty-five kilograms, and gave local vintners' organizations the right to bring legal action against individuals who failed to comply with these laws. At the end of August the government voted to exonerate small winegrowers from taxes owed between 1904 and 1906.[21] In the meantime, a second Argelliers committee (designed to replace leaders who had been arrested) laid the foundations of an organization that would protect the position of southern wine in the domestic market, combat fraud, regulate wine prices, and encourage the expansion of agricultural credit: the Confédération générale des vignerons du Midi (CGV).

The CGV, formed in September 1907, brought together local viticultural defense committees under the leadership of Ernest Ferroul and included landowners of all kinds, including large proprietors. As Harvey Smith has suggested, large estate owners, initially resistant to government controls that would restrict their use of sugar and other profitable practices, were eventually forced to accept regulation.[22] Eager to continue the interclass front for the defense of the vine, Ferroul appealed to workers and small vineyard owners to join the organization and called on "all children of the Midi" to come together to save the vineyards. Minimizing the importance of class differences, Ferroul insisted that "before we are proprietors or proletarians, we are men who need to live." The CGV would thus represent the "fraternal alliance of capital and labor."[23]

Such a position could hardly have differed more from the earlier views of this former member of the National Council of the POF. Needless to say, Ferroul's appeal fell like a bombshell on the ears of syndicalist leaders. Moreover, while small proprietors stood to benefit enormously from an organization that promised to regulate wine production and end market instability, nothing in the organization addressed the special needs of landless workers.[24] This was precisely the breach into which the unions stepped. Although the 1907 movement succeeded in momentarily bringing together small growers and large, workers, syndicalists, and artisans, the formation of the CGV called that alliance into question. Socialists now divided over the interclass partnership of labor and capital, and the labor movement attempted to steer landless workers toward affirming their own class interests.

Socialists, Syndicalists, and the CGV

From the very earliest demonstrations in 1907, Socialists expressed reservations about the interclass character of the winegrowers' revolt. In the Hérault and the Gard, Socialist federations warned workers and small vineyard owners against letting themselves be co-opted by the large proprietors who guided the movement, and refused to blindly accept Ferroul's leadership.[25] Early on, the SFIO National Council reminded its members that the reforms that demonstrators demanded would do nothing to erase the deeper causes of the crisis, a view that even Ferroul supported in Nîmes on June 2.[26] Ferroul, however, led the movement not as a member of the Socialist party, but as a nonpartisan *méridional*. The 1907 revolt in fact proved problematic for the SFIO because the diverse class participation made independent party influence of the movement very difficult.[27] In 1908 a member of the SFIO National Council took the CGV to task for encouraging workers to collaborate with proprietors, who, he charged, dominated the organization. At the Socialist congress in St-Etienne in April 1909, during a prolonged debate on the "peasant question," delegates condemned the CGV for the same reasons, and the federations of the Seine and the Hérault both moved (unsuccessfully) to encourage workers to stay out of the CGV.[28] Even Jaurès, who campaigned for the nationalization of the vineyards, argued that the 1907 movement was really about "saving the vines, and not saving the property of the vines." Jaurès had initially praised the 1907 movement and the CGV for revealing the disorganization and the exploitive nature of viticultural capitalism; eventually, though, he distanced himself from the confederation.[29] Only in the Aude did Socialists actively participate in the CGV leadership with Ferroul.

If the question of class collaboration divided Socialists, it raised even more fundamental problems for syndicalists, who debated the issue in the November 1907 congress of the FTAM. The debate brought to a head a fundamental dilemma within the rural labor movement: what was the place of the small producer in the class relations of peasant society, and to what extent did the interests of small vineyard owners really coincide with those of propertyless workers? Workers who demonstrated alongside employers in the mass meetings earlier that year, and who subsequently joined the CGV, justified their participation before their fellow syndicalists. One claimed that he supported the viticultural defense movement because "I saw in this organization from which politics was banished the image of the revolutionary union that fights against state oppression." Those workers who were landowners saw their membership in both the CGV and the FTAM as perfectly compatible: the CGV defended their interests as proprietors; unions, their interests as workers.[30]

Others were strongly opposed to the CGV, arguing that collaboration with employers was contrary to the essence of syndicalism and that workers should never forget that proprietors once used force against them. Earlier, syndicalists did not question the common interests of workers and small vineyard owners, and many of the latter, as part-time workers, felt quite at home in the unions. Indeed, Ader insisted, "the small proprietor is really a proletarian who owns only the tools of production; he shouldn't act any differently from those who possess nothing, because he suffers as much as we do from current conditions."[31] The 1907 revolt, however, had changed all that. In 1908 the FTAM took a radical step that in the end seriously weakened the labor movement: it resolved to exclude automatically any union that supported the CGV or union member who was simultaneously a member of the new organization.[32]

Two factors pushed the FTAM to take this categorical position. One was the decline of the union movement as the strike momentum receded and small proprietors or proprietor-workers rejected the radical stance of syndicalist leaders and left the unions. As Table 22 shows, membership in the FTAM had declined precipitously after 1904–1905.[33] The battle by syndicalist leaders against the CGV was part of their effort to win workers back into the unions, but it likely had precisely the opposite effect. Although we do not know how many small proprietor–workers actually left the unions in 1907 or later, it is virtually certain that a large number abandoned the labor movement for the CGV.

The second factor was the renewal of strike activity at the end of 1907 and the beginning of 1908, when employers failed to live up to earlier promises to hire workers or raise wages.[34] These events strengthened leaders' arguments that employers could not be trusted and that workers should under no circumstances collaborate with them. Thus the FTAM embarked on a strategy of defending the class interests of unpropertied workers; yet in so doing it effectively denied the complex class identity of agricultural workers in the Aude. It underestimated the number of members who were small proprietor–workers and the extent to which landless workers and small vintners continued to share common interests. By deciding to defend only some workers and by expelling those who joined the CGV, it condemned itself to a position as a minority movement.

Attempting to Rebuild the Labor Movement

During 1908 and 1909, labor activists Léon Jouhaux, Paul Ader, and François Cheytion toured the countryside, trying to win workers back to the FTAM.[35] They attempted to push the unions to undertake job actions for conditions unmet by 1907 and, in the spring of 1908, encouraged workers to demand two liters of wine as part of their daily wage. Using the argument of entitlement to the fruits of their labor, workers struck over wine in six of eight labor conflicts in the Aude in 1908. The following year workers in Coursan struck for a wine allocation, this time using force and sabotage to get farmhands to join them.[36] Meanwhile Clemenceau, as minister of the interior, had begun to crack down on the unions, arresting syndicalist leaders Griffuelhes and Monatte and calling in troops to control demonstrations and break strikes. These attacks on the labor movement drove the agricultural unions in the Aude further to the left, and different forms of militant labor activity emerged after 1907.

The 1907 shootings in Narbonne and the subsequent shooting of striking workers at Raôn l'Etape, Draveil-Vigneux, and Villeneuve-St-Georges fanned the fires of antimilitarism (already awakened during the first Moroccan crisis in 1905) among agricultural workers.[37] Antimilitarist propaganda through 1907 drew mainly on workers' hostility to the government's use of troops to silence demonstrations and break up strikes. In the fall of 1907, as the CGT stepped up its antimilitarist campaign nationally, antimilitarist groups including agricultural workers and artisans organized in Narbonnais villages like Leucate, Coursan, Fleury, in Narbonne, and in the Corbières village of St-Laurent de la Cabrérisse. These groups subscribed to such publications as Gustave Hervé's forcefully antimilitarist *Guerre sociale*, Emile Pouget's *Père Peinard*, and the anarchist *Les Temps nouveaux*. In addition, villagers came into contact with antimilitarist propaganda through songs and plays performed in cafés.[38]

Antimilitarist discourse also reached agricultural workers through the Fédération des travailleurs agricoles du Midi and its press, *Le Travailleur de la terre*. Influenced by the antimilitarist campaign of Hervé and others within the CGT, agricultural workers in lower Languedoc adopted antiwar and antimilitarist resolutions at the Narbonne congress of the FTAM in 1908. These resolutions differed from earlier expressions of antimilitarist sentiment among agricultural workers (such as support for the *sou au soldat*), in that they marked the first real expressions of antiwar and internationalist feeling. Congress speakers condemned the idea of *la patrie* as meaningless for "poor proletarians who at all latitudes, in all countries, are odiously exploited and massacred in the same way when the capitalists' interests demand it." The working class, they declared, must resist all mobilization for war with a general strike and mass insurrection.[39]

Although many workers agreed with this position, workers in the Aude responded only half-heartedly to the CGT's call for a twenty-four-hour strike for peace, with antiwar meetings, on December 16, 1912. Some four to five hundred showed up in Narbonne, a tiny gathering given the size of Narbonne's working class and the number of agricultural workers in the surrounding countryside. One is inclined to agree with Jacques Julliard that the fact that so many workers later rallied to the *union sacrée* suggests that the CGT and its member federations simply did not succeed in spreading these ideas among the rank and file at this time.[40]

Syndicalist leaders also stepped up their attacks on local Socialists in the wake of 1907 and openly criticized Ferroul as a traitor to the working class for colluding with large proprietors in the CGV.[41] One union activist, writing in *Le Travailleur de la terre*, brought together both antisocialist and antimilitarist sentiment as he criticized

> the great Socialist orators, all the party notables who, having a heritage to defend, run the whole gamut of patriotic sentiments . . . raise the specter of the Kaiser's armies overrunning our land, destroying our homes . . . while they shoot down the proletariat of the "sweetest of countries."
>
> Chalons, Martinique, Limoges, Longwy, Raôn l'Etape, Narbonne, all these towns are crushed under the boots of republican cossacks, or washed with workers' blood, while the patriotic socialists counsel strikers to . . . moral insurrection![42]

FTAM leader Paul Ader reflected these views when he rejected a proposal to run an FTAM column in *Le Midi socialiste* on the grounds that syndicalist leaders should not write for any political newspaper.[43]

Finally, after the CGT had begun to tone down its revolutionary stance after about 1909 (the so-called *rectification de tir*), the FTAM on the contrary campaigned against the dangers of reformism. At its 1909 congress, delegates from Narbonne angrily criticized the recent election of Louis Niel as secretary general of the CGT (the result of an internal struggle to eliminate "anarchist influence" from the confederation) and the ascendancy of reformists within the Federation of the Bourses du travail. Likewise, FTAM activists continued to exclude those who broke syndicalist discipline by joining the CGV and so forced small proprietors and proprietor-workers out of the unions.[44]

Attempts to rebuild the agricultural workers' unions across the region were not altogether successful. By the end of 1908, the first year of its new organizing drive, the FTAM's membership stood at 3,360, a far cry from its pre-1906 level of some 10,000 and more (see Table 22 above), though by 1911 members numbered 6,000. In the Aude, union membership recovered but was still unstable (see Table 20), fluctuating between 1909 and 1914. Union leaders there expressed continuous frustration with rank-and-file workers' apparent lack of enthusiasm. When in January 1910 syndicalists in the Aude formed a department organization grouping all labor unions, the Union départementale des syndicats ouvriers de l'Aude, agricultural workers responded feebly.[45] In areas where vineyard workers did drift back to the unions, their reengagement owed as much to the material difficulties workers continued to face after 1907 as to leaders' organizing efforts.

Strike Activity and the Standard of Living

The sound and fury of strikes and demonstrations that occurred between 1904 and 1907, although they produced tangible results, changed little in vinedressers' material situation. Neither government regulation of wine production and the wine market nor the creation of the Confédération générale des vignerons du Midi arrested the prolonged depression of the southern wine economy. Even when wine prices improved marginally, vineyard owners did not raise wages enough to match the cost of living, which had increased almost 30 percent between 1905 and 1912—almost three times that for France as a whole over the same period (see Table 17 above).[46] From 1908 to 1914, fifty-six strikes took place in the Aude, bringing almost 8,500 workers off the job. Most of these strikes attempted to restore earlier agreements that employers had broken: apart from wage increases, the most frequent demand involved the wine allocation. Many strikes (43 percent) succeeded; 39 percent ended in compromises, and 18 percent failed. But had the 1907 revolt altered the pattern of strike activity?

The "shape" of strikes in the Aude before and after 1907 was remarkably similar. It is true that more strikes ended in failure after 1907 than before (ten as opposed to four).[47] Strikes after 1907 tended to be somewhat smaller and last longer as well (Table 24; compare with Table 22). Although noticeably fewer strikes occurred after 1907, this was scarcely surprising, given the shrinking of the labor movement after 1905–1906 and again after 1907. Furthermore, although as time went on syndicalists exhibited a more revolutionary posture, their bark was louder than their bite. When, after the winegrowers' revolt, it came time to negotiate settlements, union leaders were just as prepared to accept the arbitration of justices of the peace and mayors as they had been earlier, and just as eager to obtain contracts for their members.[48] One aspect of labor strategy did change, however: as Smith has noted, unions became more careful about the timing of strikes after 1907. This shift was due both to the hard lessons of the earlier strike movement and to the awareness that, since the 1907 revolt, large proprietors (who had lost their control of the market to the government and the CGV) would be more reluctant to make concessions to workers.

Strikes in the Aude, like strikes nationally, occurred partly in relation to changes in the standard of living. The organization and mobilization of rural workers took place in a period when workers' living standard was in sharp decline (just before 1900 and after the turn of the century), and when real wages had been

Table 24. Strikes in the Aude, 1908–1914

	No. Strikes	No. Strikers	Outcome[a]			Mean Duration (days)	Mean Size
			S	F	C		
1908	8	876	4	0	4	17.0	110
1909	5	590	2	2	1	37.2	118
1910	0	—	—	—	—	—	—
1911	8	2,187	4	2	2	5.9	273
1912	13	2,163	5	2	6	9.3	166
1913	13	1,793	5	3	5	11.9	138
1914	9	737	4	1	4	4.2	82

Source: France, Ministère de commerce, Direction du travail, *Statistique des grèves et des recours à la conciliation et à l'arbitrage* (1908–1914) (Paris: Imprimerie nationale, 1909–1915).
[a]S = success, F = failure, C = compromise

falling for some time. Before and after 1907 unions tended to call strikes when rising wine prices suggested that employers might make concessions, a pattern that Jean Sagnes has noted also in the Hérault.[49] Thus, these strikes caused, rather than resulted from, an improved standard of living.[50] Similarly, both before and after 1907, once workers obtained wage improvements, labor organization often disintegrated, instead of expanding as might have been expected.[51]

Although gains made in earlier labor conflicts brought workers higher wages, real wages, which had increased from 1900 to 1905, actually fell between 1905 and 1912: workers' situation in fact deteriorated after 1905–1906. In Coursan more villagers worked in the vines than ever before, but official documents like the census no longer described vineyard workers as *cultivateurs*; rather, they used the term *journalier agricole*, a symbolic reminder of their loss of status.[52] As workers all over France began to experience the *crise de la vie chère*, and the CGT and the *bourses* stepped up their national campaigns against inflation, the first Audois consumers' cooperatives were established in Cuxac, Durban, St-Jean de Barrau, Canet, Marcorignan, and Ornaisons.[53] In this context, agitation for the wine allocation that brought

workers off the job in 1908 and 1909 took on particular significance—for it was designed to allow workers not only to enjoy the
fruits of their labors (literally), but also to maintain a certain
standard of living.

As workers' living standards continued to decline, the FTAM
launched a new campaign for a six-hour day, a 50 centime
hourly wage, and a wine allocation throughout the year. Leaders
invoked the concept of the moral economy (although they did
not use the term) by reminding workers and vineyard owners of
the mass meetings and demonstrations of 1907, "when workers'
blood ran in the defense of employers' interests." Employers,
they charged, had gone back on their word: they had cut back
wages, asked workers to put in longer hours, and refused to give
them wine. Still worse, "wine has sold . . . well, beyond all hopes,
and what have we gotten from all that? NOTHING!"[54] Nationally,
demonstrations against the rising cost of living, organized by the
CGT, brought French workers into the streets from 1910 to
1912.[55] If nothing else, these conditions aroused public sympathy for workers' demands. In the Narbonnais, when wine prices
improved at the end of 1910 employers cleverly anticipated
workers' demands and actually raised wages. Other workers,
however, had to fight for improvements. Strikes in 1911, 1912,
and 1913, timed more effectively to coincide with periods of
activity in the vines, raised wages, obtained the year-round wine
allotment, and resulted in annually renewable contracts.[56]

These successes notwithstanding, most strikes after 1907 were
defensive attempts to retrieve lost ground. Moreover, the FTAM
did not manage to bring masses of workers out in these strikes.
This situation paralleled the national decline of strike activity
between 1910 and 1913, as workers all over France sought to
hold on to their jobs rather than risk new confrontations. Only
women's strike activity proved an exception to this pattern.

Women, Unions, and Strikes

In attempting to rebuild the unions after 1907, the FTAM leadership shifted its position on women's work and ceased to argue
for women's return to hearth and home. The participation of
women in strikes and demonstrations between 1903 and 1908

deepened their commitment to securing rights for themselves and also convinced union leaders that they could be counted on to support men's labor struggles. These union men seemed to realize that by failing to organize women they were missing an important opportunity to rebuild the unions and create a mass movement of agricultural workers. As a result, from about 1909 labor activists praised women's participation in the conflicts of the past six years and agreed to organize women, "who will be very useful when we next present our collective demands."[57]

These good intentions, however, were not acted on, and ultimately the potential of unionizing women remained a lost opportunity. By 1914 women in only eight Audois villages had actually formed their own unions (108 women in Coursan unionized in 1911). Nevertheless, they continued to participate actively in local labor conflicts, as before. In the thirty-four strikes between 1911 and 1913 they counted for some 22 to 35 percent of strikers, three and four times the national average of women's strike participation in these years.[58]

Whereas earlier women had acted essentially to support men's claims, now they used the rising cost of living to justify wage increases for themselves. After all, large numbers of married women worked in the vineyards as wage workers, and they continued to occupy a vital place in the working-class household economy. Moreover, women's community ties and social networks provided them with "organization," helping them to build a collective awareness of their rights as mothers and as workers and creating a community of interests that overlapped with workplace solidarities. These same ties had facilitated women's labor activism earlier. Finally, women had the advantage of an accumulated experience of participation in protest from 1903 through 1907 that broke down some of the gender barriers of Mediterranean village society. Not that their participation in labor struggles alongside men changed male workers' essentially masculine concept of class, but the strikes did force unionists in the Aude to accept women's place in the public (and essentially male) world of labor conflict.[59] The extent to which women's work and claims were enmeshed in both community and family is illustrated by the women's strike in Coursan in 1912–1913.

Vineyard *journalières* in Coursan were one of the few groups of women to organize in the Aude. Following labor conflicts in 1911, 108 women established a section within the Syndicat des cultivateurs et travailleurs de la terre de Coursan and, in October 1912, took the radical step of attempting to negotiate a separate contract (as men had done just a year earlier). They demanded a 25 centime hourly wage (exactly half of men's wages); a 50 centime increase over the 3.50 francs for every hundred bundles of branches they gathered; and standard rates for "women's work"—sulphuring, sulfating, and harvesting. In addition, they demanded that "women's work," gathering branches and spreading chemicals, be reserved for them alone—in other words, that the gender-based division of labor in the vines be preserved to protect their jobs.[60] When vineyard owners refused to talk to the women, they refused to return to work, and brought an additional 250 nonunionized women and about 675 men off the job in a two-day sympathy strike.

In this strike, which lasted two months (longer than any other strike in the Aude), the women mobilized the support of the entire community. Male workers took up collections in Coursan and surrounding villages and held concerts to raise money. Contributions poured in from sympathetic unions as far away as Paris.[61] Even though work in the vines could not proceed until the vines had been cleared of branches, male workers refused to act as scab labor by performing women's work. Such work, they rightly protested, was not in their contract. When employers responded by imposing a lockout, the men briefly joined the strike. Thus, curiously, the gender-based division of labor served the cause of labor solidarity.[62] Although the women eventually returned to work without a settlement at the end of January, the men's support showed that they accepted women's place in the vineyard labor structure. Workers recognized that women's position in the workplace differed from men's and had to be dealt with separately. This recognition did not betoken protofeminist consciousness on the part of either male or female workers. On the contrary, the women's attempt to preserve conditions that to us seem highly exploitive is not difficult to explain.

In the first place, women faced increasing competition from unskilled male immigrants. Their attempt to secure a contract was above all aimed at protecting their position in the labor market—necessary given the importance of their wage contribution to the family in these inflationary times. In addition, many of these women were mothers as well as wage earners. Their acceptance of a secondary place in the labor hierarchy and of a secondary wage was a tacit recognition of their complex roles. Behind the insistence on maintaining a gender-based division of labor lay a demand that they be permitted to continue to fulfill their roles as mothers and as family providers—what some have called the "rights of gender"—and an assertion of their right to control the pace of work.[63]

The effort to negotiate a separate contract also implied an agreement that women would not compete with men or drive down their wages. These *journalières*, over half of whom were married, did not strike only with an eye to material gains. Their acceptance of the gender-based division of labor and, by implication, of women's culturally ascribed roles also involved an understanding that the family's control of labor power was a vital element in working-class independence and resistance to exploitation. Preservation of their husbands', fathers', and sons' jobs was also at issue. Their failure to reach a settlement points to both the difficulties unions now faced in negotiating with employers and the strength of centuries-old gendered divisions in Mediterranean villages—something that even the war did not change.

The failure of strikes like this one did not cause syndicalist leaders to modify their militant stance. Cheytion, Ader, and others continued to denounce the "yellow" CGV, and they pursued their antimilitarist campaign right up to June 1914, spurred on by the 1913 law extending military service to three years. In February 1913 Vincent Daïde, secretary of the Narbonne Bourse du travail and a strong supporter of Ferroul and the CGV, was ousted, replaced by François Cheytion.[64] Moreover, syndicalists' relations with Ferroulist Socialists remained strained well after 1907.

Socialists, Workers, and Elections in the Wake of the Winegrowers' Revolt

After 1906, the political map of the Aude changed slightly. Socialist unification, together with Socialist hostility to the Radical government's use of force against demonstrators in 1907 and against strikers in 1908 and 1910 (especially Briand's brutal repression of the 1910 railway strike), combined to end these two parties' electoral alliances.[65] Simultaneously, the wretched economic situation of workers in these years caused alienation from the "pie in the sky" promises of politicians, who either minimized workers' efforts as useless or failed to address their concerns directly.

Syndicalists had certainly done their best to encourage workers to maintain a certain distance from political parties. Moreover, their anti-electoral campaign after 1907 not only criticized the uselessness of political action (their primary argument before 1907) but now also attacked politicians' intentions given the imprisonment of labor leaders and the government's use of military force to repress strikes. In villages where important syndicalist leaders resided (such as François Cheytion's Coursan and Paul Ader's Cuxac d'Aude), abstentionism—which was especially high in Third Republic elections—was also an expression of loyalty to labor leaders, as we have already suggested.

Even though the Aude had one of the highest levels of abstention of any department in France under the Third Republic, and even if some rank-and-file syndicalists did respond to the call to boycott the ballot box, no evidence suggests that vineyard workers alone were responsible for these high levels. Workers remained divided over the wisdom of relinquishing the rights and duties of the ballot. Nor did high abstentions prevent Socialists from winning legislative elections in the Narbonnais. They may, however, indicate that if socialism was a logical choice for small winegrowers and artisans, it was not necessarily the obvious route for all unionized agricultural workers.

While die-hard syndicalists struggled to sustain both their membership and their ability to wrest concessions from employers, the moderate, pragmatic socialism of urban workers and small vineyard owners expanded. Ferroul's leadership in the 1907 movement played a crucial role in helping Audois socialists gain municipalities and extend their popular base in the west and south of the department. The Socialist Federation of the Aude now organized sections in Carcassonne, La Nouvelle, Gruissan, Fabrezan, Thezan, and Quillan.[66]

Table 25. Legislative Elections of 1910 and 1914 in the Narbonnais
(percent of votes cast)

	SFIO	Radical	Republican	Abstentions
Narbonne I				
1910	53.2	15.6	25.6	33.6
1914	59.6	20.1	18.5	39.5
Narbonne II				
1910	48.9	50.2	—	17.7
1914	40.2	57.3	—	28.7
Coursan commune				
1910	41.3	34.2	22.0	50.3
1914	68.6	7.6	20.6	58.2

Source: AD Aude 2M58, "Recensement général des votes, 1876–1914."

Although the 1907 revolt did not cause a major shift from
radicalism to socialism in the Aude (Audois Radicals defended
the interests of small winegrowers too well for that to happen),
in the legislative elections of 1910 and 1914 Socialists advanced
considerably (as in most areas of France where they presented
candidates), more than doubling their share of votes since 1906
(Table 25).[67]

In contrast to the Var, where Tony Judt has shown that radicalism gave way to socialism during the depression at the end of
the nineteenth century, radicalism in the Aude retained the
support of small winegrowers up to World War I. While Radicals
benefited from a powerful regional press and a popular base in
local clubs and societies, their defense of distressed small *vignerons* was every bit as important in gaining them political
support in the Aude.[68] Socialists, of course, benefited from these
things too, but here local traditions and loyalties to local men
influenced the vote significantly. Peasants and workers may have
identified with national political parties and issues; yet allegiance
to "favorite sons" such as Sarraut, Aldy, and Ferroul still carried
weight in the political life of rural France. This even syndicalists,
with their disdain for the electoral process, had a hard time
fighting.

The day after the 1914 legislative elections, for the last time in

his life, François Cheytion led the May Day parade around Coursan, bearing the red flag and followed by a village band playing
the "Internationale." Winding through the streets, the parade
picked up followers. After the customary speeches, all made
their way to the village square for a *bal populaire*. In retrospect it
was a poignant scene, for within two months this ardent antimilitarist had joined the *union sacrée*, along with most of the
French labor movement. Just over a year later, Cheytion lay
dead on a battlefield in the Somme, "a martyr to that odious
war."[69] The state's readiness to use violence against workers,
together with the defeats the labor movement sustained before
the war, sapped the morale of even the most radical activists. But
the *union sacrée* itself was ephemeral. Well before the end of the
war, old divisions among Socialists, syndicalists, and the state
reappeared, to reemerge after 1917 in new forms that were
deeper than ever.

Ultimately, the great winegrowers' revolt of 1907 had profound repercussions for both the agricultural labor movement
and the evolution of Socialist politics in the Aude after 1907. It
confirmed syndicalist leaders in their more radical vision of the
class relations of rural society, even if it did not significantly
change patterns of strike activity. The formation of the Confédération générale des vignerons du Midi divided both Socialists and syndicalists on the wisdom of collaborating with men
whom both groups had previously considered the class enemy.
In the Aude, Socialists' support of the viticultural defense movement and the CGV not only enabled them to win followers in the
department; it also established a historical foundation on which
Narbonnais Socialists could later build.

In contrast to what Harvey Smith has argued, the 1907 revolt
did not mark the end of class conflict in the Aude, any more than
it represented the end of syndicalism.[70] Smith contends that
unions in lower Languedoc became more moderate and more
willing to bargain with employers after 1907. While he is right
that workers learned that massive protests could lead to concessions from the state, they also learned that the state was prepared to shoot workers and break up strikes with military force.
Unlike syndicalists elsewhere who acquiesced after 1907, activ-

ists in the Aude rejected the movement's appeal to join the "fraternal alliance of capital and labor" and refused to abandon their revolutionary rhetoric even after the CGT's *rectification de tir*. This position, as we have seen, cost them members and, indeed, left them in the role of a *minorité agissante*.

The 1907 revolt not only raised the issue of class collaboration (which syndicalist leaders fixed on at the time), it also vividly illustrated the fundamental complexities of rural society and class identity in the Aude. These complexities came to the foreground immediately after the revolt, especially when it came to organizing individuals for whom the distinctions of "peasant" and "worker" were often blurred. The aftershocks of 1907 also showed how divided the class loyalties of small vineyard owners really were. Ultimately, this very complexity sapped the strength of the labor movement as much as did the persistent economic depression that finally eroded workers' ability to risk costly strikes. The withdrawal of small vineyard owners weakened the unions numerically and psychologically, and at the same time diminished their capacity to resist further proletarianization.

8
CONCLUSION:
CAPITALISM, SOCIALISM, AND
SYNDICALISM IN THE FRENCH
COUNTRYSIDE

In the nineteenth century capitalist economic relations emerged in the French countryside much as they did in the towns and cities of industrial France. Railroads and banks opened villages and towns to the larger world of commerce long before France actually developed a national market. Among the resin workers of the Landes, the lumbermen of the Cher and Nièvre, and the *vignerons* of lower Languedoc, the customary moral economy of small peasant communities gave way to the contractual relations of the cash nexus. These developments had a profound, if somewhat varied, impact on the political culture and social relations of rural society. Faced with the seemingly inevitable emergence of a new division of labor, new authority relations, and new forms of work discipline, peasants in some parts of France started out on the long (and sometimes not so long) road to becoming proletarians. Their story shows how rural workers contributed to the formation of that complex and heterogeneous phenomenon, the French working class, in the nineteenth and early twentieth centuries. More specifically, in the Aude, their story helps to explain the Midi *rouge*.

Most historians who have studied the impact of economic and social change on the French peasantry have focused on the development of political culture, ideology, and electoral politics.[1] Some have shown how left-wing politics emerged in response to both national and local political and economic trends. In lower Languedoc, however, a powerful (if short-lived) labor movement, inspired by revolutionary syndicalism, developed in competition with socialism as a response to agricultural capitalism and the class tensions it produced. The experience of peasants and workers in the Aude suggests new ways of looking at the development of left-wing politics in the countryside and at the growth of a rural labor movement among men and women whose status lay somewhere between "peasants" and "proletarians."

To begin with, the protourban winegrowing villages of the Aude could hardly have differed more from the isolated peasant communities in which, as Eugen Weber has argued, rural dwellers were insulated from national political movements at least until the 1870s. Nor is it clear that the peasants and rural workers of the Aude obediently heeded local notables when it came time to cast their ballots under the Third Republic.[2] By the 1840s and 1850s rural capitalism had brought Audois peasants into contact with a world that stretched far beyond the confines of their tiny villages, with new ideas and new politics—long before railways, roads, and schools brought the official, bourgeois Republic into their lives on a daily basis.[3]

The development of radical republican and democratic socialist (*démoc soc*) political groups in the Aude in the mid 1800s, a period of economic transformation, confirm the findings of Edward Berenson, Ted Margadant, and John Merriman. They have shown how peasants, partly through association with urban and rural artisans, took part in a national republican movement that swept France during the Second Republic and the very early days of the Second Empire. In the Aude as well, densely settled rural communities, with their traditions of sociability and shared community concerns, fostered the development of left-wing political clubs, barn meetings, and secret republican groups. Within these communities artisans and rural workers could fashion a politics separate from that of conservative rural notables. Peasants' contacts with local and regional market towns also facilitated the spread of republican and *démoc soc* ideas.

In much of rural France these left-wing groups died out when the Second Empire closed off political activity and when rural artisans made their way to the higher wages and (so they imagined) more stable employment in towns and cities in the 1850s and 1860s.[4] But the Aude experienced neither the "ruralization" of the countryside nor the end of radical, left-wing politics in this period. On the contrary, the development of vineyard capitalism created precisely the conditions in which that radical political tradition could grow and flourish. *Démoc soc* clubs and secret republican societies had roots deep enough to survive harsh Second Empire repression. Rural artisans meanwhile, who benefited from the "golden age of the vine," stayed in protourban winegrowing villages, bought land, and prospered. Eventually they joined agricultural laborers and small landowners to lay the foundations of radicalism, and then socialism, in the countryside.

Economic depression rather than prosperity, however, provided the real impetus for the flowering of left-wing politics in the Aude.[5] As economic expansion came to an end in the 1880s, small vineyard owners abandoned free-market liberalism and welcomed the Radicals' model of an interventionist state. Because Audois radicalism retained a real sympathy for the needs of small producers, it did not merely become another version opportunist republicanism, unlike radicalism elsewhere in lower Languedoc or in France as a whole. In Masonic lodges and free thought societies, radicals rubbed elbows with men who, first known as "radical socialists," later distinguished themselves by their perception of class struggle, sensitivity to the needs of the great mass of French men and women, and revolutionary goals. Still, a communal base in local political clubs, shared interests in a climate of near-perpetual agricultural depression, and a common following among impoverished small vinegrowers meant that socialism stayed close to its radical heritage in the Aude.[6] While Radicals and Socialists increasingly drew apart nationally, in the Aude they continued to cooperate electorally until the eve of World War I.

Socialists in the Aude, then, looked very different from those who waved the banner of revolution and collectivism in the Varois countryside. Tony Judt has shown how Socialists' collectivist discourse in Provence helped small-scale producers develop communal solutions to the problem of the competitive market. In the Aude, socialism lacked a strong collectivist and revolutionary component. Such rhetoric held little appeal for small property owners struggling to hold on to their small parcels of vines, so Audois Socialists steered clear of it; only after the SFIO's 1909 St-Etienne congress did they begin to talk seriously about promoting cooperatives. Moreover, Socialists in the Aude paid scant attention to the problems of rural workers until well after the revolutionary syndicalists demonstrated their capacity to mobilize the rural working class.

We have distinguished the rhetoric and programs of national party leaders from the interests of peasant producers and their local leaders. These differences, while not unusual in political and labor movements, are important. They remind us that French socialism, far from emerging as a ready-made solution to the problems of workers and peasants, developed strategically to fit local interests and local conditions.

The vineyards and protourban communities of the Aude suggest that southern French rural society was far less homogeneous than the work of Tony Judt or Eugen Weber would lead us to expect. Much as Harvey Smith and Jean Sagnes have found for the Hérault, viticultural capitalism in the Narbonnais generated a new rural working class that coexisted with the small *vignerons* and rural artisans who had been plying their trades in Audois villages for generations. The development of this new rural working class was very different from that of the urban working class, made up of artisans and industrial workers.

Indeed, modern understanding of the working class has been based largely on an industrial model. According to this model, the formation of the European working class occurred as industrial capitalism gradually deprived workers of property, skill, and control over work rhythms, knowledge, and hiring. Historians studying French workers in the nineteenth and twentieth centuries have stressed the elements of social disruption in the process of urban working-class formation: the breakdown of traditional communities, the decline of artisanal skills and customary relations within trades, changes in family relations and in the perception of women's work, and the transformation of working-class culture brought on by migration and immigration. Workers found themselves increasingly oppressed psychologically and materially until socialism and syndicalism provided a language, a consciousness, and a practice of resistance. Even though the story of class formation based on the classic industrial model has had to account for differences separating skilled and unskilled workers, labor aristocrats and proletarians, women and men, the vineyard workers of the Aude do not fit this picture.

For one thing, although contemporaries spoke about "industrial viticulture," the vineyards of the Aude exemplify a capitalist agriculture whose development transformed the social relations of production without fundamentally altering traditional forms of production. Thus, vinedressers did not suffer de-skilling from new technology as glassblowers, textile workers, iron workers, machinists, and many other industrial workers did. Rather, changes in landholding, the development of new entrepreneurial strategies, and new forms of labor control altered the relations between workers and vineyard owners. Immigration to the Aude of skilled and semiskilled vinedressers during the phylloxera crisis, while it saturated the labor market and created competition for "locals," did not destroy bonds of community or create rivalries destined to break down craft identities.

Labor solidarities and the capacity for action did not develop only at the point of production. The same characteristics of the protourban village (density of settlement and sociability, for example) that nourished Radical and Socialist political culture facilitated the development of an autonomous labor movement among agricultural workers and provided essential support in times of labor conflict. The village provided the "social and political space to resist economic change and forge political responses [broadly conceived] to shifts in [workers'] condition."[7] Workers also drew on the solidarities of vinedressers and small proprietors throughout the region. Thus community (in both the village and the larger regional sense) proved to be as important as craft or class in the rural labor movement.

What, then, did class mean to agricultural workers in rural France? Although vinedressers experienced the complementary processes of proletarianization and impoverishment, they did not constitute a "proletariat" in the same sense as unskilled urban industrial workers. The fact that many rural workers had been (or remained) landowners, or that numerous poor small vineyard owners became part-time or even full-time workers, made the class status of vinedressers extremely complex. Workers and small winegrowers shared corporate solidarity and a fierce sense of independence, as well as a common sensitivity to the consequences of prolonged agricultural depression for the "little guy." Along with this went an inherent suspicion of, if not outright hostility toward, *les grands*.

Many workers would have agreed with Jaurès that the small winegrower stood on labor's side, not capital's. But the same complexity of class that at one moment bolstered the labor movement could, when mixed with a radical and increasingly rigid syndicalist leadership, become a recipe for its decline. Here we agree with Harvey Smith that the 1907 revolt and its aftermath played a large role in the misfortunes of the regional labor movement before the war, although we disagree about the nature of that role. The 1907 revolt threw into relief the different origins and interests of the diverse membership of the labor movement, and irrevocably widened the gap between a radical activist leadership and a more moderate rank and file.

The story of the workers and winegrowers of the Aude points to several important lessons for the history of the French labor movement more generally. First, the story of class formation is incomplete without a consideration of the dynamics of gender, both in the relations of production and in the workings of the labor movement. The gender-based division of labor permitted employers to maintain control over all workers. It did so partly by institutionalizing definitions of skill and wages that kept women at the bottom of the workplace hierarchy. In this respect the estate owners of the Aude were no different from employers in other settings throughout Europe and North America. Employers could keep men's wages low (or, indeed, cut them) with impunity because they knew that either married women and older children would make up the difference through wage labor or the family would absorb the consequences by sacrifices made within a gendered domestic economy. Male syndicalists' masculine concepts of class and craft solidarity, which facilitated the organization of men, together with women's acceptance of the gender-based division of labor, prevented disruption of this system, with its multiple dimensions of human exploitation. Ultimately the institutionalization of gender differences in the workplace (and, by extension, in the unions) undermined the unions' capacity to build a mass movement in the Aude. Thus, unwittingly, men and women collaborated in the proletarianization of the rural working class.

Second, the case of the Aude reminds us that in nineteenth- and early-twentieth-century France workplace organization and electoral politics did not always overlap.[8] Syndicalist labor organization and socialism in the Aude sprang from different roots, adopted different organizational strategies, and flourished within different constituencies. It is true that syndicalist leaders in the Aude did not draw masses of workers into the unions on the basis of leaders' hostility to electoral politics. Nor did syndicalism succeed in providing a complete alternative to socialism. Workers did vote. But the fact that these two movements often found themselves at loggerheads helps us understand why, in a country with such a rich revolutionary tradition and wealth of labor and socialist leadership, no mass mobilization of the working class ever occurred.[9]

Third, the story of Audois vineyard workers warns us against overemphasizing union membership figures as a measure of the labor movement's strength. Here the Aude confirms a general pattern of twentieth-century unionization: fluctuating membership coexisting with strong support for strikes. The fluidity of union membership in the Aude and elsewhere in Mediterranean France tells us less about the failure of agricultural syndicalism than about the nature of rank-and-file participation, which shifted according to workers' capacity to pay dues and their perception of the need for union activity.[10] The ability of southern unions to influence and obtain support from nonunionized workers and the community during a strike was at least as important as the numbers of dues-paying members it could count. Indeed, as we have seen with respect to women, in closely knit vineyard villages community was just as important as the union in mobilizing the rural working class.

Fourth, the case of the Aude illustrates the disjuncture between syndicalist discourse on the one hand and the practical interests and preoccupations of workers on the other. Rural syndicalists in the Aude, like workers everywhere, walked a narrow line between long-range revolutionary aspirations and the

short-term, day-to-day issues of wages, hours, and working conditions. They affirmed the independence of the labor movement, the primacy of class struggle, and the revolutionary value
of the general strike, defended sabotage, and condemned the
legislative process. Yet even as their radical rhetoric increased in
intensity and volume, labor leaders in the Aude never actually
proposed the revolutionary expropriation of the vineyards. In
practice, labor activism turned on immediate, piecemeal reforms and the restoration of a certain moral economy that had
disappeared from the relations between labor and capital; over-
turning those relations was never a serious goal.

The coexistence of radical rhetoric with moderate pragmatic
objectives was not unusual. All over France, syndicalism in practice hardly matched its dramatic claims.[11] Most French workers
wanted bread-and-butter improvements in their working lives,
and these the unions obtained. *Tant pis pour la révolution.* For
much of the CGT's rank and file, membership in that organization did not entail a commitment to its revolutionary doctrine.[12]
Yet syndicalism was not therefore, to borrow from Stearns, a
"cause without rebels." Rather than being a coherent theory or
body of doctrine, syndicalism was the result of practice. And
syndicalist practice differed from place to place as workers strategically (and, we might add, wisely) responded to local conditions.[13]

By now historians of the French working class and socialism in
the nineteenth and early twentieth centuries have discovered a
veritable kaleidoscope of political forms and class identities. The
rural workers of the Aude are part of that fragmented picture.
They show us—in case we need reminding—that the story of
working-class movements and politics in modern France is one
of enormous diversity and difference. Indeed, it barely seems
possible to talk about either the French working class or the
French socialists (even after 1905) as a bloc, once we recognize
the variations in political culture and class identity that sprang
up across different regions and between different communities.
In one place (the Var), socialism was revolutionary and collectivist; in another (the Aude), it was relatively reformist and petty
bourgeois. In one area (the Nord), socialists sought to harness
and tame independent workers' movements; in another (the

Tarn), they nurtured workers' organizations and struggles; still elsewhere (the Aude), they fostered unions in urban areas and offered moral and occasionally material support to rural workers. These variations attest to the richness of the socialist and working-class movements and to the ability of workers and their allies to create effective organizations and strategies of contest commensurate with local conditions and requirements. Yet alongside the divisions between unions and parties, rhetoric and action, over the long term that very richness and diversity across regions and trades militated against the development of a united working-class movement.

Despite this shortcoming nationally, as a local movement and as an expression of class interest syndicalism made a real difference in the lives of vineyard workers in the Aude. Ironically, the very intransigence and combativeness that ultimately condemned Audois syndicalists to a minority position simultaneously enabled them to make tangible gains for agricultural workers, something the Socialists had not done by 1914. Moreover, it gave workers a language of struggle that contributed as much to the construction of class identity as did changes in the realm of production. Thus, the culture of syndicalism played a vital role in shaping the rural working class and in mediating the intricate relationships among peasants, workers, capital, political parties, and the state.

Notes

All translations from the French are by the author unless otherwise noted.

INTRODUCTION

1. Michael Burns, *Rural Society and French Politics: Boulangism and the Dreyfus Affair, 1886–1900* (Princeton: Princeton University Press, 1984); Tony Judt, *Socialism in Provence, 1871–1914* (New York: Cambridge University Press, 1979); and Georges Duby and Armand Wallon, eds., *Histoire de la France rurale*, vol. 3 (Paris: Seuil, 1976).

2. See Ronald Aminzade, *Class, Politics, and Early Industrial Capitalism* (Albany: SUNY Press, 1981); Yves Lequin, *Les ouvriers de la région lyonnaise, 1848–1914*, 2 vols. (Lyon: Presses universitaires de Lyon, 1977); Michael Hanagan, *The Logic of Solidarity: Artisans and Industrial Workers in Three French Towns, 1871–1914* (Urbana: University of Illinois Press, 1980); Joan W. Scott, *The Glassworkers of Carmaux* (Cambridge, Mass.: Harvard University Press, 1974); William H. Sewell, Jr., "Social Change and the Rise of Working-Class Politics in Nineteenth-Century Marseille," *Past and Present* 65 (1974): 75–109; Robert Bezucha, *The Lyon Uprising of 1834* (Cambridge, Mass.: Harvard University Press, 1974); Bernard Moss, *The Origins of the French Labor Movement: The Socialism of Skilled Workers, 1830–1914* (Berkeley and Los Angeles: University of California Press, 1976); Rolande Trempé, *Les mineurs de Carmaux, 1848–1914*, 2 vols. (Paris: Editions ouvrières, 1971); and John Merriman, *Red City: Limoges in the Nineteenth Century* (New York: Oxford University Press, 1986).

3. Leo A. Loubère, *Radicalism in Mediterranean France: Its Rise and Decline, 1848–1914* (Albany: SUNY Press, 1974). On politics and unions in the French countryside, see also Philippe Gratton, *Les luttes de classes dans les campagnes* (Paris: Anthropos, 1971); Gratton's study includes the Centre, Champagne, and the Landes, as well as Languedoc.

4. J. Harvey Smith, "Work Routine and Social Structure in a French Village: Cruzy, Hérault, in the Nineteenth Century," *Journal of Interdisciplinary History* 5 (December 1975): 357–382; Jean Sagnes, *Le mouvement ouvrier en Languedoc* (Toulouse: Edouard Privat, 1980), 30–33, 84–87; and Jean Sagnes, "Le mouvement de 1907 en Languedoc-

Roussillon: De la révolte viticole à la révolte régionale," *Mouvement social* 104 (July–Sept. 1978): 3–20.

5. Judt, *Socialism in Provence*, 142–143.

6. See John Merriman, *The Agony of the Republic* (New Haven: Yale University Press, 1978); Ted Margadant, *French Peasants in Revolt: The Insurrection of 1851* (Princeton: Princeton University Press, 1979); Edward Berenson, *Populist Religion and Left-Wing Politics in France, 1830–1852* (Princeton: Princeton University Press, 1984); Christopher Guthrie, "Political Conflict and Socioeconomic Change in the City of Narbonne, 1848–1871" (Ph.D. diss., Northern Illinois University, 1981); and Christopher Guthrie, "Reaction to the Coup d'Etat of 1851 in the Narbonnais: A Case Study of Popular Political Mobilization and Repression During the Second Republic," *French Historical Studies* 13 (Spring 1983): 18–46.

7. Edward Shorter and Charles Tilly, *Strikes in France, 1830–1968* (New York: Cambridge University Press, 1974); and Hanagan, *Logic of Solidarity*, esp. chap. 3.

8. J.-C. Toutain, *La population de la France de 1700 à 1959* (Paris: Institut de Science Economique Appliquée, 1963), 164; Rémy Pech, *Entreprise viticole et capitalisme en Languedoc-Roussillon. Du phylloxéra aux crises de mévente* (Toulouse: Presses de l'Université de Toulouse, 1975), 48, 51. In the Aude 55.4 percent of the land consisted of properties over forty hectares in size (1 hectare = 2.47 acres), owned by 5.1 percent of the owners.

9. France, Ministère de l'agriculture, Statistique agricole de la France, *Résultats généraux de l'enquête décennale de 1882* (Nancy: Berger-Levrault, 1887), 143.

10. France, Ministère de l'agriculture, Direction de l'agriculture, Office des renseignements agricoles. *La petite propriété rurale en France. Enquêtes monographiques, 1908–1909* (Paris: Imprimerie nationale, 1909), 37.

11. E. P. Thompson, *The Making of the English Working Class* (Harmondsworth, Eng.: Penguin Books, 1968), 11.

12. See, for example, Florencia Mallon, *The Defense of Community in Peru's Central Highlands: Peasant Struggle and Capitalist Transition, 1860–1940* (Princeton: Princeton University Press, 1983).

13. Loubère, *Radicalism in Mediterranean France*, 197.

CHAPTER 1

1. Charles Ballainvilliers, "Des mémoires sur le Languedoc, divisés par diocèses et subdélégations, 1788" (Manuscript no. 81, Municipal Library of Carcassonne), fol. 19.

2. This policy was designed to insure adequate grain reserves in an economy heavily dependent on grain for bread and animal feed. See V. Pellegrin, *Les grandes étapes de l'agriculture dans l'Aude* (Carcassonne: Gabelle, 1937), 18; Michel Augé-Laribé, *Le problème agraire du socialisme. La viticulture industrielle du Midi de la France* (Paris: Giard & Brière, 1907), 29; Gilbert Larguier, "Structures agraires, structures sociales d'un village narbonnais: Ouveillan (fin XVIIIᵉ siècle–début XXᵉ siècle)," in *Economie et société en Languedoc-Roussillon de 1789 à nos jours* (Montpellier: Centre d'histoire contemporaine du Languedoc-meditérranéen et du Roussillon, 1978), 158.

3. Berthomieu Tournal Girault de Saint-Fargeau, *Histoire nationale ou Dictionnaire géographique de toutes les communes du département de l'Aude* (Paris: Firmin Didot; Carcassonne: Arnaud; Narbonne: Delsols, 1830), 32. See also Archives départementales de l'Aude (hereafter cited as AD Aude) 13M61, "Vignoble départemental, cépages et produits, an XIII à 1878"; Jean Sentou, "Les facteurs de la révolution agricole dans le Narbonnais," in *France méridionale et pays ibériques: Mélanges géographiques offerts en hommage à Daniel Faucher* (Toulouse: Edouard Privat, 1949), 2:656.

4. Louis René Villermé, *Tableau de l'état physique et moral des ouvriers employés dans les manufactures de coton, de laine et de soie (1840)*, ed. Yves Tyl (Paris: Union générale des éditions, Collection 10/18, 1971), 155–157; AD Aude 11M58, "Dénombrement de la population. Etat nominatif des habitants de la commune de Coursan, 1836"; A. Ditandy, *Lectures variées sur le département de l'Aude* (Carcassonne: François Pomiés, 1875), 221–222.

5. At the outset, two points need to be made about landholding records (*cadastre foncier*) and the land market. First, the *cadastre* of any village cannot give a completely accurate picture of the land actually held by the resident population. That of Coursan, for example, shows numerous individuals from neighboring villages holding land in Coursan, and the notarial archives of Coursan also amply show that Coursannais themselves owned property all over the Narbonnais: a few ares in Narbonne, a few in Cuxac, Salles, or Ouveillan. Thus, any figures illustrating property ownership underestimate the real extent of villagers' landownership. Second, the *cadastre* provides a picture of enormous activity on the land market, a factor that needs to be borne in mind when looking at the evolution of property ownership. Individuals bought and sold property at a tremendous rate from year to year, most transactions involving only a few ares. Despite received wisdom about the stability of peasant proprietorship, then, landownership was extremely volatile in the Aude.

6. Service de cadastre de l'Aude, Narbonne (hereafter cited as SC Aude), Cadastre foncier de Coursan.

7. Archives nationales de France (hereafter cited as AN) F²⁰715, "Tableaux des prix et denrées et des salaires des ouvriers (1844, 1855)"; AN C86, *Agriculture française par MM. les Inspecteurs de l'agriculture, publié d'après les ordres de M. le Ministre de l'agriculture et du commerce. Département de l'Aude* (Paris: Imprimerie royale, 1847). See also AN C946, "Enquête sur le travail agricole et industriel, 25 mai 1848." The years 1846 and 1847 saw general economic depression in France, so wages were lower than they might have been. The depression, after abating for a while in the fall of 1847 and early 1848, resumed again after the revolution.

8. AD Aude 13M61, Prefect and sub-prefect reports for 1829; Gaston Galtier, *Le vignoble du Languedoc-méditerranéen et du Roussillon* (Montpellier: Causse, Graille & Castelnau, n.d.), 1:123n. The average income from one hectare of vines in the Narbonnais around 1829 was estimated at 434 francs; see Augé-Laribé, *Problème agraire du socialisme*, 41; Jean-François Garidou, "La viticulture audoise, 1870–1913" (Travail d'études et de recherches d'histoire, Université de Montpellier, Faculté des lettres et des sciences humaines, 1968, typescript), 9.

9. See Guillaume Bertier de Sauvigny, *La restauration* (Paris: Flammarion, 1955), 216; AD Aude 13M270–280, "Statistique générale. Etats de renseignements concernant les grains et les farineux . . . les céréales, 1815–1850"; AD Aude 13M275, "Etats de renseignements . . . 1818–1820"; Georges Barbut, *Histoire de la culture des céréales dans l'Aude de 1785 à 1900* (Carcassonne: Gabelle, 1900), 19; Sentou, "Révolution agricole," 661.

10. France, Ministère du commerce, Statistique générale, *Prix et salaires à diverses époques* (Strasbourg: Berger-Levrault, 1864), xxiv.

11. France, Ministère de l'agriculture, *Enquête agricole de 1872. Deuxième série. Enquêtes départementales, 21ᵉ circonscription* (Paris: Imprimerie nationale, 1872), 32.

12. See Robert Laurent, *Les vignerons de la Côte d'Or au XIXᵉ siècle* (Dijon: Bernigaud & Privat, 1957), 1:201n5.

13. Paul Carrière and Raymond Dugrand, *La région méditerranéenne* (Paris: Presses universitaires de France, 1960), 80; R. Pech, *Entreprise viticole*, 374.

14. Raymond Dugrand, *Villes et Campagnes en Bas-Languedoc. Le réseau urbain du Bas-Languedoc* (Paris: Presses universitaires de France, 1963), 395–402.

15. AD Aude 11M58, "Dénombrement de la population. Etats nominatifs des habitants de Coursan, 1836"; 11M101, ibid., "1876."

16. Philippe Pinchemel, *Structures sociales et dépopulation rurale dans les campagnes picardes de 1836 à 1936* (Paris: Armand Colin, 1957). The same was true of the Hérault; see Sagnes, *Mouvement ouvrier*.

17. Rémy Pech, "Aspects de l'économie narbonnaise de l'époque du phylloxéra à la crise de mévente (fin XIXe siècle): Un démarrage éphémère," in *Narbonne. Archéologie et histoire* (Montpellier: Fédération historique du Languedoc-méditerranéen et du Roussillon, 1973), 114; Robert Laurent, "La propriété foncière dans le Bittérois à la veille de la première guerre mondiale," in *Fédération historique du Languedoc-méditerranéen et du Roussillon, XLIIIe congrès, Béziers, 1970* (Montpellier: FHLMR, 1971), 415–426; Xavier Verdejo, "Les mutations de la vie rurale à Cuxac d'Aude aux XIXe et XXe siècles (entre 1789 et 1914)" (Mémoire de maîtrise d'histoire, Université de Toulouse–Le Mirail, 1983), 18, 48–62.

18. SC Aude, "Cadastre foncier de Coursan," fols. 94, 95, 100, 585, 654–655.

19. Ibid., fol. 305.

20. Ibid., fols. 94–95, 100, 300, 486, 552, 558, 585–586, 572, 610–612, 654–655, 974–975, 978–979, 983, 1158, 1431, 1536, 2274, 2277, 2279, 2280, 2285, 2286.

21. See Charles Gervais, *L'indicateur des vignobles méridionaux*, 2d ed. (Montpellier: Firmin, Montagne & Sicardi, [1903]).

22. Augé-Laribé estimated that it took four days to cultivate one hectare of vines with a horse and plow, but six days to cultivate the same area dispersed in small parcels throughout a village (*Problème agraire*, 268). See also J. Valentin, *La révolution viticole dans l'Aude, 1789–1907* (Carcassonne: Centre départemental de documentation pédagogique, 1977), vol. 2, doc. 206.

23. See André Garridou-Lagrange, *Production agricole et économie rurale en France* (Paris: Librairie générale de droit et de jurisprudence, 1939), 77; E. Flour de St-Genis, *La propriété rurale en France* (Paris: Armand Colin, 1902); Alfred de Foville, *Etudes économiques et statistiques sur la propriété foncière. Le morcellement* (Paris: Guillaumin, 1885). On property division in viticulture elsewhere, see Laurent, "Propriété foncière"; and Alain Corbin, *Archaïsme et modernité en Limousin au XIXe siècle* (Paris: Marcel Rivière, 1975), 1:259-260.

24. Augé-Laribé, *Problème agraire*, 64–65; and AD Aude 13M300, "Statistique décennale agricole. Tableaux communaux des cantons de Coursan, Durban, Ginestas et Sigean, 1882."

25. SC Aude, "Cadastre foncier de Coursan."

26. On the Bertrand brothers, see ibid., fol. 1502; R. Pech. "La formation de la bourgeoisie viticole en Narbonnais au XIXe siècle," in

Economie et société en Languedoc-Roussillon de 1789 à nos jours (Montpellier: Centre d'histoire contemporaine du Languedoc-méditerranéen et du Roussillon, 1978), 138–140; Yves Rinaudo, *Les vendanges de la république. Les paysans du Var à la fin du XIXe siècle* (Lyon: Presses universitaires de Lyon, 1982), 136–137; Yves Rinaudo, "Usure et crédit dans les campagnes du Var au XIXe siècle," *Annales du Midi* 92 (Oct.–Dec. 1980): 431–452.

27. SC Aude, Cadastre foncier de Coursan, fol. 77.

28. Smith, "Work Routine and Social Structure," 367–369.

29. Jules Guyot, *Etude des vignobles de France pour servir à l'enseignement de la viticulture et de la vinification française*, vol 1: *Régions du sud-est et du sud-ouest* (Paris: Imprimerie Impériale, 1868), 258.

30. Arthur Young, *Travels During the Years 1787, 1788, and 1789; Undertaken More Particularly with a View Towards Ascertaining the Cultivation, Wealth, Resources and National Prosperity of France*, 2d ed. (London: Printed for W. R. Richardson, Royal Exchange, 1794), 2:1.

31. AD Aude 13M282, "Tableaux de statistique agricole annuelle . . . 1856–1857."

32. For various descriptions of the work of the vineyard year and the calendar of the *vigneron*, see Alexis Riondet, *L'agriculture de la France méridionale. Ce qu'elle est; ce qu'elle a été; ce qu'elle pourrait être* (Paris: Librairie agricole de la maison rustique, 1863), 116–123; Aude, *Annuaire administratif, statistique et historique du département de l'Aude pour l'année 1869–1870* (Carcassonne: P. Labau, 1870); Guyot, *Régions du sud-est et du sud-ouest*, 9–14; Galtier, *Vignoble du Languedoc-méditerranéen* 1:240–242; Paul Marrès, *La vigne et le vin en France* (Paris: Armand Colin, 1950), 130–132; Garidou "Viticulture audoise," 21.

33. Paul Coste-Floret, *Les travaux du vignoble* (Montpellier: Camille Coulet; Paris: Masson, 1898).

34. R. Pech, *Entreprise viticole*, 39.

35. Augé-Laribé, *Problème agraire*, 51.

36. AN F¹¹2698, "Enquête agricole de 1862"; France, Ministère de l'agriculture, Statistique de la France, Agriculture, *Résultats généraux de l'enquête décennale de 1862* (Strasbourg: Berger-Levrault, 1868), 194–195; idem, Statistique agricole de la France, *Résultats généraux de l'enquête décennale de 1892* (Paris: Imprimerie nationale, 1898).

37. Augé-Laribé, *Problème agraire*, 248–249; R. Pech, *Entreprise viticole*, 376–380.

38. Will of Jean-Pierre Aribaud, Dec. 27, 1911; Notarial Archives, Coursan.

39. Paul Passama, *La condition des ouvriers viticoles dans le Minervois*

(Paris: Giard & Brière, 1906), 16; AD Aude 11M117, "Dénombrement de la population. Etats nominatifs des habitants de Coursan, 1876."

40. R. Pech, *Entreprise viticole*, 383–384; AD Aude 13M300, "Statistique agricole décennale . . . 1882."

41. R. Pech, *Entreprise viticole*, 383. According to Paul Coste-Floret, "men had the right to meat at every meal and women only had vegetables cooked with meat left over from the men" (*Travaux du vignoble*, 378). Although women's vineyard work was often as strenuous as that of men, this attitude was not unusual.

42. Coste-Floret, *Travaux du vignoble*, 378.

43. Augé-Laribé, *Problème agraire*, 260–261; R. Pech, *Entreprise viticole*, 383.

44. Passama, *Condition des ouvriers*, 49. Guyot, who held a low opinion of the farmhands, attributed their inferiority to the fact that they were not used to drinking wine and therefore lacked the benefits of the *aimable boisson* (*Régions du sud-est et du sud-ouest*, 258).

45. Abel Chatelain, "Les migrations temporaires françaises au XIXᵉ siècle" (Paper delivered to the Société de démographie historique, Jan. 1967) (Paris: Sirey, 1968), 20. On the use of this term by workers in the Hérault, see Smith, "Work Routine and Social Structure," 364.

46. Coste-Floret, *Travaux du vignoble*, 379.

47. Pierre Larue, *Le travail du sol dans les vignes* (Narbonne: F. Caillard, 1902); Passama, *Condition des ouvriers*, 61; Georges Barbut, "Le vignoble de l'Aude: Monographie du domaine de Jouarrès" (excerpt from *La Revue de viticulture*) (Paris: Bureau de *La Revue de viticulture*, 1898), 9; and AN F¹¹2698, "Enquête agricole de 1862"; Léopold Fontanilles, *Etude sur les ouvriers agricoles et leurs mouvements sociaux* (Grenoble: La Dépêche dauphinoise, 1908), 54.

48. SC Aude, "Cadastre foncier de Coursan." This figure was calculated as follows: the 1876 census listed 439 day laborers and *cultivateurs*. The "Cadastre" showed 61 individuals who could have been totally self-supporting (on the basis of the amount of land they owned in Coursan), leaving 378 full or part-time wage earners. According to the "Cadastre," 153 workers were landowners and hence part-time wage earners. Because the "Cadastre" provided occupational designations for a little more than half of all landowners, it is likely that this figure underestimates the true number of vinedressers who were also landowners.

49. Jules Rivals, *L'agriculture dans le département de l'Aude, 1899–1900* (Paris: Henri Poirre, 1901), 69.

50. In Coursan, where workers owned an average of 0.65 hectares

(65 ares) of land, income from a plot of vines would be somewhat lower, 1,095.25 francs. Costs of production included the following expenses: fertilizer (60 francs), sulphur (35 francs), pruning and other operations (40 francs), cultivation (130 francs), and the cost of bringing grapes to a neighbor's cellar for winemaking (75 francs). The estimate of 340 francs per hectare comes from the "Enquête agricole" of 1872.

51. Passama, *Condition des ouvriers*, 71–72; Smith, "Work Routine and Social Structure," 365.

52. AD Aude 11M101, "Dénombrement de la population. Etats nominatifs des habitants de Coursan, 1866"; 11M117, ibid., "1876." The shift is particularly striking here, showing the *journaliers'* decline from 33 percent of the working population in 1866 to less than 1 percent in 1876. At the same time, the number of *cultivateurs* grew by almost exactly the number of former *journaliers*, from 15 to 45 percent. This shift, linked to property ownership and the new ambiguity of the term *cultivateur*, was not unique to Coursan. See Smith, "Work Routine and Social Structure," 381.

53. AD Aude 13M282, "Tableaux de statistique agricole annuel . . . 1856–1857"; AN F^{11}2698, "Enquête agricole de 1862"; AD Aude 13M300, "Statistique agricole décennale . . . 1882"; France, Ministère de l'agriculture, *Résultats généraux de l'enquête décennale de 1862*, 204–205; ibid., *1882*, pt. 1, 382–396; pt. 2, 178–183; Augé-Laribé, *Problème agraire*, 76–77, 283–288, 290; Passama, *Condition des ouvriers*, 79–80. Real wages and standard of living are examined in Chapter 4, below. See also AN F^{12}4484, "Situation de l'industrie dans l'Aude," Prefect's report of September 22, 1888, and prefect's reports for 1871, 1872, 1880, and 1881.

54. See, for example, Hanagan, *Logic of Solidarity*, 130–132; Aminzade, *Class, Politics, and Early Industrial Capitalism*, 31–45; Joan Scott, *Glassworkers of Carmaux*, chap. 4.

55. Rémy Pech, "Le vignoble du Languedoc-Roussillon: Crise séculaire et recherche d'un nouveau souffle," *Revue française d'études politiques méditerranéennes* 23 (Nov. 1976): 19.

56. Dugrand, *Villes et campagnes*, 358; Ditandy, cited by Valentin, *Révolution viticole* 1:27.

CHAPTER 2

1. Margadant, *French Peasants in Revolt*, 55. I am using the term *protourbanization* in the same sense as Margadant and Charles Tilly have used it, to refer to the "expansion of urban influence over rural communities" (ibid.).

2. René Nelli, *Le Languedoc et le comté de Foix, le Roussillon* (Paris: Gallimard, 1958), 59–60; Charles Parain, "La maison vigneronne en France," *Arts et traditions populaires* 4 (Oct.–Dec. 1955): 289–378.

3. For the development of cafés in the 1840s and 1850s, see Merriman, *Agony of the Republic*, 97–101; for the later development of political cafés, see AD Aude 5M51, Letter from mayor of Coursan to subprefect of the Aude, Aug. 29, 1872; AD Aude 17J7, "Visites pastorales, Coursan," Report of 1878.

4. Daniel Fabre and Jacques Lacroix, *La vie quotidienne des paysans du Languedoc au XIXᵉ siècle* (Paris: Hachette, 1973), 238–240; Daniel Fabre and Charles Camberoque, *La fête en Languedoc* (Toulouse: Edouard Privat, 1978); Abel Chatelain, *Les migrations temporaires en France de 1800 à 1914* (Lille: Publications de l'Université de Lille III, 1976) 1:133.

5. Fabre and Lacroix, *Vie quotidienne*, 197–264.

6. Ibid., 249–250.

7. Rémy Pech, "L'organisation du marché du vin en Languedoc et en Roussillon aux XIXᵉ et XXᵉ siècles, *Etudes rurales* 78–80 (Apr.–Dec. 1980): 106, 111.

8. Ibid., 103–105.

9. Ibid., 105.

10. Ibid., 106.

11. Romain Plandé, *Géographie et histoire du département de l'Aude* (Grenoble: Editions françaises nouvelles, 1944), 57, 170; Bureau du greffier du tribunal de grande instance, Narbonne, Aude (hereafter referred to as TGI, Narbonne), "Etat civil de Coursan, Actes de naissance, 1851–1881"; "Actes de décès, 1851–1881." Between 1851 and 1881, Coursan had a mean crude birth rate of 22.0 and a mean crude mortality rate of 21.9; both rates were relatively low for the department and region. See Carrière and Dugrand, *Région méditerranéenne*, 24–27; Etienne Van de Walle, *The Female Population of France in the Nineteenth Century* (Princeton: Princeton University Press, 1974), 255; Dugrand, *Villes et campagnes*, 439; Verdejo, "Mutation de la vie rurale," 122; France, Ministère du commerce, Direction du travail, Statistique générale, *Annuaire statistique de la France. Première année, 1878* (Paris: Imprimerie nationale, 1878), table 1, "Mouvement général de la population en 1875."

12. France, Ministère de l'agriculture, *Enquête agricole par application du décrêt du 28 mars 1866. Enquêtes départementales, 21ᵉ circonscription* (Paris: Imprimerie nationale, 1866), 130, 132–133; Guyot, *Régions du sud-est et du sud-ouest*, 43–44; Chatelain, *Migrations temporaires* 1:120–122.

13. AD Aude 11M78, "Dénombrement de la Population. Etats nominatifs des habitants de Coursan, 1851"; 11M117, ibid., "1876."

14. R. Pech, "Aspects de l'économie narbonnaise," 114.

15. Chatelain, *Migrations temporaires* 1:144; TGI, Narbonne, "Etat civil de Coursan, Actes de mariage."

16. Cited by Fabre and Lacroix, *Vie quotidienne*, 374–375; AN F^{17}10781, "Mémoires sur les besoins de l'instruction primaire, Aude, Gard, 1860–1861"; F^{17}10529, "Etats de la situation des écoles primaires . . . 1878–1879."

17. AN F^{17}9322, "Inspection des écoles primaires, années 1855–1856. Ardèche à Bouches-du-Rhône."

18. Rémy Pech, "La vie politique dans l'Aude, 1881–1902" (Mémoire pour diplôme d'études supérieures d'Histoire, Université de Paris–Sorbonne, 1967), 45; national figures are from Toutain, *Population de la France*, 217, 227.

19. AN F^{17}10670, "Etats de la situation des écoles primaires publiques et libres et des écoles maternelles, 1888–1889. Aude à Corrèze."

20. Gérard Cholvy, "L'Indifférence religieuse et anticléricalisme à Narbonne et en Narbonnais au XIXe siècle," in *Fédération historique du Languedoc-méditerranéen et du Roussillon*, vol. 3 (Montpellier: FHLMR, 1973), 78.

21. AD Aude 17J7, "Visites pastorales, Coursan," Reports of 1864, 1880, 1882, 1885; AD Aude 5M7, Prefect's report, Nov. 20, 1859.

22. Cholvy, "Religion et société au XIXe siècle: Le diocèse de Montpellier" (Thèse de doctorat d'état, Université de Lille), 2 vols. (Lille: Services de réproduction des thèses de l'université, 1973); Raymond Huard, *Le mouvement républicain en Bas-Languedoc, 1848 à 1881* (Paris: Fondation nationale des sciences politiques, 1982), 144, 364.

23. Fabre and Lacroix, *Vie quotidienne*, 369; Cholvy, "Indifférence religieuse," 91.

24. Cholvy, "Indifférence religieuse," 75–76; Jean Rivière, *La sainteté en pays d'Aude* (Narbonne: Brille & Gautier, 1949); Rivière, "Croyances et êtres surnaturels," in Gaston Jourdianne, *Contribution au folklore de l'Aude* (1889; Paris: G.-P. Maisonneuve & Larose, 1973).

25. See Berenson, *Populist Religion and Left-Wing Politics*, 56–67, on more politicized forms of popular religion elsewhere.

26. AD Aude 5M7, Monthly prefect reports, Dec. 1855–Dec. 1860; Bimonthly reports of subprefect, 1861–1865; 5M84, Police reports, 1858–1859; 15M120, Report of *commissaire spécial*, Narbonne, to prefect, Apr. 1, 1905.

27. France, Ministère de l'agriculture, *Enquête agricole de 1872. Deuxième série*, 133.

28. Pierre Raynier, *Biographie des représentants du département de l'Aude de 1789 à 1900* (Toulouse: Passeman et Alquier, 1901), 87–88; Adolphe Robert and Gaston Cougny, *Dictionnaire des parlementaires français* (Paris: Bourloton, 1889–1891), 4:8, 312; André-Jean Tudesq, "L'opposition légitimiste en Languedoc en 1840," *Annales du Midi* 68 (Oct. 1956): 393; AD Aude 21M14, Report of subprefect to prefect of the Aude, Mar. 1841; 5M24, Prefect's reports, 1833 (*Propagande St-Simonienne*); 5M27, Report of subprefect to prefect, Nov. 2, 1840; Magali Jouffroi-Schaeffer, "L'implantation du St-Simonisme dans la ville et la région de Narbonne," in *Fédération historique du Languedoc-méditerranéen et du Roussillon, XLVe congrès*, vol. 3 (Montpellier: FHLMR, 1973), 61–72.

29. AN BB³⁰380, "Rapports mensuels du procureur général à Montpellier au ministre de la justice, Dec. 1849–1868," Report of Dec. 13, 1849.

30. See the brief account of Barbès's political activities in Jean Maitron, *Dictionnaire biographique du mouvement ouvrier français* (Paris: Editions ouvrières, 1964), vol. 1 (1789–1864), 147–149; Raynier, *Biographie*, 199–203. On political clubs and popular associations in the Midi in general, see Merriman, *Agony of the Republic*, 60–64; Maurice Agulhon, *La république au village* (Paris: Plon, 1970); AD Aude 5M31, Dossier on political disturbances in Narbonne in 1848 and political clubs in the Narbonnais, Reports of subprefect to prefect, Aug. 16, 1848–June 15, 1849.

31. By the middle of 1849, the Club de l'union had almost 1,500 members. See Guthrie, "Reaction to the Coup d'Etat of 1851," 27.

32. See, for example, Claire Goldberg Moses, *French Feminism in the Nineteenth Century* (Albany: SUNY Press, 1985).

33. AD Aude 5M31. Teachers were especially prominent.

34. Merriman, *Agony of the Republic*, 58.

35. Aminzade, *Class, Politics, and Early Industrial Capitalism*, 148.

36. Loubère, *Radicalism in Mediterranean France*, 32.

37. Roger Price, *The Second French Republic: A Social History* (Ithaca: Cornell University Press, 1972), 231–233. The *démoc soc* program was published in April 1849 in *La Réforme*.

38. Margadant, *French Peasants in Revolt*, 85–87.

39. AD Aude 2M61, "Elections à l'assemblée nationale constituante, 1848," Election propaganda of Théodore Raynal; 2M11, "Révolution de 1848, adhésions au gouvernement provisoire, organisation des municipalités, etc.," Printed broadside, "Aux Narbonnais," Mar. 10, 1848.

40. AD Aude 5M31, Police reports on local disturbances in August 1848.

41. AD Aude 2M13–14, Elections for the president of the Republic, Dec. 10, 1848; Paul Carbonnel, *Histoire de Narbonne* (Narbonne: P. Caillard, 1956), 387; Tudesq, *L'élection présidentielle de Louis-Napoléon Bonaparte, le 10 décembre 1848* (Paris: Armand Colin, 1965), 208; Price, *Second French Republic*, 208–225; Maurice Agulhon, *1848 ou l'aprentissage à la république* (Paris: Seuil, 1973), 85–87.

42. Carbonnel, *Histoire de Narbonne*, 387–388; AN BB[30]362, Report of *procureur général*, Montpellier, to minister of justice, Feb. 23, 1849. Merriman, *Agony of the Republic*, 218, also cites examples of the use of carnival as political allegory from the Var, the Jura, and the Deux-Sèvres. See also Robert Bezucha, "Masks of Revolution: A Study of Popular Culture During the Second French Republic," in *Revolution and Reaction: 1848 and the Second French Republic*, ed. Roger Price (London: Croom Helm, 1975), 236–253, for other examples, esp. p. 238 on incidents in March 1848 in Fleury, Aude.

43. Price, *Second French Republic*, 231–233.

44. M. Bichambis, *Narbonne, la robine, et les basses plaines de l'Aude* (Narbonne: J. Bousquet, 1926), 460; Price, *Second French Republic*, 238–240; Loubère, *Radicalism in Mediterranean France*, 37–40, 46.

45. Loubère, *Radicalism in Mediterranean France*, 39.

46. The term is taken from the title of Merriman's book.

47. AN BB[30]362, Report of *procureur général*, Montpellier, to minister of justice, May 7, 1851. On the dismissal of mayors, see Guthrie, "Reaction to the Coup d'Etat of 1851," 35.

48. AN BB[30]362, Reports of *procureur général*, Montpellier, to minister of justice, May 3, 1850; July 7, Aug. 7, Sept. 3, 1851. On resistance to the coup d'état in the Aude, see AD Aude 5M36, Report from subprefect to prefect of the Aude, Jan. 6, 1852; Price, *Second French Republic*, 242; Guthrie, "Reactions to the Coup d'Etat of 1851." On dress and revolutionary solidarity, see Lynn Hunt, *Politics, Culture, and Class in the French Revolution* (Berkeley and Los Angeles: University of California Press, 1984), 79–83.

49. AN BB[30]396, Dossier P440, on establishment of secret societies; Merriman, *Agony of the Republic*; Margadant, *French Peasants in Revolt*.

50. On similar rituals elsewhere, see Merriman, *Agony of the Republic*, 207; Price, *Second French Republic*, 302.

51. On the rituals and those who were arrested, see AD Aude 5M36, Letter from subprefect to prefect of the Aude, March 28, 1852; Letter from justice of the peace, Coursan, to subprefect, Nov. 17, 1852; AN BB[30]380, Report of *procureur général*, Montpellier, to minister of justice, Nov. 11, 1852; AD Aude 5M43, "Etat des individus dangereux à raison de la part qu'ils pourraient prendre à un moment donné dans

un mouvement insurrectionnel," Mar. 6, 1858; "Etat des individus n'ayant pas pu être compris dans le premier tableau . . . ," Mar. 10, 1858; 5M46, Political events, Apr. 23, 1853–Apr. 13, 1858; Letter from prefect to minister of the interior, Oct. 15, 1855; 5M48, Letter from prefect to minister of the interior, Mar. 31, 1863.

52. AD Aude 2M63, Election of deputies to the Corps législatif, May 22–24, 1869; Theodore Zeldin, *The Political System of Louis Napoleon III* (London: Macmillan, 1958), 135–136; also, on the 1869 elections, see Louis Girard, ed., *Les élections de 1869*, vol. 21 in *Bibliothèque de la révolution de 1848* (Paris: Marcel Rivière, 1960), xiv; Loubère, *Radicalism in Mediterranean France*, 93.

53. See Zeldin, *Emile Olivier and the Liberal Empire of Napoleon III* (Oxford: Clarendon Press, 1963), 154–155; A. Jeanjean and J. Rives, *La proclamation de la Troisième République dans le département de l'Aude. Essai historique* (Carcassonne: Gabelle, 1920), 11–19; AD Aude 2M16, "Plébiscite du 8 mai 1870."

54. AD Aude 5M51, Letter from prefect of the Aude to minister of the interior, Sept. 7, 1871; Letter from mayor of Coursan to sub-prefect, Aug. 31, 1872.

55. On the details of republican politics, see Carbonnel, *Histoire de Narbonne*, 408–409; AD Aude 2M65, Election of the representatives to the National Assembly, Feb. 5–8, 1871; André Siegfried, "Géographie de l'opinion politique dans le Midi sous la IIIᵉ République: l'Aude. Les élections de 1849 à 1945" (Course given at the Collège de France, 1939; unpaginated typescript, Archives départementales de l'Aude); Loubère, *Radicalism in Mediterranean France*, 116.

56. Carbonnel, *Histoire de Narbonne*, 412.

57. See "Manifeste de la Ligue du Midi pour la défense de la république du 26 septembre 1870," in Jeanne Gaillard, *Communes de province, commune de Paris, 1870–1871* (Paris: Flammarion, 1971), 113–114; Annie Genzling, "La commune de Narbonne en 1871" (Paper presented at the Colloquium on Right and Left in Languedoc-méditer-ranéen–Roussillon, Université Paul Valéry–Montpellier, June 9–10, 1973).

58. From *La Fraternité*, Mar. 18, 1871; quoted in Gaillard, *Communes de province*, 114–115. Digeon evoked a popular Christianity which portrayed a Christ in sympathy with the poor and with the working class: "Vous y apprendrez la vraie morale du Christ qui n'est en somme que celle de la sublime devise républicaine, liberté, égalité, fraternité. Le Christ . . . s'il revenait sur la terre . . . chasserait du temple les marchands de médailles et d'indulgences et maudirait les exploiteurs de miracles." This association of religious imagery with political radi-

calism is strikingly similar to what Edward Berenson has observed for an earlier period (*Populist Religion and Left-Wing Politics*).

59. Carbonnel, *Histoire de Narbonne*, 415. This was the first time the French government used colonial troops to suppress a domestic insurrection.

60. AD Aude 5M51, Letters from subprefect to prefect, Sept. 7, 1871, and Oct. 10, 1873; Letter from mayor of Coursan to subprefect, Aug. 29, 1872.

61. AD Aude 7M31, Cercles, chambrées, clubs, salons, Letter from subprefect to prefect, Mar. 14, 1872; Georges Germa, "Les élections législatives du 8 février et du 2 juillet 1871 dans l'Aude: Essai historique" (Typescript, Carcassonne, n.d.), 14; Siegfried, "Géographie de l'opinion"; Raynier, *Biographie*, 130. Fortuné Brousses was elected in a by-election in 1871; Théophile Marcou and Léon Bonnel were elected in 1873.

62. AD Aude 5M51, Prefect to minister of the interior, Dec. 10, 1873.

63. Loubère, *Radicalism in Mediterranean France*, 111–112; "Tableau comparatif des programmes radicaux (1849–1898)," in Jacques Kayser, *Les grandes batailles du radicalisme, 1820–1901* (Paris: Marcel Rivière, 1962), n.p.

64. Aude, *Délibérations du Conseil général du département de l'Aude. Procès-verbal des délibérations. Session de 1878* (Carcassonne: Pierre Polère, 1878), 779–782; Garidou, "Viticulture audoise," 37–41.

CHAPTER 3

1. J. A. Barral, *Conférence sur le phylloxéra, faite le 1er avril 1882* (Paris: Tremblay, 1882), 22.

2. Income averaged 168 million francs per year (AD Aude 13M85, "Enquête sur la situation des vignes phylloxérées").

3. France, Ministère de l'agriculture, Direction de l'agriculture, *Compte rendu des travaux de la Commission supérieure du phylloxéra (année 1882) et rapport de M. Tisserand, Conseiller d'Etat, Direction de l'Agriculture* (Paris: Imprimerie nationale, 1883), 38–39; AD Aude 13M78 "Phylloxéra. Tableaux statistiques sur la marche du phylloxéra, du 3 octobre au 16 mars 1887"; 13M300, "Statistique agricole décennale des communes, 1882"; 13M307, "Statistique agricole annuelle, commune de Coursan, 1890"; Verdejo, "Mutation de la vie rurale," 70.

4. Paul Degrully, *Essai historique et économique sur la production et le marché des vins en France* (Montpellier: Roumegous & Dehan, 1910).

5. AD Aude 14M20, Report from president of the Chamber of Commerce in Narbonne, Jan. 3, 1885.

6. R. Pech, *Entreprise viticole*, p. 60.

7. Aude, *Délibérations du Conseil général de l'Aude . . . Sessions de 1875–1878*; AD Aude 13M75, "Phylloxéra. Associations syndicales des communes, arrondissement de Narbonne, commune de Coursan. Formation d'une association syndicale pour la sulphurisation du vignoble"; Verdejo, "Mutation de la vie rurale," 67–68; France, Ministère de l'agriculture, *Compte rendu des travaux de la Commission supérieure du phylloxéra*, 33. The author of the law exonerating owners of diseased vines from taxes was Adolphe Turrel, opportunist deputy and large proprietor from Narbonne arrondissement.

8. In July 1878 the government agreed to double every sum voted by a commune or department for treatment of vines. Villages throughout the Aude voted sums ranging from 1,000 to 20,000 francs. See AD Aude 13M67, "Traitement du phylloxéra"; Comice agricole de Narbonne, *Questionnaire sur le revenu foncier des terres dans l'arrondissement de Narbonne* (Narbonne: F. Caillard, 1908), 8; Georges Barbut, *Etude sur le vignoble de l'Aude et sa production* (Carcassonne: Pierre Polère, 1912), 61–62; Barbut, "Vignoble de l'Aude."

9. Average subsidies per hectare were actually quite small (68 francs in 1881, 33 francs in 1882); see France, Ministère de l'agriculture, *Compte rendu des travaux de la Commission supérieure du phylloxéra*. See also Garidou, "Viticulture audoise," 41; Charles K. Warner, *The Winegrowers of France and the Government Since 1875* (New York: Columbia University Press, 1960), chap. 1. Small growers in the Aude continued to receive subsidies as late as 1908; see AD Aude 13M82, "Phylloxéra. Etats nominatifs communaux . . . des propriétaires . . . possédant moins que six hectares de vignes qui ont bénéficiés de l'allocation de secours du Conseil général . . . 1908.

10. Prosper Gervais, *La réconstitution du vignoble. Quantité ou qualité?* (Paris: Au siège du Syndicat central des agriculteurs de la France, 1903), 3.

11. Comice agricole de Narbonne, *Résumé des leçons pratiquées sur le greffage des vignes américaines* (Montpellier: Société centrale d'agriculture de l'Hérault, 1880).

12. On the development of Algerian vineyards during the phylloxera crisis, see Hildebert Isnard, *La vigne en Algérie. Etude géographique*, 2 vols. (Orpheys-Gap, 1954); François Raymond Peyronnet, *Le vignoble nord-africain* (Paris: Peyronnet, 1950); Romould Dejernon, *Les vignes et les vins d'Algérie*, 2 vols. (Paris: Librairie agricole de la Maison rustique, 1883–1884).

13. Warner, *Winegrowers*, 13–15. Warner states that the use of sugar in winemaking increased from eight million kilos in 1885 to thirty-nine million kilos in 1899.

14. On the increasing capital requirement of post-phylloxera vineyards, see France, Ministère de l'agriculture, *Enquête agricole de 1872. Deuxième série*, 128, 146; *Vigneron narbonnais*, Oct. 1, 1892, quoted in Garidou, "Viticulture audoise," 65; Comice agricole de Narbonne, *Questionnaire sur le revenu foncier*, 11; R. Pech, *Entreprise viticole*, 159–165; Augé-Laribé, *Problème agraire*, 138–209; Michel Augé-Laribé, "Le rôle du capital dans la viticulture languedocienne," *Revue d'économie politique* 19 (1905): 198ff.

15. Augé-Laribé, *Problème agraire*, 101; Rivals, *Agriculture dans l'Aude*, 65. "La culture viticole devient une industrie avec ses prix de revient, ses études théoriques et scientifiques, avec le perfectionnement de son machinisme, sa comptabilité . . ." (Jean Vigoroux, *Essai sur le fonctionnement économique de quelques très grandes exploitations viticoles dans la Camargue et le Bas-Languedoc* [Montpellier: Société anonyme de l'Imprimeur général du Midi, 1906], 73ff.).

16. Average annual wine imports increased from 824,383 hectoliters in 1870–1879 to 9,372,400 hectoliters in 1880–1889. See Warner, *Winegrowers*, 30; France, Ministère de l'agriculture, *Statistique agricole annuelle, 1889–1900* (Paris: Imprimerie nationale, 1889–1900); De-grully, *Essai historique et économique*, 326; R. Pech, *Entreprise viticole*, 119.

17. Prosper Gervais, "Conférence à l'exposition agricole de Béziers, 1906," *Revue de Viticulture* (1906), cited by Valentin, *Révolution viticole*, vol. 2, doc. 405.

18. Eventually small growers formed cooperatives to produce and market their wine. Nine existed in the Aude by 1914, and they became more widespread in the interwar years. See Hubert Rouger, *La France socialiste*, in *Encyclopédie socialiste, syndicale et coopérative de l'Internationale ouvrière*, ed. Adéodat Compère-Morel (Paris: Aristide Quillet, 1912), 34; Michel Augé-Laribé, "Les coopératives paysannes et socialistes de Maraussan (Hérault)," in *Le Musée social. Mémoires et documents*, 1907, 65–74. On cooperatives in the Hérault, see Sagnes, *Mouvement ouvrier*, 146–161; and on the Var, Judt, *Socialism in Provence*, 168, 266.

19. Barbut, *Etude sur le vignoble*, 5, 77; AD Aude 15M117, "Réunions publiques, meetings contre le chômage, la vie chère, etc.," Report from the *commissaire spécial* on a meeting in Narbonne, Jan. 10, 1892. The Méline tariff was not rigorously applied to Spanish wines for fear that Spain would reciprocally raise tariffs on French wine; see Eugene O. Golob, *The Méline Tariff: French Agriculture and National Economic Policy* (New York: Columbia University Press, 1944), 239.

20. AD Aude 15M117, Report of *commissaire spécial* to prefect, Dec. 24, 1893. For earlier examples of tax revolts, see Charles Tilly, Louise A. Tilly, and Richard Tilly, *The Rebellious Century, 1830–1930* (Cambridge, Mass.: Harvard University Press, 1975), 46–48 and passim; Roger Price, ed., *1848 in France* (Ithaca: Cornell University Press, 1975), 124–125.

21. AD Aude 15M117, Report of *commissaire général*, Carcassonne, to prefect, Sept. 30, 1900; Barbut, *Etude sur le Vignoble*, 77; Warner, *Winegrowers*, 18; Comice agricole de Narbonne, *Rapport sur les travaux et sur la situation économique et agricole de l'arrondissement pour l'Exercice de 1900–1901, par le Dr. Louis de Martin, président du Comice* (Narbonne: F. Caillard, 1901), 7.

22. See Charles Gide, "La crise du vin en France et les associations de vinification," *Revue d'économie politique* 15 (Mar. 1901): 218–235; Charles Gide, "La crise du vin dans le Midi de la France," *Revue d'économie politique* 21 (July 1907): 481–512; Pierre Genieys, *La crise viticole méridionale* (Toulouse: Edouard Privat, 1905); Frédéric Atger, *La crise viticole et la viticulture méridionale, 1900–1907* (Paris: Giard & Brière, 1907); Louis de Romeuf, "La crise viticole du Midi," *Revue politique et parlementaire* 60 (May 1909): 289–321.

23. AD Aude 15M117, Report of *commissaire central*, Carcassonne, to prefect, Sept. 30, 1900.

24. R. Pech, *Entreprise viticole*, 110, 114, 117, 123–125.

25. Ardouin Dumazet, *Voyages en France* (1904), cited by R. Pech, "Vie politique," 25; Romeuf, "Crise viticole," 293.

26. Warner, *Winegrowers*, 21; Romeuf, "Crise viticole," 292–293.

27. R. Pech, *Entreprise viticole*, 149.

28. Dugrand, *Villes et campagnes*, 365. In fact, the total area given over to large vineyards of forty hectares and more shrank between 1892 and 1911; see R. Pech, *Entreprise viticole*, 149.

29. See SC Aude, "Cadastre foncier de Coursan," fols. 552 (Pontserme); 974, 975, 978, 979, 983 (Lastours); 1431 (La Française); 1158 (La Ricardelle); and 446, 449, 450, 464, 466 (Laforgue).

30. See C. Gervais, *Indicateur des vignobles méridionaux*, 501–502, 507–509.

31. Barbut, "Vignoble de l'Aude," 3–4, 9; R. Pech, "Aspects de l'économie narbonnaise," 119.

32. R. Pech, *Entreprise viticole*, 297.

33. Ibid., 303, 306–310, 312.

34. Ibid., 56, 70. More vineyard workers owned land in the Hérault: 37 percent in 1882 and 31 percent in 1892; see Smith, "Work Routine and Social Structure"; and J. Harvey Smith, "Work Structure and

Labor Organization in Lower Languedoc" (Paper presented to the Annual Meeting of the Society for French Historical Studies, Washington, D.C., Apr. 1–2, 1981).

35. France, Ministère de l'agriculture, Direction de l'enseignement et des services agricoles, *Enquête sur les salaires agricoles* (Paris: Imprimerie nationale, 1912), 54; Passama, *Condition des ouvriers*, 16ff., 86–88.

36. See Rémy Pech's analysis of the efficiency of the *petit exploitant* in *Entreprise viticole*, 438–461; see also Passama, *Condition des ouvriers*. A similar process of self-exploitation in a period of economic crisis was seen in the vineyards of Catalonia, where small producers survived and could even purchase land from bankrupt large farmers; see Abraham Iszaevich, "Social Organization and Social Mobility in a Catalan Village" (Ph.D. diss., University of Michigan, 1979), cited by David Goodman and Michael Redclift, *From Peasant to Proletarian: Capitalist Development and Agrarian Transitions* (Oxford: Basil Blackwell, 1981), 13.

37. R. Pech, *Entreprise viticole*, 413, 443–444.

38. Similar changes in the composition of the labor force have been noted by Loubère, *Radicalism in Mediterranean France*, 101; and Smith, "Work Routine and Social Structure," 371.

39. AD Aude 11M28, 35, 37, 43, 48, 49, "Tableaux récapitulatifs des dénombrements, 1886, 1891, 1896, 1901, 1906"; 11M157, "Dénombrement de la Population. Etats nominatifs des habitants de Coursan, 1911." See Verdejo, "Mutation de la vie rurale," 111, 114, 122, on a similar increase in foreign-born immigrants in Cuxac.

40. Augé-Laribé, *Problème agraire*.

41. Augé-Laribé, "Les ouvriers de la viticulture languedocienne et leurs syndicats," *Le Musée social. Mémoires et documents*, 1903, 293–294.

42. For a similar process in the Hérault, see Smith, "Work Routine and Social Structure," 370–371.

43. Garidou, "Viticulture audoise," 50; Augé-Laribé, "Ouvriers de la viticulture languedocienne," 278–279; AD Aude 15M125, "Grèves agricoles, dossiers des grèves dans l'arrondissement de Narbonne, 1903–1906."

44. Forest owners in the Cher around the turn of the century also denied lumbermen customary rights to gather wood; see Gratton, *Luttes des classes*, 63.

45. R. Pech, *Entreprise viticole*, 417. On hiring and payment practices, see Gabriel-Ellen Prévot, "Les récents mouvements agraires dans le Midi de la France," *La Revue socialiste* 39 (Jan.–July 1904): 535. On group control over wages as an early element of workers' control, see David Montgomery, "Workers' Control over Machine Production in

the Nineteenth Century," *Labor History* 17 (Fall 1976): 488. Lumbermen in the Nièvre and in the Cher also exercised collective control over the wage in the late nineteenth and early twentieth centuries; see René Braque, "Aux origines du syndicalisme dans les milieux ruraux du centre de la France (Allier, Cher, Nièvre, Sud du Loiret)," *Le Mouvement social* 42 (Jan.–Mar. 1963): 99–100.

46. Chatelain observes that in some parts of lower Languedoc, "une véritable association a été organisée et le travail se faisait généralement par équipes; les déplacements s'étendaient dans plusieurs départements" (*Migrations temporaires*, 142). This was the case also for grafters in the Gard. See also Joan Scott, *Glassworkers of Carmaux*, 33; Hanagan, *Logic of Solidarity*, 63–64, 96; Odette Hardy-Hémery, "Rationalisation de technique et rationalisation du travail à la Compagnie des mines d'Anzin, 1927–1928," *Le Mouvement social* 72 (July–Sept. 1970): 3–48.

47. Augé-Laribé, "Rôle du capital," 196.

48. On the establishment of capitalist agriculture within industrial societies, see Goodman and Redclift, *From Peasant to Proletarian*, 11.

CHAPTER 4

1. Martine Ségalen, *Love and Power in the Peasant Family*, trans. Sarah Matthews (Chicago: University of Chicago Press, 1983), 108; Martine Ségalen, "Le mariage, l'amour et la femme dans les proverbes du sud de la France," *Annales du Midi* 87 (1975): 284.

2. Rivals, *Agriculture dans l'Aude*, 69.

3. Women counted for about one-third of agricultural workers at the end of the nineteenth century; see T. Deldyke, H. Gelders, and J.-M. Limbor, *La population active et sa structure* (Brussels: Université de Bruxelles, 1968), 174.

4. Ségalen, *Love and Power*, 81, 97–98.

5. On women's contribution to rural household economies more generally, see, for example, Heidi Hartmann, "Capitalism, Patriarchy, and Job Segregation by Sex," *Signs* 1 (Summer 1976): 137–169; Cynthia B. Lloyd, "The Division of Labor Between the Sexes: A Review," in *Sex Discrimination and the Division of Labor*, ed. Cynthia B. Lloyd (New York: Columbia University Press, 1974); Ségalen, *Love and Power* and "Mariage"; and Louise A. Tilly, "The Family Wage Economy of a French Textile City: Roubaix, 1872–1906," *Journal of Family History* 4 (Winter 1979): 388; Michele Barrett, *Women's Oppression Today* (London: Verso, 1980), 172–186, on domestic labor under capitalism; and Christine Delphy, *Close to Home*, trans. and ed. Diana Leonard (London: Hutchinson, 1984), 78–92.

6. On women's migration, see Chatelain, *Migrations temporaires* 1:58ff., 121, 133; Leslie Page Moch, *Paths to the City: Regional Migration in Nineteenth-Century France* (Beverly Hills, Calif.: Sage, 1983), 147–148, 186–188.

7. Yves Rinaudo has found that in the Var, wealthy landowning women lent money to peasants, and interest from these loans provided them with a steady income ("Usure et crédit," 443–444).

8. On the division of labor in the vineyards, see Fabre and Lacroix, *Vie quotidienne*, 178–196; Galtier, *Vignoble du Languedoc-méditerranéen* 1:253; Coste-Floret, *Travaux du vignoble*, 30, 76, 375–379; Augé-Laribé, *Problème agraire*, 260–261, 272; Sagnes, *Mouvement ouvrier*, 31–32; Hartmann, "Capitalism, Patriarchy, and Job Segregation," 139; Barrett, *Women's Oppression*, 152–186.

9. AN C86, "Agriculture française par MM. les Inspecteurs de l'agriculture," 260.

10. Coste-Floret, *Travaux du vignoble*, 328.

11. The Félibrige was a movement of writers and poets who promoted the Provençal literary renaissance of the 1850s.

12. Alphonse Daudet, *Letters from My Windmill*, trans. Frederick Davies (1866–1867; Harmondsworth, Eng.: Penguin Books, 1984), 153.

13. Interview with Anastasie Vergnes (née Cheytion), Coursan, Aude, Aug. 20, 1974, conducted with Rémy Pech.

14. Fabre and Lacroix, *Vie quotidienne*, 239–240. On the ambiguity of gender and power, see Ségalen, *Love and Power*.

15. See AD Aude 9M78, "Mercuriales, Etats décadaires des denrées . . . prix pratiqués sur les marchés, 1850–1905, 1912–1921."

16. In the period of vineyard expansion, women in Coursan made 50 to 60 centimes more than women in agriculture nationally; France, Ministère de l'agriculture, *Résultats généraux de l'enquête décennale de 1882*, 382.

17. Coste-Floret, *Travaux du vignoble*, 376.

18. R. Pech, *Entreprise viticole*, 383, 385–386.

19. See, for example, Christine Delphy, "Sharing the Same Table: Consumption in the Family," in *Close to Home*, 40–56; Laura Oren, "The Welfare of Women in Laboring Families: England, 1860–1950," in *Clio's Consciousness Raised*, ed. Mary Hartman and Lois Banner (New York: Harper & Row, 1974), 229–230; Lynn Hollen Lees, "Getting and Spending: The Family Budgets of English Industrial Workers in 1890," in *Consciousness and Class Experience*, ed. John Merriman (London: Holmes & Meier, 1976), 180. Paul Passama calculated food ex-

penses at 293 francs for male workers and 232 francs for female workers (*Condition des ouvriers*, 105).

20. Mean ages at first marriage have been computed from TGI, Narbonne, "Etat civil de Coursan, Actes de mariage, 1850–1910." See also Wesley D. Camp, *Marriage and the Family in France Since the Revolution* (New York: Bookman Associates, 1961), 53. Villagers in Coursan also married earlier than villagers in the Stéphanois village of Marlhes studied by James Lehning; see *The Peasants of Marlhes* (Chapel Hill: University of North Carolina Press, 1980), 70.

21. AD Aude 5M8, Prefect reports, esp. of Sept. 16, 1861, and Mar. 1 and 15, 1862.

22. AD Aude 9M78–91, "Mercuriales . . . 1850–1885." Pierre Bléton estimated that working-class families spent the majority of their income on food in the 1860s; see *La vie sociale sous le Second Empire. Un étonnant témoignage de la comtesse de Ségur* (Paris: Editions ouvrières, 1963), 76. In the prosperous expansion years of the vineyard economy, workers in the Narbonnais spent about 20 percent of their food budget on meat, 25 percent on bread, and 20 percent on wine, with rent figuring for between 15 and 18 percent of the budget. Cf. Georges Duveau, *La vie ouvrière en France sous le Second Empire* (Paris: Presses Universitaires de France, 1946), 329–386; Hanagan, *Logic of Solidarity*, 72–80.

23. In 1870, yearly expenses of carpenters in Carcassonne averaged 985 francs for a family of four, against an income of 780 francs. That summer the Corporation des ouvriers charpentiers of Carcassonne petitioned the prefect of the Aude to demand a wage increase and supplied a family budget to support their case; see AD Aude 15M134, "Dossiers des grèves des communes rurales de l'arrondissement de Carcassonne."

24. Louise A. Tilly and Joan W. Scott, *Women, Work, and Family* (New York: Methuen, 1987), 124.

25. This was true in 34 percent of all households in Coursan in 1851; AD Aude 11M78, "Dénombrement de la population. Etats nominatifs des habitants de Coursan, 1851." It is possible that the Coursan census underestimated child labor; see Louise A. Tilly, "Individual Lives and Family Strategies in the French Proletariat," *Journal of Family History* 4 (Summer 1979): 137–152.

26. See AD Aude 11M78, "Dénombrement de la population. Etats nominatifs des habitants de Coursan, 1851."

27. Etienne Van de Walle has argued that this census (as well as others between 1872 and 1896), which relied on forms given to house-

hold heads to fill out and return, underestimated women's wage-earning activities; see *Female Population*, 24.

28. AD Aude 11M35, "Tableaux récapitulatifs généraux dans le canton de Coursan, 1886." In that year 55.8 percent of women in the labor force were listed as agricultural workers, though perhaps the female agricultural labor force in Coursan was swollen by immigrants from other parts of the south. The absence of a nominative census for 1886 for the village of Coursan prevents a closer analysis of women's work patterns just as the phylloxera began to attack the Audois vineyards.

29. Interview with Anastasie Vergnes, Aug. 20, 1974. See also Gay Gullickson, "The Sexual Division of Labor in Cottage Industry and Agriculture in the Pays de Caux: Auffay, 1750–1850," *French Historical Studies* 12 (Fall 1981): 195–196; and Charles Babbage's classic account of wage differences and the division of labor in a nineteenth-century English pin factory, cited in Harvey Braverman, *Labor and Monopoly Capital* (New York: Monthly Review Press, 1974), 80.

30. AD Aude 11M35, "Tableaux récapitulatifs généraux dans le canton de Coursan, 1886." According to Passama, the wives of Spanish workers did not work the vines but hired themselves out as *domestiques de ferme* to cook or work as domestic servants on the estate vineyards; see *Condition des ouvriers*, 91.

31. Passama, *Condition des ouvriers*, 76–77; Augé-Laribé, "Ouvriers de la viticulture languedocienne," 290–291. The number of workdays diminished because replanted vineyards did not become fully productive until 1893–1894 and so temporarily required less intensive cultivation.

32. France, Ministère du travail et de la prévoyance sociale, Statistique générale, *Salaires et coût de l'existence à diverses époques jusqu'en 1910* (Paris: Imprimerie nationale, 1911), 61; Maurice Halbwachs, "Revenues et dépenses de ménages des travailleurs: Une enquête officielle de l'avant-guerre," *Revue d'économie politique* 35 (Jan.–Feb. 1921): 57. Expenses for food made up some 75 to 80 percent of working-class budgets (Passama, *Condition des ouvriers*, 110), a higher percentage than Halbwach found for French working-class households in 1907 ("Budgets des familles ouvrières et paysannes en France en 1907," *Bulletin de la statistique générale de la France* 4 [Oct. 1914]: 55).

33. The following sources have been used to estimate household budgets in the post-phylloxera years: AD Aude 9M91–106, "Mercuriales . . . 1885–1905, 1912–1921; Passama, *Condition des ouvriers*, 56, 82, 100–115, 209–212; and Augé-Laribé, "Ouvriers de la viticulture languedocienne," 290–291. Comparable budgets for agricultural

workers' households elsewhere in France in the prewar years are found in L. Dugé de Bernonville, "Enquête sur les conditions de la vie ouvrière et rurale en France, 1913–1914" (Parts 1 and 2), *Bulletin de la statistique générale de la France* 6 (Oct. 1916): 85–108; (Jan. 1917): 185–221.

34. The standard of living of French workers in the nineteenth and early twentieth centuries has been the subject of some debate, going back to the years before World War I. Albert Aftalion argued in 1912 ("Le salaire réel et sa nouvelle orientation," *Revue d'économie politique* 26 [1912]: 541–552) that the improvement in workers' real wages in the last twenty years of the nineteenth century slowed markedly in the first decade of the twentieth, but that workers' standard of living nonetheless continued to improve. Halbwachs also noted the improvement in wages and the different distribution of working-class incomes that came with increased earnings ("Budgets des familles ouvrières" and "Revenues et dépenses"). More recently, Jean l'Homme has shown that workers' purchasing power, which increased between 1882 and 1905, declined between 1905 and 1913; see "Le pouvoir d'achat de l'ouvrier français au cours d'un siècle: 1840–1940," *Mouvement social* 63 (Apr.–June 1968): 41–69. Peter Stearns, conversely, has argued that French workers' living standards declined between 1900 and 1910; see *Revolutionary Syndicalism and French Labor: Cause Without Rebels* (New Brunswick, N.J.: Rutgers University Press, 1971), app. A. Stearns's argument is supported by Jacques Rougerie, "Remarques sur l'histoire des salaires à Paris au XIXe siècle,"*Mouvement social* 63 (Apr.–June 1968): 71–108. Stearns questions the reliability of the government's price series, which, he plausibly argues, underestimated price increases and failed to weight items consumed by workers for their actual importance in the family budget (pp. 111–112). As Michael Hanagan has pointed out, until more is known about unemployment it will be difficult to assess the standard of living of French workers accurately; see *Logic of Solidarity*, 83–84n31. Stearns's observation that nationally real wages rose slightly after 1911 is not borne out by the data for the Narbonnais, where continued increases in the cost of living offset wage increases after 1905.

35. On Roubaix, see L. Tilly, "Family Wage Economy"; see also L. Tilly, "Individual Lives and Family Strategies"; and L. Tilly and Scott, *Women, Work, and Family*, chap. 6, esp. 123–136.

36. AD Aude 11M157, "Dénombrement de la Population. Etats nominatifs des habitants de Coursan, 1911."

37. Interview with Julien Coca, Coursan, Aude, June 26, 1979.

38. Interview with Mme. Cendrous, Coursan, Aude, June 26, 1979.

39. Interview with Anastasie Vergnes, Aug. 20, 1974.

40. Passama, *Condition des ouvriers*, 114.

41. AD Aude 15M125, "Grèves agricoles," Report of *commissaire spécial*, Narbonne, to prefect, Jan. 23, 1904.

CHAPTER 5

1. Loubère, *Radicalism in Mediterranean France*, 111; Monique Pech, "Les luttes politiques à Narbonne à la fin du XIXe siècle: Un exemple, le duel Ferroul-Bartissol aux élections législatives de 1898," in *Narbonne. Archéologie et histoire* (Montpellier: Fédération historique du Languedoc-méditerranéen et du Roussillon, 1973), 95-105; Rémy Pech, "Les thèmes économiques et sociaux du socialisme férrouliste à Narbonne, 1880–1914," in *Droite et gauche de 1789 à nos jours* (Montpellier: Centre d'histoire contemporaine du Languedoc-méditerranéen et du Roussillon, 1975), 255–270.

2. AD Aude 14M20, Report of M. de Beauxhostes, president of the Comice agricole de Narbonne, to the subprefect of Narbonne, Nov. 25, 1884; Report of Chamber of Commerce of Narbonne to subprefect, Jan. 3, 1885.

3. See Clemenceau's 1881 program in Jacques Kayser, *Les grandes batailles du radicalisme, 1820–1901* (Paris: Marcel Rivière, 1962), 326–329.

4. See Leo Loubère, "Left-Wing Radicals, Strikes, and the Military, 1880–1907," *French Historical Studies* 3 (Spring 1963): 96, 100; Jean-Thomas Nordmann, *Histoire des radicaux, 1820–1973* (Paris: Editions de la Table ronde, 1974), 124.

5. R. Pech, "Vie politique," 99; Madeleine Rebérioux, *La république radicale?* (Paris: Seuil, 1975), 45–46.

6. Raynier, *Biographie*, 176. In 1898 Narbonne was elected deputy from the Second District of Narbonne, and he represented the Groupe d'études sociales of Lézignan at the 1899 socialist congress in Paris, as a member of the independent Socialist Federation of the Aude. He again represented these groups in the 1900 socialist congress, but did not join the SFIO in 1905. See Maitron, *Dictionnaire biographique* 14:168.

7. R. Pech. "Vie politique," 109.

8. Maitron, *Dictionnaire biographique* 12:187.

9. AD Aude 7M25–31, "Cercles, salons, clubs, sociétés"; 15M86, "Associations professionnelles."

10. Parti ouvrier français (POF), *8e Congrès national du Parti ouvrier tenu à Lille, les 11 et 12 octobre 1890* (Lille: Imprimerie ouvrière, 1890), 3–8; POF, *9e Congrès national du Parti ouvrier tenu à Lyon du 26 au 28*

novembre 1891 (Paris: G. Delory, 1891), 1–8; POF, *10ᵉ Congrès national du Parti ouvrier tenu à Marseille du 24 au 28 septembre 1892* (Lille: Imprimerie ouvrière, 1893); POF, *12ᵉ Congrès national du Parti ouvrier tenu à Nantes du 14 au 16 septembre 1894* (Paris: G. Delory, 1894), 10. Claude Willard underestimated the extent of socialist organization in the countryside before 1898 (*Les Guesdistes. Le mouvement socialiste en France de 1893 à 1905* [Paris: Editions Sociales, 1965], 294).

11. AD Aude 5M93, Reports of *commissaire spécial*, Narbonne, to prefect of Apr. 2 and Nov. 6, 1892, on the visits of Guesde and Minck to Narbonne, and of May 29, 1893, on Millerand's visit to Narbonne; see also reports of Mar. 19 and Apr. 18 and 27, 1889.

12. Willard, *Les Guesdistes*, 288, 293; *République sociale*, May 5, 1892.

13. On Ferroul and his political career, see Maitron, *Dictionnaire biographique* 12:186–189; Reynier, *Biographie*, 157–159; M. Pech, "Luttes politiques"; and R. Pech, "Thèmes économiques et sociaux."

14. On French municipal socialism, see Joan W. Scott, "Mayors Versus Police Chiefs: Socialist Municipalities Confront the French State," in *French Cities in the Nineteenth Century*, ed. John Merriman (New York: Holmes & Meier, 1981), 230–245.

15. R. Pech, "Thèmes économiques et sociaux," 263–264; and numerous police reports in AD Aude 5M93. Both the practical experience and the spirit of municipal socialism in Narbonne contrast with those of Villeurbanne under the socialist mayor Victor Augageur; see Bernard Meuvret, *Le socialisme municipal à Villeurbanne, 1880–1892* (Lyon: Presses universitaires de Lyon, 1982).

16. AD Aude 5M93, Reports of *commissaire spécial* to prefect, Sept. 22 and Nov. 22, 1892.

17. Paul Lafargue was skeptical of Ferroul's commitment to Marxian socialism; in October 1889, a year after Ferroul had won a deputy's seat in the Chamber of Deputies, Lafargue wrote to Engels that Ferroul was a socialist "only in name" (Friedrich Engels, Paul Lafargue, and Laura Lafargue, *Correspondance*, vol. 2: *1877–1890* (Moscow: Foreign Language Publishers, 1960), 323. Claude Willard remarks that Ferroul seemed to be completely ignorant of Marxism; see *Les Guesdistes*, 294. Rémy Pech, in contrast, has argued that Ferroul became more revolutionary in the 1890s and that this cost him votes in local elections thereafter; see "Thèmes économiques et sociaux," esp. 261–262. I believe the evidence shows Ferroul's *discours* to have been more radical than his practice.

18. Aldy was a member of the POF from 1890 to 1899. Procureur de la république in Narbonne, he had served as assistant mayor of Narbonne from 1891 to 1897 and represented the canton of Narbonne

on the department General Council. See Maitron, *Dictionnaire biographique* 12:124–125; AD Aude 5M93, Report from *commissaire spécial* to prefect of socialist banquet in Lézignan, held by the Syndicat des ouvriers cultivateurs, June 3, 1892.

19. AD Aude 15M117, "Réunions publiques, meetings contre le chômage, la vie chère, etc.," Report of *commissaire spécial* to prefect on a meeting in Narbonne, Jan. 10, 1892. On the Var, see Judt, *Socialism in Provence*, 150. Judt argues that the socialists' stand against protectionism was tied to their support of low food prices for urban workers, and that this position was received favorably in the countryside as well. On Lafargue, see Pierre Barral, *Les agrariens français de Méline à Pisani* (Paris: Armand Colin, 1968), 155; see also Willard, *Les Guesdistes*, 183–184, on the 1897 Guesdist campaign against protectionism and "le pain cher."

20. AD Aude 5M93, Reports of *commissaire spécial* to prefect, Apr. 31, Sept. 30, and Oct. 18, 1896; "Manifestation à Lézignan," *La Dépêche de Toulouse*, Apr. 31, 1896; R. Pech, "Thèmes économiques et sociaux," 265.

21. Cited by M. Pech, "Luttes politiques," 100. AD Aude 2M67, Ferroul's *profession de foi*, Apr. 29, 1898; *La République sociale*, no. 454 (Mar. 17, 1898), article on the *congrès socialiste*.

22. Willard, *Les Guesdistes*, 164ff.; Leslie Derfler, "Reformism and Jules Guesde, 1891–1914," *International Review of Social History* 12 (1967): 66–80, argues that behind Guesde's "reformism" was an effort to bolster his own personal position. A more plausible understanding of Guesdist mobilization is provided by Robert P. Baker, "Socialism in the Nord, 1880–1914: A Regional View of the French Socialist Movement," *International Review of Social History* 12 (1967): 357–389.

23. *La République sociale*, no. 522 (July 20, 1899).

24. AD Aude 2M66, Reports of *commissaire spécial* to subprefect, July 30 and Aug. 13, 1893.

25. Gratton, *Luttes de classes*, 31–35. The *conseils de prud'hommes* were local arbitration councils established under the First Empire for resolving work disputes; see Jules Guesde and Paul Lafargue, *Le programme du Parti ouvrier* (Paris: N.p., [1883]), 2–5, 30–51, 116–122; Willard, *Les Guesdistes*, 366–376.

26. Harvey Goldberg, "Jaurès and the Formation of a Socialist Peasant Policy, 1885–1898," *International Review of Social History* 2 (1957): 380.

27. Lafargue, quoted by Willard, *Les Guesdistes*, 375.

28. Goldberg, "Jaurès and Socialist Peasant Policy," 381, 388; Friedrich Engels, "La question paysanne en France et en Allemagne," *Ca-*

hiers de Communisme 31 (Nov. 1955): 1476–1479: Gratton, *Luttes de classes*, 41–45; Georges Cogniot, "La question paysanne devant le mouvement ouvrier français de 1892 à 1921," *Cahiers d'histoire de l'Institut Maurice Thorez* 24 (1971): 5–21.

29. Untitled, unsigned articles in *La République sociale*, nos. 196 (May 1, 1895), 386 (Dec. 24, 1896), 486 (Nov. 10, 1898).

30. Maitron, *Dictionnaire biographique* 12: 188. The municipal elections of June 1897 were invalidated, and Ferroul was dismissed.

31. AD Aude 2M58, Election returns, Aug. 25, 1881. High abstentions (41 percent in Narbonne arrondissement), primarily among conservative voters, occurred in the absence of a conservative candidate.

32. Raynier, *Biographie*, 147–148, 176; Robert and Cougny, *Dictionnaire des parlementaires* 4:542; Maitron, *Dictionnaire biographique* 12: 215–218.

33. AD Aude 2M58, Election returns, July 23 and Aug. 9, 1883 (second ballot).

34. Under the *scrutin de liste*, political groups presented departmentwide lists of candidates rather than running separate candidates in each electoral district.

35. AD Aude 5M93, Reports from *commissaire spécial* to prefect, July 11 and Aug. 23 and 27, 1885; Siegfried, "Géographie de l'opinion," on the elections of 1885; R. Pech, "Vie politique," 135–136.

36. AD Aude 5M93, Election returns, Oct. 4 and 18, 1885. Leo Loubère has suggested that the strong radical vote in eastern wine-growing communities was helped by the immigration of workers and winegrowers who fled phylloxera in the Hérault and settled in the Aude; see *Radicalism in Mediterranean France*, 121.

37. AD Aude 2M58, Election returns, Apr. 12 and 22, 1888.

38. The Boulangists were never terribly strong in the Aude, as their poor showing in 1888 and 1889 indicates (see Table 18); the Aude would thus seem to confirm Michael Burns's findings for several other rural departments (*Rural Society and French Politics*). Ferroul's attraction to the authoritarian left did not end here; on February 7, 1895, his newspaper, *La République sociale*, welcomed Henri Rochfort, a former Blanquist who, along with Ernest Granger and Emile Eudes, had begun to move toward integral nationalism.

39. AD Aude 2M58, Election returns, Aug. 20, 1893.

40. AD Aude 2M66, Reports from *commissaire spécial* to prefect, Aug. 21–23, 1893, on the demonstration in Coursan; Letter from Mayor Abet to subprefect, Aug. 21, 1893.

41. AD Aude 2M58, Election returns, Feb. 26, May 8 and 22, 1898; 2M67, Dossier on parliamentary inquiry into fraud. Articles from *La*

Dépêche de Toulouse, Feb. 21 and 25, 1899; from *Le Télégramme*, Feb. 23, 1899; and Report from *commissaire spécial* to prefect, Feb. 21, 1899.

42. Jean-Marie Mayeur, *Les débuts de la Troisième République* (Paris: Seuil, 1973), 209. As elsewhere in France, in the Aude the Dreyfus affair did not receive much attention in either public forums or the press; see Burns, *Rural Society and French Politics*; R. Pech, "Vie politique," 267.

43. *La République sociale*, no. 462 (May 12, 1898); AD Aude 2M67, Report of *commissaire spécial* to prefect, Feb. 21, 1899. Monique Pech speculates that anarchists in Coursan counseled abstention; see "Luttes politiques," 97.

44. Alain Lancelot has suggested that people tend not to vote in the absence of a significant political choice between candidates; see *Abstentionnisme électoral en France* (Paris: Armand Colin, 1968), 99–100.

45. AD Aude 2M66, Dossiers on candidates in the 1893 elections; Report of Apr. 16, 1893. The case of Henri Rouzeaud is notable here. Willard suggests that by this time in parts of the Aude, Guesdism had become completely intermixed with radicalism (*Les Guesdistes*, 295).

46. There has been a lively debate over the timing and extent of peasants' integration into national politics, beginning with Eugen Weber's *Peasants into Frenchmen: The Modernization of Rural France, 1870–1914* (Stanford: Stanford University Press, 1976) and Margadant's *French Peasants in Revolt*, and continuing with Berenson's *Populist Religion and Left-Wing Politics* and Weber's "Comment la politique vint aux paysans: A Second Look at Peasant Politics," *American Historical Review* 87 (1982): 357–389. See also Edward Berenson, "Politics and the French Peasantry," *Social History* 12 (May 1987): 213–229. The case of the Aude suggests that although rural dwellers were very much a part of national political movements by the 1840s, this did not mean local personalities still did not exert considerable influence on local political life.

47. AD Aude 5M93, Report of *commissaire spécial* to prefect, Aug. 20, 1893; 5M95, ibid., Oct. 30, 1893.

48. *La République sociale*, no. 634 (Jan. 23, 1902).

49. Ibid.; Aldy's *profession de foi, La République sociale*, no. 647 (Apr. 24, 1902).

50. On the Var, see Judt, *Socialism in Provence*, 323–336. Judt's interpretation has recently been challenged by Yves Rinaudo, who claims that socialists in the Var were not revolutionary collectivists; rather, they adjusted their socialism to the rural world, "respectueux de la petite propriété et soucieux d'éviter la révolution violente" (*Vendages*,

192). Rinaudo also emphasizes the links of Varois socialism with its left radical past (pp. 241, 254n1). See also Sagnes, *Le Mouvement ouvrier*, 57–64.

51. Willard, *Les Guesdistes*, 285; Judt, *Socialism in Provence*, 218.

52. Judt, *Socialism in Provence*, 143.

53. Although a few cooperatives existed in the Aude before World War I, they became well established only in the interwar years (late 1930s). In the Var, by contrast, thirty-four cooperative wineries had been established by 1914; see ibid., 167–168.

CHAPTER 6

1. Gérard Walter, *Histoire des paysans de France* (Paris: Flammarion, 1963), 427–428; Gratton, *Luttes de classes*, 145; France, Ministère de commerce, Direction du travail, *Statistique des grèves et des Recours à la conciliation et à l'arbitrage, 1903* (Paris: Imprimerie nationale, 1903).

2. Passama, *Condition des ouvriers*, 41.

3. AD Aude 15M117, Report from *commissaire spécial*, Narbonne, to prefect, Oct. 21, 1896.

4. Ibid., Oct. 21, 1896; Mar. 13, 1897; Jean-François Garidou, "Les mouvements ouvriers agricoles dans l'Aude, 1900–1910," in *Carcassonne et sa région* (Carcassonne: Gabelle, 1970), 317; Gratton, *Luttes de classes*, 141; Augé-Laribé, "Ouvriers de la viticulture languedocienne," 308; Verdejo, "Mutation de la vie rurale," 208–209.

5. AD Aude 15M30, Report to Ministry of the Interior from the municipality of Narbonne outlining Bourse activities, 1902.

6. AD Aude 15M90, Dossiers of formation and composition of workers' organizations.

7. Report of delegate from Carcassonne to First Congress of the Fédération des travailleurs agricoles du Midi, 1903; cited by Pierre Vilar, Introduction to Gratton, *Luttes de classes*, 13.

8. AD Aude 15M117 and 125, Police reports on strike of December 13, 1904.

9. See AD Aude 11M157, "Dénombrement de la population. Etats nominatifs des habitants de Coursan, 1911"; Maitron, *Dictionnaire biographique*, vol. 11, pt. 3, p. 201; TGI Narbonne, "Etat civil de Coursan, Actes de naissances, 1880–1914"; interviews with Anastasie Vergnes (née Cheytion), sister of François Cheytion and Marius Cheytion, Coursan, June 28, 1973, and Aug. 20, 1974.

10. Archives départementales de l'Hérault 15M49, Letters from prefect of the Hérault to mayor of Montpellier, Apr. 13 and 14, 1902;

Letter from Cheytion to prefect of the Hérault declaring his candidacy, Apr. 8, 1902; 15M50, *La Dépêche de Toulouse*, Apr. 28, 1902, election returns.

11. See Fédération des travailleurs agricoles du Midi, *Compte rendu des travaux du 3e Congrès de la Fédération des travailleurs agricoles du Midi* (Perpignan: D. Muller, 1906), 54 (hereafter cited as FTAM, *3e Congrès*).

12. On unions' ambivalence or hostility to working women generally, see Louise A. Tilly, "Paths of Proletarianization: Organization of Production, Sexual Division of Labor, and Women's Collective Action," *Signs* 7 (1981): 400–417; Marie-Hélène Zylberberg-Hocquard, *Femmes et féminisme dans le mouvement ouvrier français* (Paris: Editions ouvrières, 1981), 91–93, 184–195; Charles Sowerwine, "Workers and Women in France Before 1914: The Debate over the Couriau Affair," *Journal of Modern History* 55 (Sept. 1983): 411–441. By 1911 women in France counted for under 10 percent of the unionized workers (36 percent of the labor force was female); see Madeleine Guilbert, *Les femmes et l'organisation syndicale en France avant 1914* (Paris: Centre national de la recherche scientifique, 1966), 28; Zylberberg-Hocquard, *Femmes et féminisme*, 108, 152.

13. FTAM, *3e Congrès*, 49.

14. See, for example, Louis Amphoux, "Crimes impunis," *Le Paysan*, no. 3 (July 1905); and B. Fournie, "Suppression du travail de la femme agricole," *Le Paysan*, no. 7 (July 1906).

15. For membership in Audois unions, see AD Aude 15M90, 99, 100, and 117; also Prévot, "Récents mouvements agraires"; Gratton, *Luttes de classes*, 133–197; Mayeur, *Débuts de la Troisième République*, 188–189. Average union membership in France has been calculated from the following sources: France, Ministère du travail et de la prévoyance sociale, *Annuaire des syndicats professionnels, industriels, commerciaux et agricoles, déclarés conformément à la loi du 21 mars 1884* (Paris: Imprimerie nationale, 1912), xxxii; Toutain, *Population de la France*, tables 61–63, p. 165. See also Stearns, *Revolutionary Syndicalism and French Labor*, 23; and Michelle Perrot, *Les ouvriers en Grève, 1871–1890* (Paris: Mouton, 1974), 2:447.

16. See Baker, "Socialism in the Nord."

17. Rebérioux, *République radicale?* 167.

18. AD Aude 15M99, Dossiers on the formation of workers' organizations and unions.

19. P. Picard and M. Picard, *Terre de luttes (les précurseurs, 1848–1939). Histoire du mouvement ouvrier dans le Cher* (Paris: Editions sociales, 1977); Gratton, *Luttes de classes*, 59–106, for lumbermen of central France; William McMechan, "A Syndicalist Response to Social-

ism: The French Building Trades, 1906–1914" (Paper presented at the Annual Meeting of the American Historical Association, Dallas, 1977).

20. Jacques Julliard, "Théorie syndicaliste révolutionnaire et pratique gréviste," *Mouvement social* 65 (1968): 55–69; on contracts in the Aude, see France, Ministère de commerce, *Statistique des grèves*, for 1900–1915.

21. Hanagan, *Logic of Solidarity*, 15.

22. A. Souchon, *La crise de la main d'oeuvre agricole en France* (Paris: Rousseau, 1914), 21; R. Pech, *Entreprise viticole*, 416–420; Montgomery, "Workers' Control over Machine Production," 488.

23. AD Aude 6M360–361, "Documents anarchistes"; 7 M 114, "Police des spectacles."

24. Aminzade, *Class, Politics, and Early Industrial Capitalism*, 77.

25. E. P. Thompson, "The Moral Economy of the English Crowd in the Nineteenth Century," *Past and Present* 50 (Feb. 1971): 76–106; Tilly, Tilly, and Tilly, *Rebellious Century*, 85; James C. Scott, *The Moral Economy of the Peasant* (New Haven: Yale University Press, 1976). See also William Reddy, "The Language of the Crowd in Rouen, 1752–1871," *Past and Present* 74 (Feb. 1977): 62–89.

26. James Scott, *Moral Economy*, 184–185 et seq.

27. AD Aude 15M125, "Grèves agricoles, Dossiers des grèves . . . pour l'arrondissement de Narbonne, 1903–1906," Letter from subprefect of the Aude to prefect, Jan. 8, 1904; 15M121, "Grèves et grèves agricoles, Télégrammes de presse," Letter of prefect to minister of the interior on strikes, Feb. 1, 1904. These reports suggest that local government authorities were initially sympathetic to the situation of vineyard workers.

28. Gratton, *Luttes de classes*, 145–146; R. E. Mataillon, *Les syndicats ouvriers dans l'agriculture* (Paris: Bonvalot-Jouve, 1908), 49; France, Ministère de commerce, *Statistique des grèves, 1904*, 433–444; reports in *Le Petit Méridional*, Jan. 4, 7, and 9, 1904; Prévot, "Récents mouvements agraires."

29. See AD Aude 15M125, "Grèves agricoles"; *Le Petit Méridional*, Jan. 11 and 14, 1904.

30. AD Aude 15M121, Prefect's reports to minister of the interior, Jan. 21 and Feb. 1, 1904; 15M125, Police report on the strike of January 23, 1904; 15M126, Deposition of *curé* of Coursan, Jan. 15, 1904. The red flag first appeared with the May First demonstrations at the end of the nineteenth century; in earlier demonstrations workers used the tricolor, as a symbol of 1789. See Perrot, *Ouvriers en grève*, 2: 567; article from *La Dépêche de Toulouse*, cited in Walter, *Histoire des paysans*, 428.

31. J. Harvey Smith, "Agricultural Workers and the French Wine-Growers Revolt of 1907," *Past and Present* 79 (1978): 107; AD Aude 15M121, Report of prefect to minister of the interior, Feb. 1, 1904.

32. AD Aude 15M126, "Grèves agricoles, Dossiers des grèves dans la localité de l'arrondissement de Narbonne," Article from *Le Petit Méridional*, Jan. 11, 1904; Prévot, "Récents mouvements agraires," 544–545. From 1905, when the CGT began to step up its campaign for the eight-hour day, vineyard workers argued for a six-hour day on the grounds that it would help reduce unemployment; see Fédération des travailleurs agricoles du Midi, *Compte rendu des travaux du 2ᵉ Congrès national des travailleurs agricoles et partis similaires organisé par la Section de l'Aude* (Narbonne: J. Boulet, 1904), 35; FTAM, *3ᵉ Congrès*, 46. These demands were very different from those raised by workers in Cruzy, Hérault, for example, who attempted to defend "the right of the small producer to free sale on the market of natural wines at a reasonable profit" (Smith, "Work Routine and Social Structure," 375).

33. Tilly, Tilly, and Tilly, *Rebellious Century*; Laura Levine Frader, "Grapes of Wrath: Vineyard Workers, Labor Unions, and Strike Activity in the Aude, 1860–1913," in *Class Conflict and Collective Action*, ed. Louise A. Tilly and Charles Tilly (Beverly Hills, Calif.: Sage, 1981), 196.

34. AN BB¹⁸2296 (437A05), Report of *procureur général*, Montpellier, to minister of the interior, Nov. 25, 1905.

35. On artisans' contributions, see *La République sociale*, Jan. 28, 1904.

36. *Le Petit Méridional*, Jan. 14, 1904.

37. See Perrot, *Ouvriers en grève* 2: 527; AD Aude 15M117, Report of *commissaire spécial*, Narbonne, to prefect, Nov. 18, 1901.

38. France, Ministère de commerce, *Statistique des grèves, 1904*, 8–11, 32–35; AD Aude 15M125, "Grèves agricoles," Circular from minister of the interior on the January strike; 15M126, "Grèves agricoles," Article from *Le Petit Méridional*, Jan. 22, 1904.

39. Mataillon, *Syndicats ouvriers*, 54.

40. Michel Augé-Laribé, "Les résultats des grèves agricoles dans le Midi de la France," *Le Musée Social*, Oct. 1904, 287ff.

41. On the March and April strikes, see Mataillon, *Syndicats ouvriers*, 56–61; AD Aude 15M126, "Grèves agricoles," Dossier on April strike in Coursan; France, Ministère de commerce, *Statistique des Grèves, 1904*, 32–35.

42. On the formation of the FTAM, see Gratton, *Luttes de classes*, 143–144; Mataillon, *Syndicats ouvriers*, 256ff.; AD Aude 15M101, "Statuts de la Fédération . . . du département de l'Aude"; Fédération des

travailleurs agricoles du Midi, *Compte rendu des travaux du 1er Congrès national des travailleurs agricoles et partis similaires organisé par la Fédération des travailleurs agricoles de l'Hérault* (Béziers: J.-B. Perdraut, 1903), 10–11, 39–42, 75, 78.

43. FTAM, *3e Congrès*, 53–55.

44. Gratton, *Luttes de classes*, 152; Augé-Laribé, "Résultats des grèves agricoles," 290ff.; Mataillon, *Syndicats ouvriers*; FTAM, *3e Congrès*, 45.

45. See AD Aude 15M121, Report of *commissaire central*, Narbonne, to prefect, Nov. 23, 1904.

46. In a straw poll taken prior to the strike call, 29 out of 132 unions opposed the strike, 72 supported it, and 31 did not respond. See AD Aude 15M121, "Grèves et grèves agricoles," Circular signed by Paul Ader; Appeal from Federation strike committee; Mataillon, *Syndicats ouvriers*, 61. The following standard conditions were adopted:

1. A six-hour minimum, eight-hour maximum work day.
2. A minimum wage of 50 centimes an hour.
3. Sulfating to last no more than eight hours, for 4 francs and two liters of wine.
4. Harvest and pressing days fixed at eight hours for 4.50 francs and three liters of wine.
5. Overtime at harvest to be paid at 75 centimes an hour.
6. Women to earn half as much as men in both money and wine.
7. No overtime or piecework, except during harvest.
8. *Mésadiers* to earn 35 francs a month for six hours of work per day, and 45 francs a month for eight hours of work per day.
9. Workers to be paid on Saturday at their place of work.
10. Travel time to work to be paid by the patron; return from work paid by the worker.
11. Two liters of good wine to be given to men throughout the year.
12. After a rain work to begin three days later.
13. Workers to be paid for each hour of work they begin.
14. Workers may not be fired for striking or for membership in a union.

See FTAM, *2e Congrès*, 36–38; AD Aude 15M121, "Grèves et grèves agricoles," Report from *commissaire spécial* to prefect, Apr. 1, 1905.

47. AN BB[18]2272 (230A04), "Grèves artisanales, agricoles, etc.," Reports from *procureur général*, Montpellier, to minister of justice, Jan. 24, Feb. 19, and March 15, 1905; Telegram from *procureur général*, Narbonne, to minister of justice, Dec. 24, 1904.

48. AD Aude 15M120, "Grèves agricoles, Articles de presse," Newspaper accounts in *Le Petit Méridional*, Dec. 4 and 6, 1904; *La Dépêche de*

Toulouse, Dec. 5, 1904; *L'Humanité*, Dec. 8, 1904; Poster from the FTAM calling on shopkeepers for support; 15M121, "Grèves et grèves agricoles," Telegram, Dec. 8, 1904.

49. On municipal protests against troops, see AN F⁷13626, Articles from *La Petite République*, Dec. 8, 1904; *L'Humanité*, Dec. 8, 1904; AD Aude 15M120, "Grèves agricoles"; Article from *Le Petit Méridional*, Dec. 13, 1904.

50. Paul Ader, "La grève générale des travailleurs agricoles du Midi," *Le Mouvement socialiste* 147 (Jan. 15, 1905): 133–134.

51. AD Aude 15M120, "Grèves agricoles," *La Dépêche de Toulouse*, Dec. 11, 1904.

52. AD Aude 15M117, "Réunions publiques, meetings contre le chômage, la vie chère, etc.," Report from prefect to minister of the interior, Dec. 13, 1904; 15M126, "Grèves agricoles, Dossiers des grèves," Additional police reports, Dec. 3 and 4, 1904. François Cheyton was one of those arrested for stealing provisions, which he turned over to the strike committee.

53. Ader, "La grève générale," 137.

54. On the first incident in Coursan, see AD Aude 15M117, "Réunions publiques, meetings contre le chômage, la vie chère, etc.," Report from prefect to minister of the interior, Dec. 17, 1904; 15M120, "Grèves agricoles, Articles de presse," *Le Républicain de Narbonne*, Apr. 2, 1905; 15M121, "Grèves et grèves agricoles. Etat concernant les faits de grève"; 15M126, "Grèves agricoles," Police report, Dec. 13, 1904. This form of action was, as far as we know, never taken by male strikers. For other examples, see Frank Snowden, "Violence and Social Control in Southern Italy, Apulia, 1900–1922" (Paper presented to the Social History Seminar, Centre for the Study of Social History, University of Warwick, Mar. 1983); Stearns, *Revolutionary Syndicalism and French Labor*, 68; Perrot, *Ouvriers en grève*, 505. On the incident in Salles, see AD Aude 15M120, "Grèves agricoles, Articles de Presse," *La Dépêche de Toulouse*, Mar. 9 and 10, 1905.

55. France, Ministère de commerce, *Statistique des Grèves, 1904*, 493–494; AD Aude 15M120, "Grèves agricoles, Articles de presse," *La Dépêche de Toulouse*, Dec. 17, 1904; *Le Petit Méridional*, Dec. 17, 18, and 19, 1904; *Le Télégramme*, Dec. 20, 1904.

56. See FTAM, *3ᵉ Congrès*, 45.

57. See Gabriel-Ellen Prévot, "Après la grève agricole," *L'Humanité*, Dec. 19, 1904; Gabriel-Ellen Prévot, "Les Grèves agraires du Midi: La grève générale agricole du Midi," *La Revue socialiste* 41 (Jan. 1905): 107–108 (also cited in Gratton, *Luttes de classes*, 163). On syndicalist critiques, see FTAM, *3ᵉ Congrès*, 28.

58. Fédération des travailleurs agricoles du Midi, *Compte rendu des travaux du 4e Congrès de la Fédération des travailleurs agricoles et partis similaires du Midi* (Paris: Maison des Fédérations, Service de l'imprimerie, 1906), 14.

59. Shorter and Tilly, *Strikes in France*, 83–85, 92. A longer discussion of the relationship of strike activity in the Aude to standard of living and the 1907 revolt follows in Chapter 7.

60. See Gratton, *Luttes de classes*, 169–171. The third congress of the FTAM had adopted resolutions favoring legislation on work accidents, arbitration councils, and retirement legislation for agricultural workers; see FTAM, *3e Congrès*, 51–54; FTAM, *4e Congrès*, 68–70.

61. FTAM, *3e Congrès*, 46–47. On the argument for a six-hour day to reduce unemployment, see *Le Paysan* 2, no. 1 (Jan. 1906).

62. AD Aude 15M117, Report of prefect, April 17, 1905.

63. AD Aude 5M66, Poster, "Aux viticulteurs."

64. AD Aude 5M66, "La Défense du Midi," in *Le Petit Méridional*, June 22, 1905; Articles in *Le Télégramme*, June 23 and July 11, 1905; *Le Radical du Midi*, July 2, 1905; *L'Express du Midi*, June 25, 1905; Extract from the deliberations of the Narbonne town council, June 24, 1905; 5M51, Prefect's report of June 22, 1905. See also *Action viticole* (newspaper published by the Société des syndicats agricoles), July 1905.

65. See FTAM, *2e Congrès*, 23–24.

66. Gratton, *Luttes de classes*, 172.

67. Julliard, "La CGT devant la guerre, 1900–1914," *Le Mouvement social* 49 (1964): 47–62.

68. AD Aude 15M107, "Réunions corporatives à la Bourse du travail."

69. AD Aude 15M120, "Grèves agricoles, Articles de presse," Article in *La Dépêche de Toulouse*, Mar. 23, 1905; FTAM, *3e Congrès*, 89; Article in *Le Paysan*, no. 6 (Oct. 1905), by Marius Reynaud, secretary of the Syndicat des cultivateurs et travailleurs de la terre de Cuxac.

70. Mataillon, *Syndicats ouvriers*, 294; Henri Dubief, *Le syndicalisme révolutionnaire* (Paris: Armand Colin, 1969), 148. The resolution of the Coursan union was printed in *Le Paysan* 2, no. 2 (Feb. 1906). For other examples of antimilitarist sentiment in the Aude, see *Le Paysan*, no. 6 (Oct. 1905).

71. FTAM, *1er Congrès*, 76–77.

72. L. Pieux fils, "Syndicalisme et gouvernements," *Le Paysan* 1, no. 4 (July 1905), 3.

73. Ferroul, writing in *La République sociale*, Apr. 25, 1895.

74. *Le Paysan* 2, no. 4 (Apr. 1906).

75. *La Dépêche de Toulouse*, Apr. 20, 1906.

76. FTAM, *4e Congrès*, 76–77; Dubief, *Syndicalisme révolutionnaire*, 75–97.

77. Dubief, *Syndicalisme révolutionnaire*, 82, 84.

78. Since the 1906 FTAM congress (August) and the CGT Amiens congress (October) both took place after the legislative contest of that year, they could have had no influence on the 1906 balloting; here we are assessing the influence of pre–May 1906 electoral propaganda.

79. AD Aude 7M37, "Cercles, chambrées, etc., 1900–1909." On the department federation of the SFIO, see AN F[7]12497, "Activité socialiste dans les départements, 1900–1914. Ain à Calvados."

80. Quote from Roger Magraw, *France, 1815–1914: The Bourgeois Century* (London: Fontana, 1984), 252.

81. AN F[7] 12544, "Elections législatives de 1906," Report from Commissariat spécial des Chemins de fer to director of the Sûreté générale, Paris, Apr. 8, 1906; *La Dépêche de Toulouse*, Apr. 11, 1906, editorial entitled "Pour les élections."

82. AD Aude 2M58, "Recensement général des votes de 1876 à 1914, Elections législatives de 1906"; and Loubère, *Radicalism in Mediterranean France*, 210–213.

83. For a similar conclusion relating to the 1910 elections, see Gratton, *Luttes de classes*, 206. Abstentions in the May 1906 elections were 20 percent nationally and averaged 25–30 percent in the Aude; see Lancelot, *Abstentionisme électoral*, 56–59; and below.

84. Madeleine Rebérioux, Review of *Les ouvriers en grève*, by Michelle Perrot, *Le Mouvement social* 93 (Oct.–Dec. 1975): 114.

CHAPTER 7

1. Jean Fournel, *Avec ceux d'Argelliers. Une acte d'énergie méridionale* (Montpellier: Editions languedociennes, 1908), 19; Félix Napo, *1907. La révolte des vignerons* (Toulouse: Edouard Privat, 1971), 36–41.

2. J. Harvey Smith, "La Crise d'une économie régionale: La monoculture viticole et la révolte du Midi (1907)," *Les Annales du Midi* 92 (1980): 319.

3. The literature on 1907 includes Maurice LeBlond, *La crise du Midi* (Paris: Bibliothèque Charpentier, 1907); Guy Bechtel, *1907. La grande révolte du Midi* (Paris: Laffont, 1976); Smith, "Agricultural Workers"; Sagnes, "Mouvement de 1907"; André Marty, *A la gloire des lutteurs de 1907* (Paris: Editions Norman Béthune, 1972); and numerous dossiers in Series M of AD Aude, especially 5M66–67, and in Series F[7] of AN.

4. AD Aude 5M67, "Crise viticole et événements de 1907," Article

in *Le Petit Méridional*, July 7, 1905; Report of subprefect to prefect, Nov. 7, 1905; 5M66, "Crise viticole et événements de 1907," Reports of prefect to minister of the interior, Oct. 9, 1906, and Apr. 26, 1907; Report of subprefect to prefect, May 2, 1907; and *Le Tocsin*, no. 3 (May 5, 1907), on hostility to tax collectors.

5. AD Aude 15M132, "Grèves agricoles. Dossiers des grèves des communes rurales de l'arrondissement de Narbonne . . . 1906–1908," Diverse reports on strikes in Salles, Fleury, Marcorignan, etc.; 5M10, Monthly prefect reports, Report of subprefect to prefect, Feb. 1, 1907; AN F⁷12794, "Troubles causés par les événements de 1907," Prefect reports of May 6 and 17, 1907.

6. Napo, *1907*, 207–227.

7. César Boyer and J. Payret, *Aux pays de gueux. Les grands meetings du Midi* (Paris: N.p., 1907), 35; Félix Napo, *1907. La révolte des vignerons*, 2d ed. (Toulouse: Edouard Privat, 1982), 71.

8. See, for example, the account in Jules Maffre, "Les événements de 1907 dans l'Aude et la région méridionale," in *Carcassonne et sa région. Actes du congrès d'études regionales tenus à Carcassonne en mai 1968* (Carcassonne: Gabelle, 1970), 337.

9. See Napo, *1907* (1st ed.), 70, 74; Rinaudo, *Vendanges*, 48–49; and photographs of women in the 1907 mass meetings in R. Pech, *Entreprise viticole*, and in Jacques Durand and André Hampartzoumian, *Le Languedoc au temps des diligences* (Montpellier: Images d'oc, 1978). On the issues of health and additives, see Jacques Duhr, "Comment on fraude et nous empoisonne," *Le Journal*, June 24, 1907, who presents a ghastly list of chemical additives; "Du vin naturel," *Le Tocsin*, no. 2 (April 28, 1907); and various articles in AD Aude 5M66.

10. Smith shows that large landowners unsuccessfully tried to steer the movement in a direction compatible with their own entrepreneurial strategies; see "Crise d'une économie régionale," 326–332. On the participation of large proprietors in the Aude, see AD Aude 5M66, Report of subprefect to prefect, Apr. 26, 1907; AN F⁷12794, Report of subprefect to prefect, Apr. 26, 1907; Report of prefect to minister of the interior, undated but almost certainly June 12, 1907; Fournel, *Avec ceux d'Argelliers*, 29–30; Louis Blanc, *Souvenirs de 1907. Légende pour les Jacques* (Olonzac, Hérault: Confédération générale des vignerons du Midi, 1948), 14; Sagnes, "Mouvement de 1907," 13–14.

11. AD Aude 5M67, Report from prefect to minister of the interior, May 30, 1907; Articles from *Le Petit Méridional*, July 13, 1907, and *Le Courrier de l'Aude*, July 15, 1907; 5M68, Telegram from prefect to the minister of the interior, June 15, 1907.

12. Sagnes, "Mouvement de 1907," 16; Verdejo, "Mutation de la vie

rurale," 218; Ader, "Le Midi bouge," *Le Travailleur de la terre*, no. 1
(June, 1907). *Le Travailleur de la terre* served as the official newspaper of
the Union fédérative terrienne, which loosely united all the agricultural workers' federations then in existence, the Fédération nationale
des bûcherons, the Fédération nationale horticole, the Fédération agricole de la région du Nord, and the FTAM. Paul Ader was editor.

13. Sagnes, "Mouvement de 1907," 16; "Les ouvriers agricoles de
Bessan," *Le Travailleur de la terre*, no. 2 (July 1907).

14. Fédération des travailleurs agricoles du Midi, *Compte rendu des
travaux du 5ᵉ Congrès de la Fédération des travailleurs agricoles et partis
similaires du Midi* (Béziers: Imprimerie ouvrière du Centre—ouvriers
syndiqués et fédérés, 1907), 44–45; Smith, "Agricultural Workers,"
114–115. In the Aude workers did not organize and influence the mass
meetings to the extent that Smith suggests.

15. *Le Tocsin* no. 1 (Apr. 21, 1907). This paper was published by the
Argelliers Viticultural Defense Committee. I am grateful to Deke Dusinberre and Jean-Paul Socard for their assistance in translating the
manifesto.

16. Napo, *1907* (1st ed.), 63–69; see also Charles Tilly's rough
classification of rural reactions to capitalism and state making in "Proletarianization and Rural Collective Action in East Anglia and Elsewhere, 1500–1900," *Peasant Studies* 10 (Fall 1982): 5–32.

17. AN F⁷12794, Anonymous report of events of 1907; AN
F⁷12920; Napo, *1907* (1st ed.), 53–54; Sagnes, "Mouvement de 1907,"
20; on resignations in the Aude, AD Aude 5M72–82. Figures differ on
the number of municipalities that resigned. In AN F⁷12794, a report
from the prefect to the minister of the interior, Oct. 12, 1907, states
that 246 municipalities resigned; Sagnes reports 231. Some villages
remained on strike until October; others withdrew their resignations
by the end of August. On the renewal of resignations, see "Les maires
de l'arrondissement de Narbonne," *Le Temps*, July 7, 1907; and AN
F⁷12794, *Le Petit Méridional*, Aug. 9, 1907.

18. AD Aude 5M69, Commission d'enquête parlementaire et visite
dans le département des délégués du Ministère du l'intérieur, Article
from *La Dépêche de Toulouse*, June 19, 1907.

19. See Boyer and Peyret, *Aux pays de gueux*, 157–158; Bechtel,
1907, 176–214; Napo *1907* (1st ed.), 78–80, 108–123; Marty, *A la
gloire des lutteurs*, 27–28. On the events in Narbonne, see AN F⁷12920,
Emeutes provoquées dans le Midi par la crise viticole de 1907, Reports
of prefect to minister of the interior, June 21 and 26, 1907; Report of
subprefect to prefect, June 21, 1907; Reports of *commissaire spécial* to

prefect, June 22 and 24, 1907; "Le redempteur [Albert] emprisonné" and "Les collisions à Narbonne," both in *L'Eclair*, June 27, 1907. See also accounts in Napo, *1907*, 108–123.

20. On the mutiny of the seventeenth, see Napo, *1907*, 127–132; and Marty, *A la gloire des lutteurs*, 31–35; AN F⁷12920, Report from subprefect to prefect, June 21, 1907; Article in *Le Journal*, June 21, 1907.

21. Napo, *1907*, 177; Warner, *Winegrowers*, 40–41.

22. Smith, "Crise d'une économie régionale," 332.

23. For Ferroul's appeal, see *Le Petit Méridional*, Aug. 14, 1907.

24. According to the rules of the CGV, members received a number of votes proportional to the size of their vineyards. This meant that large owners would automatically carry the most weight, while landless vineyard workers (and even very small owners) would have virtually no voice in the organization. For CGV rules, see AD Aude 15M109, "Syndicats professionnels. Dossier général des unions des syndicats. Confédération générale des vignerons à Narbonne, 1907–1934."

25. Sagnes, "Mouvement de 1907," 14–15.

26. Napo, *1907*, 70.

27. See Rebérioux, "Jaurès et la nationalisation de la vigne," *Bulletin de la Société des études jaurésiennes* 17 (1965): 8. This was Jaurès's response to those who accused the SFIO of being unable to take control of the movement.

28. Citoyenne Sorgue (Antoinette Cauvin), member of the National Council of the SFIO, criticized the class collaborationism of the CGV. See AD Aude 15M94, Report of *commissaire central* to prefect on her address in Carcassonne, Mar. 24, 1908; 15M117, Report of police in Narbonne to subprefect, Mar. 23, 1908. Sorgue accused the CGV of yellow unionism and urged those workers who had joined to leave. On Sorgue, see Maitron, *Dictionnaire biographique* (pt. 3: *1871–1914*), 15: 175; Charles Sowerwine, *Sisters or Citizens: Women in the French Socialist Party* (London: Cambridge University Press, 1982), 116–117, 222n27. See Parti socialiste (SFIO), *6ᵉ Congrès national de la SFIO tenu à St-Etienne les 11, 12, 13, 14 avril 1909* (Paris: Au siège du Conseil national, 1909), 260; AD Aude 5M94, "Police générale," Article entitled "La CGV," in *Le Midi socialiste*, Apr. 16, 1909; Sagnes, *Le Mouvement ouvrier*, 114–117; Sagnes, *Jean Jaurès et le Languedoc viticole* (Montpellier: Presses de Languedoc, 1988), 68–71.

29. On Jaurès's program, see Rebérioux, "Jaurès et nationalisation," 4; Napo, *1907*, 83–84; Sagnes, *Jean Jaurès*, 63–64. On his approval of the CGV, see AD Aude 5M95, Articles in *La Dépêche de*

Toulouse, Oct. 20 and 21, 1907, reporting on Jaurès's visit to Narbonne. Jaurès took a more noncommittal position on the CGV during the SFIO St-Etienne congress; see SFIO, *6e Congrès,* 261–262.

30. See FTAM, *5e Congrès,* 47–48; Smith, "Agricultural Workers," 113. I disagree with Smith about the similarity between the CGV and the CGT; the two organizations were utterly different in their membership, aims, and methods. Smith downplays the importance of the debate over the CGV that took place within the Socialist party and the labor movement.

31. FTAM, *5e Congrès,* 46. See also Paul Ader, "La jaunisse dans le Midi," *Le Travailleur de la terre,* nos. 4 (Sept. 1907), 9 (Feb. 1908), 21 (Feb. 1909), 23 (Apr. 1909), and 24 (May 1909). For Ader's sympathy with small proprietors, see FTAM, *5e Congrès,* 50.

32. Fédération des travailleurs agricoles du Midi, *Compte rendu du 6e Congrès de la Fédération des travailleurs agricoles et partis similaires du Midi* (Montpellier: Imprimerie coopérative ouvrière, 1909), 49–51.

33. Both Smith ("Agricultural Workers," 109) and Gratton (*Luttes de classes,* 306) argue that rank-and-file workers reacted against syndicalist leaders' antiparliamentary rhetoric; as we have seen, syndicalists made no secret of these views during the years of peak unionization.

34. AD Aude 15M132, Grèves agricoles; Garidou, "Viticulture audoise," 123–124; FTAM, *6e Congrès,* 48.

35. See *La Voix du peuple,* no. 481 (Dec. 12, 1909); *Le Travailleur de la terre,* no. 21 (Dec. 1909).

36. See AD Aude 15M132, Placard, "Aux travailleurs agricoles"; Article by Paul Ader in *Le Travailleur de la terre,* no. 15 (Apr. 1908); AN F[7]13626, Report of prefect to minister of the interior, Aug. 24, 1908. In Coursan, striking workers cut the bridles and harnesses of farmhands' horses and, on one estate, set fire to haystacks; see AD Aude 15M133, "Grèves agricoles . . . 1909–1913," Police report, Apr. 20, 1909; AN BB[18]2409[2] (856A09), "Violences à Coursan par les ouvriers agricoles ayant fête le 1er mai"; F[7]13626, Clipping from *La Voix du peuple,* July 11, 1909.

37. See Roland Andréani, "L'antimilitarisme en Languedoc avant 1914," *Revue d'histoire moderne et contemporaine* 20 (Jan.–Mar. 1973): 106; Roger Magraw, "Pierre Joigneaux and Socialist Propaganda in the French Countryside, 1849–1851," *French Historical Studies* 10 (1978): 623.

38. AN F[7]12794, "Troubles causés par les événements de 1907–1908," Telegram from prefect to minister of the interior, Sept. 3, 1907; AD Aude 6M631, Anarchistes, Report from *commissaire spécial* to pre-

fect, Nov. 19, 1907; Report of subprefect to prefect on antimilitarist group in Coursan, Oct. 2, 1907; 7M114, "Police administrative, police des spectacles," Placard dated Jan. 24, 1907, "Réglementation des cafés concerts," issued by prefect of the Aude; see also 6M360, "Documentation anarchiste," Report of prefect to minister of the interior on regulation of plays with antimilitarist themes in the Aude, Feb. 29, 1912.

39. FTAM, *6e Congrès*, 40, 43–45.

40. See Julliard, "CGT Devant la Guerre," 47–62; AN F⁷13338, "Agitation contre la Loi de trois ans," Report of *commissaire de police* to subprefect, Dec. 16, 1912.

41. See, for example, AD Aude 5M10, Report of prefect to minister of the interior, Jan. 9, 1909, on a meeting of vineyard workers in Coursan at the end of December 1908.

42. A. Travert, "Douce patrie," *Le Travailleur de la terre*, no. 9 (Feb. 1908).

43. Fédération des travailleurs agricoles du Midi, *Compte rendu des travaux du 7e Congrès de la Fédération des travailleurs agricoles et partis similaires de la région du Midi* (Montpellier: Imprimerie coopérative ouvrière, 1909), 62. From about 1908 on, the Socialist press, including *L'Humanité*, opened its columns to syndicalists, in an effort to reach out to the labor movement.

44. Ibid., 21; Fédération des travailleurs agricoles du Midi, *Compte rendu des travaux du 8e Congrès de la Fédération des travailleurs agricoles et partis similaires de la région du Midi* (Montpellier: Imprimerie coopérative ouvrière, 1910), 26–33.

45. AN F⁷13599, "Bourse du Travail, Union départementale des syndicats," Newspaper articles: "L'Union départementale de l'Aude," *La Voix du peuple*, Mar. 13–20, 1910; "Union des syndicats de l'Aude," *La Voix du peuple*, Feb. 15–18, 1913; "Congrès de l'Union départementale," *La Voix du peuple*, June 14–21, 1914.

46. See "Propagande rurale," *Le Travailleur de la terre*, no. 31 (Dec. 1909); AD Aude 5M10, Report of prefect to minister of the interior, Jan. 7, 1909.

47. There was a less marked increase in the proportion of unsuccessful strikes in this period than that found nationally by Shorter and Tilly; see *Strikes in France*, 370. Our findings also differ somewhat from Smith's for lower Languedoc generally; see "Agricultural Workers," 123–125.

48. Our findings differ from those of Smith, who has argued that the unions became more accommodating and more adept at bargaining with employers after 1907, having learned the rules of the game; see "Agricultural Workers," 124–125. It is true that unions were more

successful at winning annually renewable contracts after 1907 than earlier; however, as is shown above, unions in the Aude fought for and won contracts well before 1907.

49. Sagnes, "Les grèves dans l'Hérault de 1890 à 1938," in *Economie et société en Languedoc-Roussillon de 1789 à nos jours* (Montpellier: Centre d'histoire contemporaine de Languedoc-méditerranéen et du Roussillon, 1978), 268–269.

50. Shorter and Tilly (*Strikes in France*, 76–103), Hanagan (*Logic of Solidarity*, 72–80), and Perrot (*Ouvriers en grève* 1:114–149 esp.) suggest, on the contrary, that workers struck when living standards were improving.

51. See Shorter and Tilly, *Strikes in France*, 76.

52. Smith has found that this was true for Cruzy, Hérault, as well; see "Work Routine and Social Structure," 381.

53. See FTAM, *4ᵉ Congrès*, 34, 44–45; "Agitation syndicale, la propagande rurale," *La Voix du peuple*, no. 481 (Dec. 12, 1909); Paul Ader, "La vie chère," *Le Travailleur de la terre*, no. 40 (Sept. 1910); Léon Violes, "La pacte de famine," *Le Travailleur de la terre*, no. 41 (Oct. 1910); Comité confédéral, "Contre la vie chère," *Le Travailleur de la terre*, no. 41 (Oct. 1910); Jean-Marie Flonneau, "La crise de la vie chère, 1910–1914," *Le Mouvement social* 72 (July–Sept. 1970): 58, and especially Flonneau's discussion of inflation, pp. 49–58.

54. FTAM, *8ᵉ Congrès*, 18–19.

55. AD Aude 15M117, Reports of *commissaire central* to prefect, Sept. 25, 1910; Oct. 9 and Nov. 5, 1911; and June 25, 1912; Reports of subprefect to prefect, Oct. 18, 1911, and June 23, 1912.

56. AD Aude 15M133, Questionnaires from Direction du travail, Feb. 28 and Sept. 8, 1911; Police report, Sept. 4, 1911; *Le Petit Méridional*, Sept. 4, 1911: France, Ministère de commerce, *Statistique des grèves* for 1911–1913.

57. FTAM, *7ᵉ Congrès*, 26; "Congrès régional de Coursan," *Le Travailleur de la terre*, no. 32 (Jan. 1910).

58. See France, Ministère de commerce, *Statistique des grèves* for 1911–1913; Guilbert, *Femmes et l'organisation syndicale*, 204.

59. This did not happen all over France, of course; see Sowerwine, "Workers and Women." On male workers' concept of class as essentially masculine, see Joan W. Scott, "Language, Gender, and Working-Class History," *International Labor and Working-Class History* 31 (Spring 1987): 9.

60. On the women's section of the union and the women's strike, see AD Aude 15M133, Questionnaire from Direction du travail, Telegram from subprefect to prefect, Nov. 28, 1912; Police reports to prefect,

Nov. 12, 1912, and Jan. 21, 1913; Articles in *La Dépêche de Toulouse*, Jan. 13, 1913; 15M102, Etats des syndicats; AN F[7]13626, Report of *commissaire central* to *directeur de sûreté générale*, Aug. 1912.

61. See *Le Travailleur de la terre*, no. 70 (Mar. 1913).

62. AD Aude 15M133, "Dossiers des grèves des communes rurales de l'arrondissement de Narbonne, 1908–1913," *Le Petit Méridional*, Jan. 17–19 and 24, 1913; *La Dépêche de Toulouse*, Jan. 17 and 19, 1913.

63. See Temma Kaplan, "Female Consciousness and Collective Action: The Case of Barcelona, 1910–1918," *Signs* 7 (Spring 1982): 545.

64. AD Aude 15M107, "Réunions corporatives à la bourse du travail," *Le Midi socialiste*, Feb. 16–19, 1913.

65. See Ferroul's and Aldy's vehement denunciations of radical "labor policy" at meetings organized by the Socialist Federation of the Aude in 1909, in AN F[7]12794, Report from *commissaire central* to prefect, Jan. 11, 1909.

66. AN F[7]12794, Telegram from prefect to minister of interior, Sept. 6, 1907; AD Aude 5M10 Reports from subprefect to prefect, Aug. 9 and Sept. 4, 1908; 5M117, Report from subprefect to prefect, Oct. 18, 1911; Hubert Rouger, *La France socialiste*, 35.

67. Sagnes, "Mouvement de 1907," 28; AD Aude 2M58, "Recensement général des votes."

68. Sagnes, "Mouvement de 1907," 29.

69. Inscription on Cheytion's tombstone (d. Nov. 3, 1915) in the cemetery in Coursan, erected by the Bourse du travail de Narbonne and the Syndicat des cultivateurs de Narbonne.

70. Smith, "Agricultural Workers."

CHAPTER 8

1. See, for example, Berenson, *Populist Religion and Left-Wing Politics*; Burns, *Rural Society and French Politics*; Loubère, *Radicalism in Mediterranean France*; Margadant, *French Peasants in Revolt*; and Weber, *Peasants into Frenchmen*.

2. See, for instance, Weber, "Comment la politique vint aux paysans."

3. Here I agree with Charles Tilly's analysis in "Did the Cake of Custom Break?" in *Consciousness and Class Experience*, ed. John Merriman (New York: Holmes & Meier, 1979), 17–44.

4. See, for instance, Burns, *Rural Society and French Politics*.

5. See Loubère, *Radicalism in Mediterranean France*.

6. Both Loubère and Jean-Marie Mayeur have pointed to the close association of radicalism and socialism in rural areas elsewhere; see

ibid., 205; Mayer, *Débuts de la Troisième République*, 79. See also Judt, *Socialism in Provence*, 228, who identifies more definite lines of difference between radicalism and socialism in the Var.

7. Ira Katznelson, "Constructing Cases and Comparisons," in *Working-Class Formation: Nineteenth-Century Patterns in Western Europe and the United States*, ed. Ira Katznelson and Aristide Zolberg (Princeton: Princeton University Press, 1986), 33.

8. On this point more generally, see ibid., 25.

9. On this point more generally, see Katznelson and Zolberg, *Working-Class Formation*.

10. See Jean-Daniel Reynaud, *Les syndicats en France*, vol. 1 (Paris: Seuil, 1975), 140–142.

11. See Stearns, *Revolutionary Syndicalism and French Labor*.

12. Zolberg, "How Many Exceptionalisms?" in Katznelson and Zolberg, *Working-Class Formation*, 403. Jacques Julliard has pointed out that the CGT's revolutionary rhetoric was more the creation of the rank and file than the doctrine of syndicalist leaders. In the Aude it was the opposite. See Julliard, *Autonomie ouvrière. Etudes sur le syndicalisme et l'action directe* (Paris: Gallimard–Le Seuil, 1988), 15–16.

13. See also Julliard, "Théorie syndicaliste révolutionnaire."

Bibliography

ARCHIVAL SOURCES

Archives municipales de Coursan (unclassified)
Listes nominatives communales des recensements quinquennaux, 1911, 1920.
Contrat du Travail, octobre 1911.
Ibid., octobre 1912.
Déclaration de Récolte, 1915.

Archives départementales de l'Aude (AD Aude)
Série J. Evêché.
17J7   Visites pastorales, Coursan. 1864–1891.
Série M. Personnel et administration générale.
2M. Politique.
2M11–14   Révolution de 1848. Adhésions au gouvernement provisoire, organisation des municipalités, élection du président de la République, recensement général des votes.
2M15   Scrutin du 21 novembre 1852 sur le rétablissement de l'Empire.
2M16   Plébiscite du 8 mai 1870.
2M58   Recensement général des votes pour l'élection des membres à la Chambre de députés, 1876–1914.
2M61   Recensement des votes pour l'élection des membres à l'Assemblée nationale, mars–avril 1848 et mai 1849.
2M62   Elections des députés au corps législatif, 1852–1864.
2M63   Elections au corps législatif du 23 mai 1869.
2M65   Election de six membres à l'Assemblée nationale du 8 février 1871.
2M66–74   Elections législatives, 1876–1914.
2M344–359   Régistres des Tableaux communaux indiquant la population des habitants et des électeurs, l'électif du Conseil municipal.
5M. Police générale.
5M7   Rapports périodiques du préfet, 1855–1860.
5M8   Ibid., 1861–1865.
5M9   Rapports mensuels du préfet, 1890–1896.
5M10–11   Ibid., 1907–1911.

5M23–27   Rapports périodiques du préfet.

5M31   Attentat contre le roi, troubles à Narbonne, 1846.

5M33   Rapports du préfet, sociétés secrets, 1851–1852.

5M34   Voyage du prince-président, son passage à Narbonne, 1852.

5M36   Condamnés politiques, mesures de police, 1852–1853.

5M38–41   Dossiers individus des condamnés politiques, 1851–1881.

5M43   Documentation relative aux mesures d'expulsion et de l'internement, de surveillance. Etat des individus dangereux. 1853–1859.

5M44–45   Condamnés politiques, 1852–1859.

5M46   Menées légitimistes dans le département.

5M48   Evénements politiques diverses; Coursan, tentative criminelle de déraillement près de Coursan sous la ligne de chemin de fer du Midi, 1859.

5M51   Narbonne, rapport du commissaire de la police de Narbonne aux préfets pour signaler réunions clandestines, 1867–1872.

5M66   Rapports mensuels du préfet et des sous-préfets, divers comptes rendus de police . . . concernant la défense des intérêts de la viticulture méridionale, 1905–1907.

5M67   Dossier des documents et rapports de la période précédante les meetings de protestation, 1907.

5M68   Dossier des meetings de Coursan, Narbonne, etc., 1907.

5M69   Commission d'enquête parlementaire et visite dans le département des délégués du ministre de l'intérieur, 1907.

5M70   Grève administrative des municipalités, 1907.

5M71   Ingérences politiques dans le mouvement viticole du Parti socialiste et des syndicats et menaces de grève, 1907.

5M72   Démissions et retraites de démissions des municipalités, 1907.

5M73   Communes ayant refusés la réception de l'envoi par la préfecture de la circulaire de Clemenceau, 1907.

5M74   Rapports et messages officiels, articles de presse relatifs à M. Marcellin Albert, 1907.

5M75   Dossiers des démissions des membres des collectivités départementales, 1907.

5M79–81   Lettres individuelles des démissions renouvellées, par commune, 1907.

5M82   Grève de l'impôt. Documentation générale en matière de défense du Midi viticole. 1907.

5M83–86   Rapports périodiques du préfet, 1851–1867.

5M88–97   Police générale, rapports, enquêtes de police sur l'activité des partis politiques incidents à la suite de congrès, meetings ou réunions publiques à caractère politique, 1896, 1885–1929.

5M99   Propagande des partis politiques: comptes rendus, rapports et instructions concernant les partis, 1898–1939.

6M. Sûreté générale.

6M360–361   Documents anarchistes.

7M. Repression du vagabondage et de la mendicité.

7M24   Enquêtes communales . . . l'extinction du vagabondage . . . 1900.

7M25–33   Cercles, chambrées, clubs, salons, sociétés politiques et agricoles, 1834–1901.

7M37   Cercles, chambrées, etc., arrondissement de Carcassonne, 1900–1909.

7M114   Police des spectacles.

9M. Subsistances.

9M78–106   Mercuriales. Etats décadaires des denrées, grains, céréales, légumes secs et viandes. Quantités et prix pratiqués à la vente sur les marchés. 1850–1905, 1912–1921.

11M. Mouvement de la population.

11M7–10   Etats récapitulatifs de statistique annuelle de la population du département, 1851–1865, 1887–1893, 1894–1899, 1900–1906.

11M15–17   Tableaux communaux de statistique numérique du dénombrement de 1856 par catégories diverses concernant les ménages, la population sur diverses formes professionnelles, confessionnelles, et culturelles suivant l'âge, le sexe et la population par état civil.

11M28   Tableaux récapitulatifs sommaires de la population par commune, 1886.

11M35   Tableaux récapitulatifs généraux dans le canton de Coursan, 1886.

11M37   Tableaux récapitulatifs généraux du dénombrement de 1891.

11M43   Ibid., 1896.

11M48   Tableaux récapitulatifs du dénombrement de 1901.

11M49   Ibid., 1906.

11M58   Dénombrement de la population. Etats nominatifs des habitants de Coursan, 1836.

11M67   Ibid., 1846.

11M78　　Ibid., 1851.

11M93　　Ibid., 1861.

11M101　　Ibid., 1866.

11M108　　Ibid., 1872.

11M117　　Ibid., 1876.

11M157　　Ibid., 1911.

13M. Agriculture.

13M61　　Vignoble départemental, cépages et produits. An XIII–1878.

13M62　　Viticulture. Vignoble départemental. Phylloxéra. Documentation générale. 1873–1886.

13M63　　Phylloxéra. Comité départemental de défense et comité d'études et de vigilance. 1873–1879.

13M64　　Phylloxéra. Organisation de défense, désignation des délégués. 1879–1881.

13M65　　Comité d'études et vigilance. 1876–1886.

13M67　　Traitement du phylloxéra. Commission de contrôle de l'emploi des crédits attribués au département . . . pour le traitement des vignobles phylloxérés, 1878–1883.

13M75　　Phylloxéra. Association syndicale des communes d'Argens, Bizanet, Castelnau, Coursan . . . , 1883–1884.

13M78　　Phylloxéra. Tableaux statistiques sur la marche du phylloxéra du 3 octobre au 16 mars 1887.

13M82　　Phylloxéra. Etats nominatifs communaux par ordre topographique et par arrondissement chef-lieu des propriétaires de vignobles . . . qui ont bénéficiés de l'allocation de secours du Conseil général. . . . 1908.

13M85　　Enquête sur la situation des vignes phylloxérées.

13M86　　Crise viticole. Délibérations municipales. 1900–1906.

13M235　　Comice agricole de l'arrondissement de Narbonne, 1856–1915.

13M270–280　　Statistique générale. Etats de renseignements concernant les grains et les farineux . . . les céréales, 1815–1850.

13M281　　Tableaux récapitulatifs cantonaux . . . de recensement général des produits végétaux récoltes . . . , 1851.

13M282　　Tableaux de statistique agricole annuelle par arrondissement . . . des relevés cantonaux de la production en céréales et pommes de terre . . . des prix et salaires moyens . . . , 1856–1857.

13M284　　Etats cantonaux des salaires agricoles . . . , 1860–1861.

13M287　　Rapports des sous-commissions . . . relatives à la situation et aux besoins de l'agriculture . . . , 1866–1867.

13M289–296 Tableaux récapitulatifs . . . de la culture de la vigne, 1868–1880.

13M300 Statistique agricole décennale. Tableaux communaux des cantons de Coursan, Durban, Ginestas et Sigean. 1882.

13M303 Statistique agricole annuelle communale, 1888.

13M307 Ibid., 1890.

13M313 Tableaux récapitulatifs de statistique annuelle agricole, 1893–1901.

13M318 Ibid., 1905.

13M323 Ibid., 1910.

14M. Commerce et industrie.

14M20 Enquête parlementaire particulière à la crise agricole et industrielle à la condition des ouvriers, 1881–1885.

15M. Travail.

15M16 Enquête administrative de la préfecture . . . sur la durée normale de la journée agricole, 1907.

15M30 Bourses du travail, 1892–1921.

15M86 Associations professionnelles. Documentation. 1845–1939.

15M98–104 Etats des syndicats professionnels industriels, commerciaux et agricoles, 1891–1919.

15M107 Réunions corporatives à la Bourse du travail. Comptes rendus de police et rapports du préfet. 1905–1928.

15M109 Syndicats professionnels. Dossier général des unions des syndicats (C.G.V. à Narbonne 1907–1934).

15M117 Réunions publiques, meetings contre le chômage, la vie chère, l'insuffisance des salaires, le contrat de travail, 1892–1914.

15M120 Grèves agricoles. Articles de presse. Affiches et placards. 1904–1905.

15M125 Grèves agricoles. Dossiers des grèves . . . pour l'arrondissement de Narbonne. 1903–1906.

15M131 Dossiers des grèves des communes rurales de l'arrondissement de Narbonne, 1905.

15M132 Ibid., 1906–1908.

15M133 Ibid., 1908–1913.

Série T. Instruction publique.

T 559 Statistique de la fréquentation scolaire; gratuite des admissions, 1862–1871.

T 535 Ecoles libres.

T 539 Laïcisation des écoles, 1851–1859.

T 540 Crêches, écoles enfantines, salles d'asile, 1839–1905.

Archives départementales de l'Hérault
15M. Politique.
>   15M49–50   Elections législatives de 1902. Liste des candidats, résultats.

Archives nationales de France (AN)
Série C. Archives parlementaires, Assemblée nationale.
>   C86   *Agriculture française par MM. les Inspecteurs de l'agriculture, publié d'après les ordres de M. le Ministre de l'agriculture et du commerce. Département de l'Aude.* Paris: Imprimerie royale, 1847.

>   C946   *Enquête sur le travail agricole et industriel, 25 mai 1848.* Paris: Imprimerie royale, 1849.

Série F^7. Police générale.
>   F^{7}12497   Activité socialiste dans les départements, 1900–1914.

>   F^{7}12541   Elections législatives de 1902. Dossiers départementaux.

>   F^{7}12544   Elections législatives de 1906. Dossiers départementaux.

>   F^{7}12773   Grèves. Instructions ministerielles; plans de protection . . . emploi des troupes . . . , 1849–1914.

>   F^{7}12794   Troubles causés par les événements de 1907.

>   F^{7}12887   Documents relatifs au Parti socialiste Guesdiste, 1895–1900.

>   F^{7}12920   Emeutes provoquées dans le Midi par le crise viticole de 1907.

>   F^{7}13053   Documents généraux. Listes d'anarchistes et notes sur les groupements anarchistes. 1897–1921.

>   F^{7}13268   Manifestations du 1er mai, 1909–1910.

>   F^{7}13338   Agitation contre le Loi de trois ans.

>   F^{7}13567   Bourses du travail: historique, renseignements généraux . . . propagande révolutionnaire et antimilitariste, 1893–1916.

>   F^{7}13624   Fédérations et syndicats d'agriculture.

>   F^{7}13626   Mouvement syndicaliste agricole, 1904–1936.

Série F^{11}. Subsistance.
>   F^{11}2698   Enquête agricole de 1862. Questionnaires.

Série F^{12}. Commerce et industrie.
>   F^{12}4484   Situation de l'industrie dans l'Aude.

Série F^{17}. Instruction.
>   F^{17}9322   Inspection des écoles primaires, années 1855–1856. Ardèche à Bouches-du-Rhône.

F^{17}10529　Etats de situation des écoles primaires publiques et libres et des écoles maternelles, 1878–1879. Aude à Corse.

F^{17}10670　Etats de situation des écoles primaires publiques et libres et des écoles maternelles, 1888–1889, Aude à Corrèze.

F^{17}10781　Mémoires . . . sur les besoins de l'instruction primaire. Aude, Gard. 1860–1861.

Série F^{20}. Statistique.

F^{20} 715　Tableaux des prix et denrées et des salaires des ouvriers, 1844, 1855.

Série BB^{18}. Ministère de la justice: correspondance générale de la Division criminelle.

BB^{18}2272　Grèves agricoles, 1904.

BB^{18}2296　(437 A 05) Grèves dans le ressort de Montpellier.

BB^{18}2324　Antimilitarisme, 1906.

BB^{18}2329　(326 A 06) Grèves dans le ressort de Montpellier.

BB^{18}2375　Placards. Fédération des travailleurs de la terre. 1908.

BB^{18}2406　Incidents à Coursan. Poursuits à Narbonne contre Cheytion et autres pour entraves à la liberté du travail. 1909.

BB^{18}2409　Violences à Coursan par ouvriers agricoles fêtant le 1er mai, 1909.

BB^{18}2478　Discours antimilitaristes à Coursan par le sieur Reynes, 1912.

Série BB^{30}. Versements de 1904, 1905, 1908, 1929, 1933, 1936, 1941, 1943, 1944.

BB^{30}362　Rapports mensuels du procureur générale à Montpellier au Ministère de la justice.

BB^{30}380　Ibid.

BB^{30}396　Dossier P. 440.

Service de cadastre de l'Aude (SCA). Narbonne, Aude. Cadastre foncier de Coursan. 1830–1914

Bureau de greffier du Tribunal de grande instance, Narbonne, Aude
Etat civil du village de Coursan.

Actes de naissance, 1850–1913.

Actes de mariage, 1850–1913.

Actes de décès, 1850–1913.

INTERVIEWS

All interviews were conducted with Rémy Pech in Coursan, Aude.

Léon Bedry. Proprietor in Coursan. August 20, 1974.

Victorin Cabrié. Vineyard worker in Coursan. June 28, 1973.

Mme. Cendrous. Coursan. June 26, 1979.

Marius Cheytion and Anastasie Vergnes (née Cheytion). Brother and sister of François Cheytion. June 28, 1973.

Julien Coca. Deputy mayor and head of vineyard workers' union in Coursan, June 26, 1979.

Alphonse Fau and Simone Fau. Small proprietors in Coursan. June 28, 1973.

Jacques Quilis. Former *chef de colle* on domaine of Celeyran, Salles d'Aude. June 29, 1973.

Mme Rouaix. Former day laborer; wife of François Rouaix, union activist. August 7, 1973.

Anastasie Vergnes (née Cheytion). Sister of François Cheytion and former day laborer. August 20, 1974.

PARTY AND FEDERATION CONGRESSES

Fédération des travailleurs agricoles du Midi. *Compte rendu des travaux du 1er Congrès national des travailleurs agricoles et partis similaires organisé par la Fédération des travailleurs agricoles de l'Hérault.* Béziers: J.-B. Perdraut, 1903.

—————. *Compte rendu des travaux du 2e Congrès national des travailleurs agricoles et partis similaires organisé par la Section de l'Aude.* Narbonne: J. Boulet, 1904.

—————. *Compte rendu des travaux du 3e Congrès de la Fédération des travailleurs agricoles du Midi.* Perpignan: D. Muller, 1906.

—————. *Compte rendu des travaux du 4e Congrès de la Fédération des travailleurs agricoles et partis similaires du Midi.* Paris: Maison des fédérations, Service de l'imprimerie, 1906.

—————. *Compte rendu des travaux du 5e Congrès de la Fédération des travailleurs agricoles et partis similaires du Midi.* Bourges: Imprimerie ouvrière du Centre–Ouvriers syndiqués et fédérés, 1907.

—————. *Compte rendu des travaux du 6e Congrès de la Fédération des travailleurs agricoles et partis similaires du Midi.* Montpellier: Imprimerie coopérative ouvrière, 1909.

—————. *Compte rendu des travaux du 7e Congrès de la Fédération des travailleurs agricoles et partis similaires de la région du Midi.* Montpellier: Imprimerie coopérative ouvrière, 1909.

—————. *Compte rendu des travaux du 8e congrès de la Fédération des travailleurs agricoles et partis similaires de la région du Midi.* Montpellier: Imprimerie coopérative ouvrière, 1910.

Parti ouvrier français. *7e Congrès national du Parti ouvrier à Roubaix du samedi 29 mars au lundi 7 avril 1884.* Roubaix: Imprimerie ouvrière, 1884.

————. *8ᵉ Congrès national du Parti ouvrier tenu à Lille, les 11 et 12 octobre 1890.* Lille: Imprimerie ouvrière, 1890.

————. *9ᵉ Congrès national du Parti ouvrier tenu à Lyon du 26 au 28 novembre 1891.* Paris: G. Delory, 1891.

————. *10ᵉ Congrès national du Parti ouvrier tenu à Marseille du 24 au 28 septembre 1892.* Lille: Imprimerie ouvrière, 1893.

————. *11ᵉ Congrès national du Parti ouvrier tenu à Paris du 7 au 9 octobre 1893.* Paris: G. Delory, 1893.

————. *12ᵉ Congrès national du Parti ouvrier tenu à Nantes du 14 au 16 septembre 1894.* Paris: G. Delory, 1894.

Parti socialiste (SF10). *Compte rendu du 3ᵉ Congrès national de la SFIO tenu à Limoges du 1ᵉʳ au 4 novembre 1906.* Paris: Au siège du Conseil national, 1907.

————. *Compte rendu du 4ᵉ Congrès national de la SFIO tenu à Nancy du 11 au 14 août 1907.* Paris: Au siège du Conseil national, 1908.

————. *6ᵉ Congrès national de la SFIO tenu à St-Etienne les 11, 12, 13, 14 avril 1909.* Paris: SFLO, Au siège du Conseil national, 1909.

CONTEMPORARY NEWSPAPERS AND JOURNALS

La Dépêche de Toulouse
L'Echo de l'Aude
L'Emancipation sociale
L'Humanité
Le Journal
Le Midi socialiste
Le Mouvement socialiste
Le Paysan
Le Petit Méridional
Le Radical du Midi
La Réforme sociale
La République sociale
La Revue socialiste
Le Socialisme
Le Télégramme
Le Tocsin
Le Travailleur de la terre
La Voix du peuple

CONTEMPORARY PRINTED SOURCES

Ader, Paul. "La grève générale des travailleurs agricoles du Midi." *Le Mouvement socialiste* 147 (Jan. 15, 1905): 128–139.

————. "Le Midi bouge." *Le Travailleur de la terre*, no. 1 (June, 1907).

————. "L'organisation rurale dans le Midi viticole." *Le Mouvement socialiste* 145 (Dec. 15, 1904): 265–281.

Aftalion, Albert. "Le salaire réel et sa nouvelle orientation." *La Revue d'économie politique* 26 (1912): 541–552.

Ardouin-Dumazet, V.-E. "Le travail des femmes à la campagne." *La Réforme sociale*, Dec. 1909, 657–746.

Atger, Frédéric. *La crise viticole et la viticulture méridionale, 1900–1907.* Paris: Giard & Brière, 1907.

————. "La production légale de la viticulture et la crise viticole." Thèse de Doctorat de droit, Université de Montpellier, 1907.

Aude. *Almanach-Annuaire de l'Aude pour l'année 1891.* Carcassonne: Gabelle, Bonnafous, 1890.

————. *Almanach de l'atelier pour le département de l'Aude, 1876.* Paris: M. Dauchez, 1875.

————. *Almanach du laboureur et du vigneron pour le département de l'Aude, 1876.* Paris: M. Dauchez, 1875.

————. *Annuaire administratif, statistique et historique du département de l'Aude pour l'année 1869–1870.* Carcassonne: P. Labau, 1870.

————. *Annuaire du département de l'Aude pour 1856.* Carcassonne: C. Labau, 1856.

————. *Annuaire statistique et administratif de l'Aude pour 1841.* Carcassonne: C. Labau, 1841.

————. *Annuaire statistique et administratif de l'Aude pour 1844.* Carcassonne: C. Labau, 1844.

————. *Annuaire statistique du département de l'Aude pour 1851.* Carcassonne: C. Labau, 1851.

————. *Conseil général de l'Aude. Session extraordinaire. Procès-verbal de la séance du 9 mars 1889 adopté par la Commission départementale dans sa séance du 23 mars 1889.* Carcassonne: C. Labau, 1889.

————. *Délibérations du Conseil général du département de l'Aude. Procès-verbal des délibérations* (sessions of 1850–1880). Carcassonne: Pierre Polère, 1850–1880.

————. *Petit annuaire statistique, administratif, ecclésiastique, militaire et commercial pour 1854.* Carcassonne: Pierre Polère, 1854.

Audiganne, Armand. *Les populations ouvrières et les industries de la France dans le mouvement social du XIXᵉ siècle.* 2 vols. Paris: Capelle, 1854.

Augé-Laribé, Michel. "L'agriculture capitaliste et les exploitations paysannes." *Le Mouvement socialiste*, June 1912, 5–29.

————. "Les coopératives paysannes et socialistes de Maraussan (Hérault)." In *Le Musée social. Mémoires et documents*, 1907, 65–74.

———. "Deuxième congrès des syndicats d'ouvriers agricoles." *Le Musée social. Annales*, 1904, 393–402.

———. "Les grèves d'ouvriers agricoles dans le Languedoc." *Le Musée social. Annales*, 1904, 39–50.

———. "Les ouvriers de la viticulture languedocienne et leurs syndicats." *Le Musée social. Mémoires et documents*, 1903, 265–328.

———. *La politique agricole en France, 1880–1940*. Paris: Presses universitaires de France, 1950.

———. *Le problème agraire du socialisme. La viticulture industrielle du Midi de la France*. Paris: Giard & Brière, 1907.

———. "Les résultats des grèves agricoles dans le Midi de la France." *Le Musèe social*, Oct. 1904, 273–320.

———. "Le rôle du capital dans la viticulture languedocienne." *Revue d'économie politique* 19 (1905): 193–222.

Ballainvilliers, Charles. "Des mémoires sur le Languedoc, divisés par diocèses et subdélégations, 1788." Manuscrit no. 81. Municipal Library of Carcassonne.

———. "Un traité sur le commerce de Languedoc, 1788." Manuscrit no. 82. Municipal Library of Carcassonne.

Barbut, Georges. *La coopération et les coopératives dans l'Aude*. Carcassonne: Pierre Polère, 1908.

———. *Enquête sur la production du vin dans l'Aude en 1899*. Carcassonne: Gabelle, 1900.

———. *Etude sur le vignoble de l'Aude et sa production (récolte de 1912)*. Carcassonne: Pierre Polère, 1912.

———. *Etude sur le vignoble de l'Aude et sa production (récolte de 1913)*. Carcassonne: Pierre Polère, 1913.

———. *Histoire de la culture des céréales dans l'Aude de 1785 à 1900*. Carcassonne: Gabelle, 1900.

———. *Notes sur l'économie rurale de l'Aude*. Carcassonne: Gabelle, 1909.

———. *La vigne et le vin dans l'Aude en 1907*. Carcassonne: Gabelle, 1907.

———. *La vigne et le vin dans l'Aude en 1910–1923*. Carcassonne: Gabelle, 1910–1923.

———. "Le vignoble de l'Aude: Monographie du domaine de Jouarres" (excerpt from *La Revue de viticulture*). Paris: Bureau de *La Revue de viticulture*, 1898.

Barbut, Georges, and André Marty. *Les syndicats agricoles et les caisses de crédit agricoles*. Carcassonne: Gabelle, 1901.

Barral, J. A. *Conférence sur le phylloxéra*, faite le 1ᵉʳ avril 1882. Paris: J. Tremblay, 1882.

————. *Enquête sur la situation de l'agriculture en France en 1879, faite à la demande de M. le ministre de l'agriculture et du commerce par la Société nationale de l'agriculture.* 2 vols. Paris: Bouchard-Huzard, 1880.

————. *La lutte contre le phylloxéra.* Paris: C. Marpon & E. Flammarion, 1883.

Barral, J. A., and Henri Sagnier. *Dictionnaire d'agriculture. Encyclopédie agricole complète.* 4 vols. Paris: Hachette, 1889–1892.

Baudrillart, Henri. *Les populations agricoles de la France.* Paris: Guillaumin, 1893.

Benoist, Charles. *La crise d'état moderne. L'organisation du travail.* 2 vols. Paris: Plon-Nourrit, 1905–1914.

Bibliothèque du mouvement socialiste. *Le Parti socialiste et la Confédération générale du travail.* Paris: Bibliothèque du mouvement socialiste, 1908.

Blanqui, Adolphe. "Tableau des populations rurales de la France en 1850." *Journal des Economistes* 28 (Jan. 1851): 9–27; 30 (Sept. 1851): 1–15.

Bouffet, Félix. "Les grèves agricoles du Midi, leurs causes et leurs remèdes." *La Réforme sociale,* June 16, 1905, 917–938.

Bourrel, Charles. "Excursion du 29 juin 1902 à Coursan, à Fleury et à la mer." *Bulletin de la Société d'études scientifiques de l'Aude* 14 (1903): 63–74.

Bousquet, Adrien. *Le régime économique du vin. Le marché des vins.* Paris: Larose, 1904.

Boyer, César, and J. Payret. *Aux pays de gueux. Les grands meetings du Midi.* Paris: N.p., 1907.

Bruneton, F. "Les grèves agricoles dans le Midi." *Emancipation,* Jan. 15, 1905, 6–8.

Castel, P. *Enquête sur les vignobles du département de l'Aude, reconstitués en plantes américaines.* Carcassonne: N.p., 1889.

Casteran, A. *Mémoires de Marcellin Albert en l'Algérie.* Paris: Librairie universelle, 1911.

Chevallier, Emile. *Les salaires au XIXᵉ siècle.* Paris: Librairie nouvelle de jurisprudence, 1887.

Comice agricole de Narbonne. *Questionnaire sur le revenu foncier des terres dans l'arrondissement de Narbonne.* Narbonne: F. Caillard, 1908.

————. *Rapport addressé au Conseil général de l'Aude sur le revenu foncier des terres dans l'arrondissement de Narbonne.* Narbonne: F. Caillard, 1908.

————. *Rapport sur les travaux et sur la situation économique et agricole de l'arrondissement pour l'exercice 1900–1901, par le Dr. Louis de Martin, président du Comice.* Narbonne: F. Caillard, 1901.

————. *Résumé des leçons pratiquées sur le greffage des vignes américaines.* Montpellier: Société centrale d'agriculture de l'Hérault, 1880.

Compère-Morel, Adéodat. *Les propos d'un rural.* Preface by Paul Lafargue. 4th ed. Paris: Librairie du Parti socialiste, 1908.

————. *La question agraire et le socialisme en France.* Paris: Marcel Rivière, 1912.

————. *Le socialisme agraire.* Paris: Marcel Rivière, 1920.

Convert, François. "Les caisses de retraits ouvriers et l'agriculture: Enquête parlementaire." *Le Musée Social. Annales,* 1902, 65–78.

————. *L'industrie agricole.* Paris: Librairie J.-B. Ballière, 1901.

————. *Les ouvriers agricoles et les salaires en présence de l'invasion du phylloxéra.* Montpellier: Imprimerie centrale du Midi–Hamlin, 1878.

————. "Les variations des prix: Les impôts, les salaires." *Journal d'agriculture pratique* 49 (Dec. 2, 1880): 781–783.

————. "Les variations des prix des vins." *Journal d'agriculture pratique* 40 (Sept. 30, 1880): 463–469.

————. "La viticulture et la vinification de 1780 à 1870." *Revue de viticulture* 12 (1899): 409–413, 493–495, 577–582.

Cost of Living in French Towns. Report of an Enquiry by the Board of Trade into Working-Class Rents, Housing, and Retail Prices, Together with the Rates of Wages in Certain Occupations in the Principal Industrial Towns of France. With an Introductory Memorandum and a Comparison of Conditions in France and the U.K. House of Commons Sessional Papers, vol. 91. London: Darling, 1909.

Coste-Floret, Paul. *L'avenir du marché des vins.* Montpellier: Serre & Roumegous, 1903.

————. *Les bouilleurs de cru.* Montpellier: Serre & Roumegous, 1905.

————. *Les travaux du vignoble.* Montpellier: Camille Coulet; Paris: Masson, 1898.

Coulet, Elie. *Le mouvement syndical et coopératif dans l'agriculture française.* Montpellier: Camille Coulet; Paris: Masson, 1898.

Coursan. *Rapport de l'administration municipale de Coursan fait en Conseil municipal de ladite commune dans le séance du 27 décembre 1877.* France: A. Capelle, 1878.

D'Angeville, A. *Essai sur la statistique de la population française.* Introduction by Emmanuel Le Roy Ladurie. 1836; Paris: Mouton, 1969.

Daudet, Alphonse. *Letters from My Windmill.* Translated by Frederick Davies. 1866–1867; Harmondsworth, Eng.: Penguin Books, 1984.

Degrully, Paul. *Essai historique et économique sur la production et le marché des vins en France.* Montpellier: Roumegous & Dehan, 1910.

Dejernon, Romould. *Les vignes et les vins d'Algérie*. 2 vols. Paris: Librairie agricole de la Maison rustique, 1883–1884.

Descamps, Paul. *Populations viticoles. Evolution du type du vigneron et la crise actuelle*. Paris: Bureau de la science sociale, 1907.

Ditandy, A. *Lectures variées sur le département de l'Aude*. Carcassonne: François Pomiés, 1875.

Dutil, Léon. *L'état économique du Languedoc à la fin de l'Ancien Régime, 1750–1789*. Paris: Hachette, 1911.

Félice, Raoul de. *Les naissances en France. La situation, ses conséquences, ses causes*. Paris: Hachette, 1910.

Flour de St-Génis, E. *La propriété rurale en France*. Paris: Armand Colin, 1902.

Foex, Gustave. *Cours complet de viticulture*. Montpellier: Camille Coulet; Paris: Masson, 1895.

Fontanilles, Léopold. *Etude sur les ouvriers agricoles et leurs mouvements sociaux*. Grenoble: La dépêche dauphinoise, 1908.

Fourès, Auguste. *Les hommes de l'Aude*. 2 vols. Narbonne: F. Caillard, 1889–1891.

Fournel, Jean. *Avec ceux d'Argelliers. Une acte d'énergie méridionale*. Montpellier: Editions languedociennes, 1908.

Foville, Alfred de. *Etudes économiques et statistiques sur la propriété foncière. Le morcellement*. Paris: Guillaumin, 1885.

France. Ministère de l'agriculture. Direction de l'agriculture. *Agriculture française par MM. les inspecteurs de l'agriculture publié après les ordres de M. le ministre de l'agriculture et du commerce. Département de l'Aude*. Paris: Imprimerie royale, 1847.

———. *Atlas de statistique agricole. Résultats généraux des statistiques agricoles décennales de 1882 et de 1892*. Paris: Imprimerie nationale, 1897.

———. *Compte rendu des travaux de la Commission supérieure du phylloxéra (année 1882) et rapport de M. Tisserand, conseiller d'état, Direction de l'agriculture*. Paris: Imprimerie nationale, 1883.

———. *Statistique agricole annuelle, 1889–1900*. 12 vols. Paris: Imprimerie nationale, 1889–1900.

———. *Enquête agricole par application du décrêt du 28 mars 1866. Enquêtes départementales, 21e circonscription*. Paris: Imprimerie nationale, 1866.

———. *Enquête agricole de 1872. Deuxième série. Enquêtes départementales, 21e circonscription*. Paris: Imprimerie nationale, 1872.

———. Direction de l'enseignement et des services agricoles. *Enquête sur les salaires agricoles*. Paris: Imprimerie nationale, 1912.

———. Office des renseignements agricoles. *La petite propriété rurale en*

France. *Enquêtes monographiques, 1908–1909.* Paris: Imprimerie nationale, 1909.

————. *Rapport sur les travaux administratifs entrepris contre le phylloxéra et sur la situation du vignoble français et étranger pendant l'année 1887.* Paris: Imprimerie des journaux officiels, 1888.

————. Statistique agricole de la France. *Résultats généraux de l'enquête décennale de 1882.* Nancy: Berger-Levrault, 1887.

————. *Résultats généraux de l'enquête décennale de 1892.* Paris: Imprimerie nationale, 1898.

————. Statistique de la France. Agriculture. *Résultats généraux de l'enquête décennale de 1862.* Strasbourg: Berger-Levrault, 1868.

————. Ministère de commerce. Direction du Travail. *Album graphique de la statistique générale de la France. Résultats statistiques du recensement de 1901.* Paris: Imprimerie nationale, 1907.

————. Office du Travail. *Bulletin de l'Office du travail, no. 3, mars 1903.* Paris: Imprimerie nationale, 1903.

————. *Bordereaux des salaires pour diverses catégories d'ouvriers en 1900 et 1901.* Paris: Imprimerie nationale, 1902.

————. *Statistique annuelle du mouvement de la population, 1901.* Vol. 13. Paris: Imprimerie nationale, 1902.

————. *Statistique des grèves et des recours à la conciliation et à l'arbitrage* (1890–1913). Paris: Imprimerie nationale, 1890–1913.

————. Statistique générale. *Bulletin de la Statistique générale de la France.* 4 vols. Paris: Félix Alcan, 1911.

————. *Prix et salaires à diverses époques.* Strasbourg: Berger-Levrault, 1864.

————. *Annuaire statistique de la France. Première année, 1878.* Paris: Imprimerie nationale, 1878.

————. Ministère du travail et de la prévoyance sociale. *Annuaire des syndicats professionnels, industriels, commerciaux et agricoles, déclarés conformément à la loi du 21 mars 1884* (1900–1914). Paris: Imprimerie nationale, 1900–1914.

————. Statistique générale. *Résultats statistiques du recensement général de la population.* Paris: Imprimerie nationale, 1913.

————. *Salaires et coût de l'existence à diverses époques jusqu'en 1910.* Paris: Imprimerie nationale, 1911.

————. *Statistique annuelle, 1882.* Paris: Imprimerie nationale, 1885.

Genieys, Pierre. *La crise viticole méridionale.* Toulouse: Edouard Privat, 1905.

Germa, Georges. "Les élections législatives du 8 février et du 2 juillet 1871 dans l'Aude: Essai historique." Carcassonne, n.d. Typescript.

Gervais, Charles. *L'indicateur des vignobles méridionaux*, 2d ed. Montpellier: Firmin, Montagne & Sicardi, [1903].

Gervais, Henri. *La rémunération du travail dans la viticulture méridionale*. Paris: Arthur Rousseau, 1908.

Gervais, Prosper. *La réconstitution du vignoble. Quantité ou qualité?* Paris: Au siège du Syndicat central des agriculteurs de France, 1903.

————. *La situation de la viticulture méridionale*. Paris: Bureau de *La Revue de viticulture*, 1906.

Ghesquière, Henri, and Adéodat Compère-Morel. *L'action syndicale. Discours des citoyens Ghesquière et Compère-Morel à la Chambre des députés, le 2 décembre 1911*. Lille: Imprimerie ouvrière M. Dhoosche, 1911.

Gide, Charles. "La crise du vin en France et les associations de vinification." *Revue d'économie politique* 15 (Mar. 1901): 218–235.

————. "La crise du vin dans le Midi de la France." *Revue d'économie politique* 21 (July 1907): 481–512.

La grande encyclopédie. Vol. 4. Paris: H. Lamirault, 1887.

Guérin, Urbain. "Enquête de la Société des agriculteurs de France et de la Société d'économie sociale sur la condition des ouvriers agricoles." *La Réforme sociale*, Oct. 1894, 531–542.

Guesde, Jules, and Paul Lafargue. *Le programme du Parti ouvrier*. Paris: N.p., [1883].

Guyot, Jules. *Etude des vignobles de France pour servir à l'enseignement de la viticulture et de la vinification française*. Vol. 1: *Régions du sud-est et du sud-ouest*. Paris: Imprimerie impériale, 1868.

Guyot, Jules, A. Riondet, and M. A. Pellicot. *De la culture de la vigne dans le Midi. Lettres de M. Riondet . . . et de M. le Dr. Jules Guyot*. Toulon: E. Aurel, 1861.

Larue, Pierre. *Le travail du sol dans les vignes*. Narbonne: F. Caillard, 1902.

————. *La vinification à Cuxac en 1902*. Narbonne: F. Caillard, 1903.

Lavergne, Léonce de. *Economie rurale de la France*. Paris: Guillaumin, 1877.

LeBlond, Maurice. *La crise du Midi*. Paris: Bibliothèque Charpentier, 1907.

Lecouteux, Edouard. *Cours d'économie rurale*. Paris: Librairie agricole de la Maison rustique, 1889.

Le Play, Pierre Guillaume Frédéric. *L'organisation de la famille selon le vrai modèle signalé par l'histoire de toutes les races et tous les temps*. Tours: A. Mame, 1884.

————. *Les ouvriers européens*. 6 vols. Tours: A. Mame, 1877–1879.

Levasseur, Emile. *Histoire des classes ouvrières et de l'industrie en France de 1789 à 1870*. 2 vols. Paris: Rousseau, 1903.

Marqfoy, Gustave. *De l'abaissement des tarifs de chemin de fer en France*. Paris: Librairie nouvelle, 1863.

Marx, Karl. *Class Struggles in France*. 1895; New York: International Publishers, 1934.

———. *The Eighteenth Brumaire of Louis Bonaparte*. 1852; New York: International Publishers, 1969.

Mataillon, R. E. *Les syndicats ouvriers dans l'agriculture*. Paris: Bonvalot-Jouve, 1908.

Meinadier, Albert. *La Compagnie des chemins de fer de Paris à Lyon et à la Méditerranée*. Paris: Hachette, 1908.

Mommeja, Fernand. *A travers le Midi. Avril–Octobre 1907*. Paris: Roustan, 1908.

Moreau de Jonnès, Alexandre. *Statistique de l'agriculture de la France*. Paris: Guillaumin, 1848.

Moureau, Marceau. *La coopérative de Lézignan. De l'isolement au groupement chez les vignerons du Narbonnais*. Paris: Arthur Rousseau, 1911.

Nicole, Marcel. *Les communautés de laboureurs dans l'ancien droit*. Dijon: Lamarche, E. Nourry, 1902.

Nuville, L. *Des accidents du travail agricole*. Paris: Marcel Rivière, 1908.

Passama, Paul. *La condition des ouvriers viticoles dans le Minervois*. Paris: Giard & Brière, 1906.

Paysan, Jacques, and François Paysan. *Les prolétaires de la Glèbe. Etudes sur la misère du peuple des campagnes*. Limoges: Imprimerie nouvelle, 1911.

Perrossier, E. *La commune de 1871 à Narbonne*. Tulle: J. Mazeyrie, 1900.

Prévot, Gabriel-Ellen. "Après la grève agricole." *L'Humanité*, Dec. 19, 1904.

———. "Le congrès des travailleurs agricoles du Midi." *La Revue socialiste* 42 (Sept. 1905): 363–367.

———. "Les grèves agraires du Midi: La grève générale agricole du Midi." *La Revue socialiste* 41 (Jan. 1905): 106–109.

———. "Mouvement agraire: A propos de la crise viticole." *La Revue socialiste* 42 (Aug. 1905): 231–232.

———. "Mouvement agraire: Le cinquième congrès national des syndicats agricoles mixtes." *La Revue socialiste* 41 (June 1905): 748–753.

———. "Mouvement agraire: La viticulture méridionale." *La Revue socialiste* 41 (Mar. 1905): 374–375.

———. "Les récents mouvements agraires dans le Midi de la France," *La Revue socialiste* 39 (Jan.–July 1904): 533–558.

Pullès, Henri. "Compte rendu sur le logement de la classe ouvrière agricole." *Mémoires de la Société des arts et sciences de Carcassonne* 6 (1890–1892): 199–204.

Rappoport, Charles. *Pourquoi nous sommes socialistes.* In *Encyclopédie socialiste, syndicale et coopérative de l'Internationale ouvrière,* ed. Adéodat Compère-Morel. Paris: Aristide Quillet, 1913.

Raynier, Pierre. *Biographie des représentants du département de l'Aude de 1789 à 1900.* Toulouse: Passeman & Alquier, 1901.

Razimbaud, Jules. *La crise viticole. Discours prononcés à la Chambre des députés.* Paris: Bernard Grasset, 1910.

Riondet, Alexis. *L'agriculture de la France méridionale. Ce qu'elle a été; ce qu'elle est; ce qu'elle pourrait être.* Paris: Librairie agricole de la Maison rustique, 1863.

Rivals, Jules. *L'agriculture dans le département de l'Aude, 1899–1900.* Paris: Henri Poirre, 1901.

———. *L'âme terrienne (Argelliers, 1907).* Carcassonne: Pierre Polère, 1914.

Robert, Adolphe, and Gaston Cougny. *Dictionnaire des parlementaires français.* 5 vols. Paris: Bourloton, 1889–1891.

Rocquigny, Henri de Fayel, comte de. *Les syndicats agricoles et leur œuvre.* Paris: Armand Colin, 1900.

Romeuf, Louis de. "La crise viticole du Midi." *Revue politique et parlementaire* 60 (May 1909): 289–321.

Rouger, Hubert. *La France socialiste.* In *Encyclopédie socialiste, syndicale et coopérative de l'internationale ouvrière,* ed. Adéodat Compère-Morel. Paris: Aristide Quillet, 1912.

Rousseau, Charles. *Enquête sur les vignobles du département de l'Aude reconstitués en plantes américaines.* Carcassonne: François Pomiés, 1888.

Saint-Fargeau, Berthomieu Tournal Girault de. *Histoire nationale ou Dictionnaire géographique de toutes les communes du département de l'Aude.* Paris: Firmin Didot; Carcassonne: Arnaud; Narbonne: Delsols, 1830.

Saporta, Antoine de. *La vigne et le vin dans le Midi de la France.* Paris: J.-B. Ballière, 1894.

Semichon, Lucien. *Le progrès de la vinification dans l'Aude.* Montpellier: Camille Coulet, 1897.

Société centrale de l'agriculture de l'Aude. *Enquête sur les vignobles du département de l'Aude reconstitués en plantes américaines.* Carcassonne: François Pomiés, 1888.

Souchon, A. *La crise de la main d'oeuvre agricole en France.* Paris: Rousseau, 1914.

————. "Le syndicalisme chez les ouvriers de l'agriculture." *La Réforme sociale* 96 (Dec. 16, 1909): 721–729.

Stroumsa, Vitalis. *Excursion dans les vignobles des environs de Perpignan, Narbonne et Béziers.* Montpellier: Grollier, 1886.

Syndicat professionnel des intérêts vinicoles de l'Aude. *Réponses au questionnaire de la Commission parlementaire d'enquête sur la viticulture.* Carcassonne: Gabelle, 1907.

Taillander, L. "Les salaires des ouvriers agricoles." *Le Musée social. Annales*, 1902, 178–186.

Tardy, Louis. "Une nouvelle coopérative vinicole: Les 'vignerons libres' de Maraussan (Hérault)." *Le Musée social. Annales*, 1902, 214–217.

Tisserand, M. *Rapport sur les travaux administratifs entreprises contre le phylloxéra et sur la situation des vignobles en France et en Algérie pendant les années 1888 et 1889.* Paris: Imprimerie nationale, 1890.

Vendémiaire. Bulletin officiel de la Confédération générale des vignerons des syndicats et de leurs adhérants (1ere année). Narbonne: Bousquet, 1907.

Vigouroux, Jean. *Essai sur le fonctionnement économique de quelques très grandes exploitations viticoles dans la Camargue et le Bas-Languedoc.* Montpellier: Société anonyme de l'Imprimeur général du Midi, 1906.

Visite des délégués de Narbonne à son majesté l'empereur Napoléon III. Paris: Firmin Didot, 1853.

Young, Arthur. *Travels During the Years 1787, 1788, and 1789; Undertaken More Particularly with a View Toward Ascertaining the Cultivation, Wealth, Resources, and National Prosperity of France.* 2d ed. 2 vols. London: Printed for W. R. Richardson, Royal Exchange, 1794.

Zévaès, Alexandre. *Histoire des partis socialistes. Les Guesdistes.* Paris: Marcel Rivière, 1911.

MODERN PRINTED SOURCES (AFTER 1914)

Acker, J. *L'organisation et l'action syndicale ouvrière dans l'Aude.* Paris: Domat-Montchréstien, 1932.

Aguet, Jean-Pierre. *Les grèves sous la monarchie de juillet 1830–1847.* Geneva: Droz, 1954.

Agulhon, Maurice. *1848 ou l'apprentissage à la république.* Paris: Seuil, 1973.

————. *La république au village.* Paris: Plon, 1970.

Agulhon, Maurice, Gabriel Desert, and Robert Specklin. *Histoire de la France rurale.* 4 vols. Paris: Seuil, 1976.

Almairic, Yvon. "Le village de la plaine viticole du Bas-Languedoc." *Folklore* 5 (Autumn 1944): 125–139.

Aminzade, Ronald. *Class, Politics and Early Industrial Capitalism*. Albany: SUNY Press, 1981.

Andréani, Edgar. *Grèves et fluctuations. La France de 1890 à 1914*. Paris: Cujas, 1968.

Andréani, Roland. "L'antimilitarisme en Languedoc avant 1914." *Revue d'histoire moderne et contemporaine* 20 (Jan.–Mar. 1973): 104–123.

Armengaud, André. *La population française au XIXe siècle*. Paris: Presses universitaires de France, 1971.

Atlas de géographie économique du département de l'Aude dressé sous la direction de M. le Dr. Jean Durand . . . par le Commandant Z. Khanzadian. Paris: Imprimerie artistique arménienne, 1928.

Atlas historique de la France contemporaine, 1800–1965. Paris: Armand Colin, 1966.

Baker, Robert P. "Socialism in the Nord, 1880–1914: A Regional View of the French Socialist Movement." *International Review of Social History* 12 (1967): 357–389.

Barral, Pierre. *Les agrariens français de Méline à Pisani*. Paris: Armand Colin, 1968.

Barrett, Michele. *Women's Oppression Today*. London: Verso, 1980.

Bechtel, Guy. *1907. La grande révolte du Midi*. Paris: Laffont, 1976.

Beltramone, André. *La mobilité géographique d'une population*. Paris: Gauthier-Villars, 1966.

Berenson, Edward. "Politics and the French Peasantry." *Social History* 12 (May 1987): 213–229.

———. *Populist Religion and Left-Wing Politics in France 1830–1852*. Princeton: Princeton University Press, 1984.

Bergé, Pierre. *Le marché des vins du Midi*. Paris: Presses universitaires de France, 1927.

Bertier de Sauvigny, Guillaume de. *La Restauration*. Paris: Flammarion, 1955.

Bezucha, Robert. *The Lyon Uprising of 1834*. Cambridge, Mass.: Harvard University Press, 1974.

Bichambis, M. *Narbonne, la Robine et les basses plaines de l'Aude*. Narbonne: J. Bousquet, 1926.

Blanc, Louis. *Souvenirs de 1907. Légende pour les Jacques*. Olonzac, Hérault: Confédération générale des vignerons du Midi, 1948.

Blanchard, Marcel. *Essais historiques sur les premiers chemins de fer du Midi languedocien et de la vallée du Rhône*. Montpellier: Imprimerie de la presse, 1935.

Bléton, Pierre. *La vie sociale sous le Second Empire. Un étonnant témoignage de la comtesse de Ségur*. Paris: Editions ouvrières, 1963.

Bloch, Marc. *French Rural History: An Essay on Its Basic Characteristics.* Trans. Janet Sondheimer. London: Routledge & Kegan Paul, 1966.

Bois, Paul. *Paysans de l'ouest.* Paris: Flammarion, 1971.

Bouillaguet-Bernard, Patricia, and Annie Ganvin. "Les effets de la restructuration de l'appareil de production sur le travail féminin et les perspectives de l'activité féminine." *Problèmes économiques,* no. 1669 (Apr. 16, 1980): 18–26.

Bourgeois-Pichat, Jean. "Evolution générale de la population française depuis le XVIIIᵉ siècle." *Population* 6 (Oct.–Dec. 1951): 635–663.

———. "Note sur l'évolution générale de la population française depuis le XVIIIᵉ siècle." *Population* 7 (Apr.–June 1952): 320–329.

Bouvier, Jean. "Le mouvement ouvrier et conjonctures économiques." *Le Mouvement social* 48 (July–Sept. 1964): 3–30.

Braque, René. "Aux origines du syndicalisme dans les milieux ruraux du centre de la France (Allier, Cher, Nièvre, Sud du Loiret)." *Le Mouvement social* 42 (Jan.–Mar. 1963): 79–116.

Braverman, Harry. *Labor and Monopoly Capitalism.* New York: Monthly Review Press, 1974.

Breugel, Irene. "Women as a Reserve Army of Labor: A Note on Recent British Experiences." *Feminist Review* 3 (1979): 12–23.

Burns, Michael. *Rural Society and French Politics: Boulangism and the Dreyfus Affair, 1886–1900.* Princeton: Princeton University Press, 1984.

Camp, Wesley D. *Marriage and the Family in France Since the Revolution.* New York: Bookman Associates, 1961.

Caralp, R. "Le transport férroviaire des vins du Languedoc vers Paris." *Revue de géographie de Lyon* 26 (1951): 273–296.

Carbonnel, Paul. *Histoire de Narbonne.* Narbonne: P. Caillard, 1956.

Carrière, M. "Le ramado de Coursan." *Folkore de l'Aude,* 1938, 13–14.

Carrière, Paul, and Raymond Dugrand. *La région méditerranéenne.* Paris: Presses universitaires de France, 1960.

Charles, Jean. *Les débuts du mouvement syndical à Besançon. La Fédération ouvrière, 1891–1914.* Paris: Editions sociales, 1962.

Chatelain, Abel. *Les migrations temporaires en France de 1800 à 1914.* 2 vols. Lille: Publications de l'Université de Lille III, 1976.

———. "Les migrations temporaires françaises au XIXᵉ siècle." Paper delivered to the Société de démographie historique, Jan. 1967. Paris: Sirey, 1968.

———. "Les ouvriers migrants temporaires en Côte-d'Or au XIXᵉ siècle." *Annales de Bourgogne* 23 (1951): 266–281.

———. "Valeur des recensements de la population française au XIXᵉ siècle." *Revue de géographie de Lyon* 29 (1954): 273–280.

Cholvy, Gerard. "L'indifférence religieuse et anticléricalisme à Narbonne et en Narbonnais au XIXᵉ siècle." In *Fédération historique du Languedoc-méditerranéen et du Roussillon, XLVᵉ congrès,* 3:73–93. Montpellier: FHLMR, 1973.

———. "Religion et société au XIXᵉ siècle: Le diocèse de Montpellier." Thèse de doctorat d'état, Université de Lille. 2 vols. Lille: Services de réproduction des thèses de l'université, 1973.

Clapham, J. H. *The Economic Development of France and Germany.* New York: Cambridge University Press, 1966.

Clough, Shepard B. *France: A History of National Economics, 1789–1939.* New York: Scribner, 1939.

Cogniot, Georges. "La question paysanne devant le mouvement ouvrier français de 1892 à 1921." *Cahiers d'histoire de l'Institut Maurice Thorez* 24 (1971): 5–21.

Collins, E.J.T. "Labor Supply and Demand in European Agriculture, 1800–1880." In *Agrarian Change and Economic Development,* ed. E. L. Jones and S. J. Woolf, 61–94. London: Methuen, 1969.

Compère-Morel, Adéodat. "Le programme socialiste des réformes agraires." In *Les documents du socialisme,* ed. Albert Thomas. Paris: Marcel Rivière, 1919.

Corbin, Alain. *Archaïsme et modernité en Limousin au XIXᵉ siècle.* 2 vols. Paris: Marcel Rivière, 1975.

Costeplane, Gibert. "Note sur le folklore de Lastours (Aude)." *Folklore* 18 (Summer 1965): 17–19.

Cousteix, Pierre. "Le mouvement ouvrier Limousin de 1870 à 1939." *Actualité d'histoire* 20–21 (Dec. 1957): 27–95.

Cros-Mayrevieille, G. "L'évolution économique de Narbonne." *Bulletin de la Commission archéologique de Narbonne* 17 (1926): 102–159.

Debant, Robert. "Un périodique d'opposition à la fin de la monarchie de juillet: *La revue de l'Aude,* 1845–1846." In *Carcassonne et sa région. Actes du congrès d'études régionales tenus à Carcassonne en Mai 1968.* Carcassonne: Gabelle, 1970.

Deldyke, T., H. Gelders, and J.-M. Limbor. *La population active et sa structure.* Brussels: Université de Bruxelles, 1968.

Delphy, Christine. *Close to Home.* Translated and edited by Diana Leonard. London: Hutchinson, 1984.

Derfler, Leslie. "Reformism and Jules Guesde, 1891–1914." *International Review of Social History* 12 (1967): 66–80.

Dommanget, Maurice. *Histoire du premier mai.* Société universitaire d'éditions et de librairie, 1953.

Drogat, N. "Le travail féminin à la campagne." *Travaux de l'action populaire* 11 (Aug. 1947): 585–599.

Dubief, Henri. *Le syndicalisme révolutionnaire*. Paris: Armand Colin, 1969.

Duby, Georges, and Armand Wallon, eds. *Histoire de la France rurale*. Vol. 3. Paris: Seuil, 1976.

Dugé de Bernonville, L. "Enquête sur les conditions de la vie ouvrière et rurale en France en 1913–1914" (Parts 1 and 2). *Bulletin de la statistique générale de la France* 6 (Oct. 1916): 85–108; (Jan. 1917): 185–221.

Dugrand, Raymond. "La propriété foncière des citadins en Bas-Languedoc." *Bulletin de l'Association de géographes français* 256–260 (May–June 1956): 133–145.

———. *Villes et campagnes en Bas-Languedoc. Le réseau urbain du Bas-Languedoc*. Paris: Presses universitaires de France, 1963.

Dupeux, George. *Aspects de l'histoire sociale et politique du Loire-et-Cher, 1848–1914*. Paris: Mouton, 1962.

Durand, Jacques, and André Hampartzoumian. *Le Languedoc au temps des diligences*. Montpellier: Images d'oc, 1978.

Dussourd, Henriette. *Au même pot et au même feu. Etude sur les communautés familiales agricoles du centre de la France*. Moulins: A. Potier, 1962.

Duveau, Georges. *La vie ouvrière en France sous le Second Empire*. Paris: Presses universitaires de France, 1946.

Elwitt, Sanford. *The Making of the Third Republic*. Baton Rouge, La.: Louisiana State University Press, 1975.

Engels, Friedrich. "La question paysanne en France et en Allemagne." *Les Cahiers du Communisme* 31 (Nov. 1955): 1467–1488.

Engels, Friedrich, Paul Lafargue, and Laura Lafargue. *Correspondance*. Vol. 2: *1877–1890*. Moscow: Foreign Language Publishers, 1960.

Fabre, Daniel, and Charles Camberoque. *La fête en Languedoc*. Toulouse: Edouard Privat, 1978.

Fabre, Daniel, and Jacques Lacroix. *La vie quotidienne des paysans du Languedoc au XIXᵉ siècle*. Paris: Hachette, 1973.

Faucher, Daniel. "Aspects sociologiques du travail agricole." *Etudes rurales* 13–14 (Apr.–Sept. 1964): 125–131.

Faucher, Daniel, Elie Lambert, and Jean Fourcassie. *Visages du Languedoc*. Strasbourg: Imprimerie strasbourgeoise, 1965.

Faure, Marcel. *Les paysans dans la Société française*. Paris: Armand Colin, 1966.

Fédération des travailleurs de l'agriculture, des forêts et similaires de France. *Histoire du mouvement syndical des ouvriers agricoles forestiers et similaires*. Orléans: Imprimerie la laborieuse, 1952.

Fénélon, Paul. *Vocabulaire de géographie agraire*. Gap: Louis-Jean, 1970.

Flonneau, Jean-Marie. "La crise de la vie chère, 1910–1914." *Le Mouvement social* 72 (July–Sept. 1970): 49–81.

Frader, Laura Levine. "Grapes of Wrath: Vineyard Workers and Strike Activity in the Aude, 1860–1913." In *Class Conflict and Collective Action*, ed. Louise A. Tilly and Charles Tilly, 185–206. Beverly Hills, Calif.: Sage, 1981.

Gaillard, Jeanne. *Communes de province, commune de Paris, 1870–1871*. Paris: Flammarion, 1971.

Gallon, G. "Mouvement de la population dans le département de l'Aude (1821–1920) et depuis la fin de cette période." *Bulletin de la Société d'études scientifiques de l'Aude* 35 (1931): 128–170.

Galtier, Gaston. *Le vignoble du Languedoc-méditerranéen et du Roussillon*. 3 vols. Montpellier: Causse, Graille & Castelnau, n.d.

Garidou, Jean-François. "La viticulture audoise 1870–1913." Travail d'études et de recherches d'histoire, Université de Montpellier, Faculté des lettres et des sciences humaines, 1968.

Garridou-Lagrange, André. *Production agricole et économie rurale en France*. Paris: Librairie générale de droit et de jurisprudence, 1939.

Genzling, Annie. "La Commune de Narbonne en 1871." Paper presented at the Colloquium on Right and Left in Languedoc-méditerranéen–Roussillon, Université Paul-Valéry–Montpellier, June 9–10, 1973.

Gilbert, Urbain. "Quelques aspects populaires de manifestations viticoles de 1907." In *Carcassonne et sa région*. Actes des congrès d'études régionales tenus à Carcassonne en Mai 1968, 325–333. Carcassonne: Gabelle, 1970.

Girard, Louis. "L'affaire du chemin de fer Cette-Marseille (1861–1863)." *Revue d'histoire moderne et contemporaine* 11 (Jan.–Mar. 1955): 107–126.

———. *Les élections de 1869*. Vol. 21 of *Bibliothèque de la révolution de 1848*. Paris: Marcel Rivière, 1960.

Glass, D. V., and D.E.C. Eversley. *Population in History*. Chicago: Aldine, 1965.

Godechot, Jacques, and Suzanne Moncassin. *Démographie et subsistances en Languedoc du XVIIIᵉ siècle au début du XIXᵉ siècle*. Paris: Imprimerie nationale, 1965.

Goetz-Girey, R. "Les ouvriers-paysans." In *Mélanges économiques dédiés à M. le professeur René Gonnard*, 149–159. Paris: Librairie générale de droit et de jurisprudence, 1946.

Goldberg, Harvey. "Jaurès and the Formation of a Socialist Peasant Policy, 1885–1898." *International Review of Social History* 2 (1957): 372–391.

————. *Jean Jaurès*. Madison: University of Wisconsin Press, 1962.

————. "The Myth of the French Peasant." *American Journal of Economics and Sociology* 13 (July 1954): 363–378.

Golob, Eugene O. *The Méline Tariff: French Agriculture and National Economic Policy*. New York: Columbia University Press, 1944.

Goodman, David, and Michael Redclift. *From Peasant to Proletarian: Capitalist Development and Agrarian Transitions*. Oxford: Basil Blackwell, 1981.

Goubert, Pierre. "Local History." *Daedalus* 100 (Winter 1971): 113–127.

Gratton, Philippe. *Les luttes de classes dans les campagnes*. Paris: Anthropos, 1971.

————. *Les paysans français contre l'agrarisme*. Paris: François Maspero, 1972.

Guilbert, Madeleine. *Les femmes et l'organisation syndicale avant 1914*. Paris: Centre national de recherche scientifique, 1966.

Gullickson, Gay. "The Sexual Division of Labor in Cottage Industry and Agriculture in the Pays de Caux: Auffay, 1750–1850." *French Historical Studies* 12 (Fall 1981): 177–199.

Guthrie, Christopher. "Political Conflict and Socioeconomic Change in the City of Narbonne, 1848–1871." Ph.D. diss., Northern Illinois University, 1981.

————. "Reaction to the Coup d'Etat of 1851 in the Narbonnais: A Case Study of Popular Political Mobilization and Repression During the Second Republic." *French Historical Studies* 13 (Spring 1983): 18–46.

Halbwachs, Maurice. "Budgets des familles ouvrières et paysannes en France en 1907." *Bulletin de la statistique générale de la France* 4 (Oct. 1914): 47–83.

————. "Revenues et dépenses de ménages des travailleurs: Une enquête officielle d'avant-guerre." *Revue d'économie politique* 35 (Jan.–Feb. 1921): 50–59.

Halévy, Daniel. *Visites aux paysans du centre*. Paris: Bernard Grasset, 1921.

Hanagan, Michael. *The Logic of Solidarity: Artisans and Industrial Workers in Three French Towns, 1871–1914*. Urbana: University of Illinois Press, 1980.

Hardy-Hémery, Odette. "Rationalisation de technique et rationalisation du travail à la Compagnie des mines d'Anzin, 1927–1928." *Le Mouvement social* 72 (July–Sept. 1970): 3–48.

Hareven, Tamara, and Maris Vinovskis. "Marital Fertility, Ethnicity and Occupation in Urban Families: An Analysis of South Boston and the South End in 1880." *Journal of Social History* 9 (1975): 69–93.

Hartmann, Heidi. "Capitalism, Patriarchy, and Job Segregation by Sex." *Signs* 1 (Summer 1976): 137–169.

Henry, Louis. "Historical Demography." *Daedalus* 97 (Spring 1968): 385–396.

———. *Manuel de démographie historique*. Paris: Droz, 1967.

Henry, Louis, and Michel Fleury. *Des régistres paroissaux à l'histoire de la population. Nouveau manuel de dépouillement et d'exploitation de l'état-civil ancien*. Paris: Institut national d'études démographiques, 1965.

Higonnet, Patrice L. R. *Pont-de-Montvert: Social Structure and Politics in a French Village, 1700–1914*. Cambridge, Mass.: Harvard University Press, 1971.

Histoire du mouvement anarchiste en France, 1889–1914. Paris: Société universitaire d'éditions et de librairie, 1951.

Howorth, Jolyon. *Edouard Vaillant. La création de l'unité socialiste en France*. Paris: Edi-Syros, 1982.

———. "French Workers and German Workers: The Impossibility of Internationalism, 1900–1914." *European History Quarterly* 15 (1985): 71–97.

Huard, Raymond. *Le mouvement républicain en Bas-Languedoc, 1848–1881*. Paris: Fondation nationale des sciences politiques, 1982.

Hunt, Lynn. *Politics, Culture, and Class in the French Revolution*. Berkeley and Los Angeles: University of California Press, 1984.

Hutton, Patrick. *The Cult of the Revolutionary Tradition: The Blanquists in French Politics, 1864–1893*. Berkeley and Los Angeles: University of California Press, 1981.

Isnard, Hildebert. *La vigne en Algérie. Etude géographique*. 2 vols. Orpheys-Gap: N.p., 1954.

Jeanjean, A., and J. Rives. *La proclamation de la Troisième République dans le département de l'Aude. Essai historique*. Carcassonne: Gabelle, 1920.

Jones, Peter. "Parish, Seigneurie, and Community of Inhabitants in Southern Central France During the 18th and 19th Centuries." *Past and Present* 91 (1981): 74–108.

———. "Political Commitment and Rural Society in the Southern Massif Central." *European Studies Review* 10 (1980): 337–356.

Jouffroi-Schaeffer, Magali. "L'implantation du St-Simonisme dans la ville et la région de Narbonne." In *Fédération historique du Languedoc-méditerranéen et du Roussillon, XLVᵉ congrès*, 3:61–72. Montpellier: FHLMR, 1973.

Judt, Tony. *Socialism in Provence, 1871–1914*. New York: Cambridge University Press, 1979.

Julliard, Jacques. *Autonomie ouvrière. Etudes sur le syndicalisme et l'action directe*. Paris: Gallimard–Le Seuil, 1988.

————. "La CGT devant la guerre, 1900–1914." *Le Mouvement social* 49 (1964): 47–62.

————. "Théorie syndicaliste révolutionnaire et pratique gréviste." *Le Mouvement social* 65 (1968): 55–69.

Kaplan, Temma. "Female Consciousness and Collective Action: The Case of Barcelona." *Signs* 7 (Spring 1982): 545–566.

Katznelson, Ira, and Aristide Zolberg, eds. *Working-Class Formation: Nineteenth-Century Patterns in Western Europe and the United States*. Princeton: Princeton University Press, 1986.

Kayser, Jacques. *Les grandes batailles du radicalisme, 1820–1901*. Paris: Marcel Rivière, 1962.

Kriegel, Annie. "Histoire ouvrière aux XIXe et XXe siècles" (Parts 1 and 2). *Revue historique*, nos. 232 (Oct.–Dec. 1963): 447–478; 235 (Apr.–June 1966): 455–490.

Lacombe, Christian. "Desserte secondaire des pays de l'Aude par voie ferrée." In *Carcassonne et sa région. Actes des congrès d'études régionales tenus à Carcassonne en mai 1968*, 341–348. Carcassonne: Gabelle, 1970.

Lair, Maurice. *Le socialisme et l'agriculture française*. Paris: Plon, 1922.

Lancelot, Alain. *L'abstentionnisme électoral en France*. Paris: Armand Colin, 1968.

Landauer, Carl. "The Guesdists and the Small Farmer: The Early Erosion of French Marxism." *International Review of Social History* 6 (1961): 212–225.

————. "The Origin of Socialist Reformism in France." *International Review of Social History* 12 (1967): 81–107.

Larguier, Gilbert. "Structures agraires, structures sociales d'un village narbonnais: Ouveillan (fin XVIIIe siècle–début XXe siècle)." In *Economie et société en Languedoc-Roussillon de 1789 à nos jours*, 143–167. Montpellier: Centre d'histoire contemporaine de Languedoc-méditerranéen et du Roussillon, 1978.

Laurent, Robert. *Esquisse méthodologique pour l'étude d'un vignoble*. In *Actes du 86e congrès nationale des sociétés savantes*, 259–266. Montpellier: N.p., 1961.

————. "La propriété foncière dans le Bittérois à la veille de la première guerre mondiale." In *Fédération historique du Languedoc-méditerranéen et du Roussillon, XLIIIe congrès, Béziers, 1970*, 415–426. Montpellier: FHLMR, 1971.

————. *Les vignerons de la Côte d'Or au XIXe siècle*. 2 vols. Dijon: Bernigaud & Privat, 1957.

Lees, Lynn Hollen. "Getting and Spending: The Family Budgets of English Industrial Workers in 1890." In *Consciousness and Class Experience*, ed. John Merriman, 169–186. London: Holmes & Meier, 1979.

Lehning, James. *The Peasants of Marlhes*. Chapel Hill: University of North Carolina Press, 1980.

Lequin, Yves. *Les ouvriers de la région lyonnaise, 1848–1914*. 2 vols. Lyon: Presses universitaires de Lyon, 1977.

————. "Sources et méthodes de l'histoire des grèves, l'exemple de l'Isère." *Cahiers d'histoire* 12 (1967): 215–231.

LeRoy Ladurie, Emmanuel. *Les paysans de Languedoc*. Paris: Flammarion, 1969.

L'Homme, Jean. "Le pouvoir d'achat de l'ouvrier français au cours d'un siècle: 1840–1940." *Le Mouvement social*, no. 63 (Apr.–June 1968): 41–69.

L'Huillier, Fernand. *La lutte ouvrière à la fin du Second Empire*. Paris: Armand Colin, 1957.

Ligou, Daniel. *Histoire du socialisme en France, 1871–1961*. Paris: Presses universitaires de France, 1962.

Litchfield, Burr. "The Family and the Mill: Cotton Mill Work, Family Work Patterns, and Fertility in Mid-Victorian Stockport." In *The Victorian Family*, ed. Anthony S. Wohl, 180–196. London: Croom Helm, 1978.

Lloyd, Cynthia B. "The Division of Labor Between the Sexes: A Review." In *Sex Discrimination and the Division of Labor*, ed. Cynthia B. Lloyd. New York: Columbia University Press, 1975.

Locke, Robert R. *French Legitimists and the Politics of Moral Order in the Early Third Republic*. Princeton: Princeton University Press, 1974.

Lombard, Henri. *Monoculture de la vigne et évolution rurale dans la vallée de la Cèze (Gard)*. Montpellier: Causse, Graille & Castelnau, 1951.

Loubère, Leo A. "Coal Miners, Strikes, and Politics in Lower Languedoc, 1880–1914." *Journal of Social History* 2 (Fall 1968): 25–50.

————. "The Emergence of the Extreme Left in Lower Languedoc, 1848–1851: The Social and Economic Factors in Politics." *American Historical Review* 73 (Apr. 1968): 1019–1051.

————. "Left-Wing Radicals, Strikes, and the Military, 1880–1907." *French Historical Studies* 3 (Spring 1963): 93–105.

————. *Radicalism in Mediterranean France: Its Rise and Decline, 1848–1914*. Albany: SUNY Press, 1974.

————. "Les radicaux d'extrême gauche en France et les rapports entre patrons et ouvriers, 1871–1900." *Revue d'histoire économique et sociale* 1 (1964): 89–103.

McBride, Theresa. *The Domestic Revolution*. London: Croom Helm, 1976.

McMechan, William. "A Syndicalist Response to Socialism: The French Building Trades, 1906–1914." Paper presented at the Annual Meeting of the American Historical Association, Dallas, 1977.

Maffre, Joseph. "Les événements de 1907 dans l'Aude et la région méridionale." In *Carcassonne et sa région. Actes des congrès d'études régionales tenus à Carcassonne en mai 1968*, 335–340. Carcassonne: Gabelle, 1970.

Magraw, Roger. *France, 1815–1914: The Bourgeois Century*. London: Fontana, 1984.

———. "Pierre Joigneaux and Socialist Propaganda in the French Countryside, 1849–1851." *French Historical Studies* 10 (1978): 599–640.

Maitron, Jean. "Un 'anar,' qu'est-ce que c'est?" *Le Mouvement social* 83 (Apr.–June 1973): 23–45.

———. *Dictionnaire biographique du mouvement ouvrier français*. 15 vols. Paris: Editions ouvrières, 1974.

Manuel, Frank. "The Luddite Movement in France." *Journal of Modern History* 10 (June 1938): 180–211.

Margadant, Ted. *French Peasants in Revolt: The Insurrection of 1851*. Princeton: Princeton University Press, 1979.

Marrès, Paul. "L'évolution de la viticulture dans le Bas-Languedoc." *Bulletin de la Société languedocienne de géographie* 6 (1935): 26–58.

———. "Le prolétariat viticole: Aspects humains de la crise viticole." *Bulletin de la Société languedocienne de géographie* 6 (1935): 125–140.

———. *La vigne et le vin en France*. Paris: Armand Colin, 1950.

Marty, André. *A la gloire des lutteurs de 1907*. Paris: Editions Norman Béthune, 1972.

———. *L'histoire véritable et vécue d'un beau chant populaire, "Gloire du 17ᵉ."* Paris: Editions de l'avant-garde, 1952.

Mayeur, Jean-Marie. *Les débuts de la Troisième République*. Paris: Seuil, 1973.

Mendras, Henri. *The Vanishing Peasant: Innovation and Change in French Agriculture*. Translated by Jean Lerner. Cambridge, Mass.: MIT Press, 1970.

Merriman, John. *The Agony of the Republic*. New Haven: Yale University Press, 1978.

———. *Red City: Limoges in the Nineteenth Century*. New York: Oxford University Press, 1986.

Meuvret, Bernard. *Le socialisme municipal à Villeurbanne, 1880–1982*. Lyon: Presses universitaires de Lyon, 1982.

Milhaud, Jules. "Le prix de vin et les revenues viticoles." *Etudes et conjonctures: Union française* 2 (Feb. 1948): 65–74.

———. "Viticulture et la lutte des classes dans le Midi." *Cahiers internationaux, Revue internationale du monde de travail* 88 (July–Aug. 1957): 66–72.

Moch, Leslie Page. *Paths to the City: Regional Migration in Nineteenth-Century France*. Beverly Hills, Calif.: Sage, 1983.

Montgomery, David. "Workers' Control over Machine Production in the Nineteenth Century." *Labor History* 17 (Fall 1976): 485–509.

More, C. H. *Skill and the English Working Class*. London: Croom Helm, 1980.

Moses, Claire Goldberg. *French Feminism in the Nineteenth Century*. Albany: SUNY Press, 1985.

Moss, Bernard. *The Origins of the French Labor Movement: The Socialism of Skilled Workers, 1830–1914*. Berkeley and Los Angeles: University of California Press, 1976.

Napo, Félix. *1907. La révolte des vignerons*. Toulouse: Edouard Privat, 1971; 2d ed. 1982.

Nelli, René. *Le Languedoc et le comté de Foix, le Roussillon*. Paris: Gallimard, 1958.

Nordmann, Jean-Thomas. *Histoire des radicaux, 1820–1973*. Paris: Editions de la Table ronde, 1974.

Oren, Laura. "The Welfare of Women in Laboring Families: England, 1860–1950." In *Clio's Consciousness Raised*, ed. Mary Hartman and Lois Banner, 226–244. New York: Harper & Row, 1974.

Parain, Charles. "La maison vigneronne en France." *Arts et traditions populaires* 4 (Oct.–Dec. 1955): 289–378.

Pech, Monique. "Essai sur la crise économique de la viticulture languedocienne en 1907, antécédents et causes." Thèse de diplôme d'études supérieurs, Faculté des lettres, Université de Paris-Sorbonne, 1967.

———. "Les luttes politiques à Narbonne à la fin du XIXe siècle: Un exemple, le duel Ferroul-Bartissol aux élections législatives de 1898." In *Narbonne. Archéologie et histoire*, 95–105. Montpellier: Fédération historique du Languedoc-méditerranéen et du Roussillon, 1973.

Pech, Rémy. "Aspects de l'économie narbonnaise de l'époque du phylloxéra à la crise de mévente (fin XIXe siècle): Un démarrage éphémère." In *Narbonne. Archéologie et histoire*, 107–122. Montpellier: Fédération historique du Languedoc-méditerranéen et du Roussillon, 1973.

———. "Les Caractères économiques et sociaux du socialisme férrouliste à Narbonne (1880–1914)." Paper presented at the Colloquium on Right and Left in Languedoc-méditerranéen–Roussillon, Université Paul-Valéry, Montpellier, June 9–10, 1973.

———. *Entreprise viticole et capitalisme en Languedoc-Roussillon. Du phylloxéra aux crises de mévente.* Toulouse: Presses de l'Université de Toulouse, 1975.

———. "La formation de la bourgeoisie viticole en Narbonnais au XIXe siècle." In *Economie et société en Languedoc-Roussillon de 1789 à nos jours*, 133–141. Montpellier: Centre d'histoire contemporaine du Languedoc-méditerranéen et du Roussillon, 1978.

———. "L'organisation du marché du vin en Languedoc et en Roussillon aux XIXe et XXe siècles." *Etudes rurales* 78–80 (Apr.–Dec. 1980): 99–111.

———. "Les thèmes économiques et sociaux du socialisme férrouliste à Narbonne, 1880–1914." In *Droite et gauche de 1789 à nos jours*, 133–141. Montpellier: Centre d'histoire contemporaine du Languedoc-méditerranéen et du Roussillon, 1975.

Pech, Rémy. "La vie politique dans l'Aude, 1881–1902." Mémoire pour diplôme d'études supérieures d'histoire, Université de Paris-Sorbonne, 1967.

———. "Le vignoble du Languedoc-Roussillon: Crise séculaire et recherche d'un nouveau souffle." *Revue française d'études politiques méditerranéennes* 23 (Nov. 1976): 17–38.

Pellegrin, V. *Les grandes étapes de l'agriculture dans l'Aude.* Carcassonne: Gabelle, 1937.

Pennetier, Claude. *Le socialisme dans le Cher, 1851–1921.* Paris: Delayance, 1982.

Perrot, Michelle. "Grèves, grévistes et conjoncture: Vieux problèmes, travaux neufs." *Le Mouvement social* 63 (Apr.–June 1968): 109–124.

———. *Les ouvriers en grève, 1871–1890.* 2 vols. Paris: Mouton, 1974.

———. "Le problème des sources pour l'étude du militant ouvrier du XIXe siècle." *Le Mouvement social* 33–34 (Oct. 1960–Mar. 1961): 21–34.

Peyronnet, François Raymond. *Le vignoble nord-africain.* Paris: Peyronnet, 1950.

Le phylloxéra de la vigne. Rabat: Direction générale de l'agriculture, du commerce et de la colonisation, 1935.

Pierrard, Pierre. *La vie ouvrière à Lille sous le Second Empire.* Paris: Bloud & Gay, 1965.

Pigenet, P., M. R. Rygiel, and M. Picard. *Terre de luttes (les précurseurs, 1848–1939). Histoire du Mouvement Ouvrier dans le Cher.* Paris: Editions sociales, 1977.

Pinchemel, Philippe. *Structures sociales et dépopulation rurale dans les campagnes picardes de 1836 à 1936*. Paris: Armand Colin, 1957.

Plandé, Romain. *Géographie et histoire du département de l'Aude*. Grenoble: Editions françaises nouvelles, 1944.

Pradal, Mme. "Les migrations intérieures de Caunes, Ginestas et Coursan en 1872." Mémoire pour Diplôme d'études supérieures, Université de Toulouse, Institut d'études politiques, 1970.

Price, Roger. *The Second French Republic: A Social History*. Ithaca: Cornell University Press, 1972.

———, ed. *1848 in France*. Ithaca: Cornell University Press, 1975.

———, ed. *Revolution and Reaction: 1848 and the Second French Republic*. London: Croom Helm, 1975.

Rebérioux, Madeleine. *La république radicale?* Paris: Seuil, 1975.

———. "Jaurès et la nationalisation de la vigne." *Bulletin de la Société des études Jaurésiennes* 17 (1965): 2–9.

Reddy, William. "The Language of the Crowd in Rouen, 1752–1871." *Past and Present* 74 (Feb. 1977): 62–89.

———. *The Rise of Market Culture: The Textile Trade and French Society, 1750–1900*. New York: Cambridge University Press, 1984.

Reeves, Maud Pember. *Round About a Pound a Week*. 1913; London: Virago, 1980.

Renaud, Jean-Daniel. *Les syndicats en France*. Vol. 1. Paris: Seuil, 1975.

Ridley, F. F. *Revolutionary Syndicalism in France: The Direct Action of Its Time*. New York: Cambridge University Press, 1970.

Rinaudo, Yves. "Usure et crédit dans les campagnes du Var au XIXe siècle." *Annales du Midi* 92 (Oct.–Dec. 1980): 431–452.

———. *Les vendanges de la république. Les paysans du Var à la fin du XIXe siècle*. Lyon: Presses universitaires de Lyon, 1982.

Rivière, Jean. "Croyances et êtres surnaturels." In Gaston Jourdianne, *Contribution au folklore de l'Aude*. 1889; Paris: G.-P. Maisonneuve & Larose, 1973.

———. *La sainteté en pays d'Aude*. Narbonne: Brille & Gautier, 1949.

Roubin, Lucienne. *Chambrettes des provencaux. Une maison des hommes en Méditerranée septrionale*. Paris: Plon, 1970.

Rougerie, Jacques. "Remarques sur l'histoire des salaires à Paris au XIXe siècle." *Le Mouvement social* 63 (Apr.–June 1968): 71–108.

Rude, Fernand. *Le mouvement ouvrier à Lyon de 1827 à 1832*. Paris: Domat-Monchréstien, 1944.

Sagnes, Jean. "Les grèves dans l'Hérault de 1890 à 1938." In *Economie et société en Languedoc-Roussillon de 1789 à nos jours*, 251–274. Montpellier: Centre d'histoire contemporaine du Languedoc-méditerranéen et du Roussillon, 1978.

———. "Le mouvement de 1907 en Languedoc-Roussillon: De la révolte viticole à la révolte régionale." *Le Mouvement social* 104 (July–Sept. 1978): 3–20.

———. *Le mouvement ouvrier en Languedoc*. Toulouse: Edouard Privat, 1980.

———. *Jean Jaurès et le Languedoc viticole*. Montpellier: Presses du Languedoc, 1988.

Schöttler, Peter. "Politique ou lutte des classes: Notes sur le syndicalisme 'apolitique' des bourses du travail." *Le Mouvement social* 116 (July 1981): 3–20.

Scott, James C. *The Moral Economy of the Peasant*. New Haven: Yale University Press, 1976.

Scott, Joan W. *The Glassworkers of Carmaux*. Cambridge, Mass.: Harvard University Press, 1974.

———. "Language, Gender, and Working-Class History." *International Labor and Working-Class History* 31 (Spring 1987): 1–13.

———. "Mayors Versus Police Chiefs: Socialist Municipalities Confront the French State." In *French Cities in the Nineteenth Century*, ed. John Merriman, 230–245. New York: Holmes & Meier, 1981.

———. "Les verriers de Carmaux, 1856–1895." *Le Mouvement social* 76 (July–Sept. 1971): 67–93.

Seager, Frederick. *The Boulanger Affair*. Ithaca: Cornell University Press, 1969.

Ségalen, Martine. *Love and Power in the Peasant Family*. Translated by Sarah Matthews. Chicago: University of Chicago Press, 1983.

———. "Le mariage, l'amour et la femme dans les proverbes du sud de la France." *Annales du Midi* 87 (1975): 265–288.

Sentenac, Paul. *La lame et le fourreau*. Paris: Sansot, 1921.

Sentou, Jean. "Les facteurs de la révolution agricole dans le Narbonnais." In *France méridionale et pays ibériques. Mélanges géographiques offerts en hommage à Daniel Faucher*, 2:651–666. Toulouse: Edouard Privat, 1949.

Sewell, William H., Jr. "La classe ouvrière de Marseille sous la Seconde République: Structure sociale et comportement politique." *Le Mouvement social* 76 (July–Sept. 1971): 27–65.

———. "Social Change and the Rise of Working-Class Politics in Nineteenth-Century Marseille." *Past and Present* 65 (1974): 75–109.

———. "Social Mobility in a Nineteenth-Century European City: Some Findings and Implications." Paper presented at the Conference on International Comparisons of Social Mobility in Past Societies, Institute for Advanced Study, Princeton, June 15–17, 1972.

Sheppard, Thomas F. *Loumarin in the Eighteenth Century: A Study of a French Village*. Baltimore: Johns Hopkins University Press, 1971.

Shorter, Edward, and Charles Tilly. "The Shape of Strikes in France, 1830–1960." *Comparative Studies in Society and History* 13 (Jan. 1971): 60–86.

———. *Strikes in France, 1830–1968*. New York: Cambridge University Press, 1974.

Siegfried, André. "Géographie de l'opinion publique dans le Midi sous la IIIᵉ République: l'Aude. Les élections de 1849 à 1945." Course given at the Collège de France, 1939. Typescript.

Sion, Jules. "La structure agraire de la France méditerranéenne." *Bulletin de la Société languedocienne de géographie* 8 (1937): 109–131.

Smith, J. Harvey. "Agricultural Workers and the French Wine-Growers Revolt of 1907." *Past and Present* 79 (1978): 100–125.

———. "La crise d'une économie régionale: La monoculture viticole et la révolte du Midi (1907)." *Annales du Midi* 92 (1980): 317–334.

———. "Village Revolution: The Agricultural Workers of Cruzy (Hérault), 1850–1910." Ph.D. diss. University of Wisconsin, 1972.

———. "Work Routine and Social Structure in a French Village: Cruzy, Hérault, in the Nineteenth Century." *Journal of Interdisciplinary History* 5 (Dec. 1975): 357–382.

———. "Work Structure and Labor Organization in Lower Languedoc." Paper presented at the Annual Meeting of the Society for French Historical Studies, Washington, D.C., April 1–2, 1981.

"Souvenirs d'un compagnon du tour de France." *Folklore* 19 (Winter 1966): 2–32.

Spitzer, Alan B. "Anarchy and Culture: Fernand Pelloutier and the Dilemma of Revolutionary Syndicalism." *International Review of Social History* 8 (1963): 379–388.

Soboul, Albert. "The French Rural Community of the 18th and 19th Centuries." *Past and Present* 10 (Nov. 1956): 78–95.

Sowerwine, Charles. *Sisters or Citizens: Women in the French Socialist Party*. London: Cambridge University Press, 1982.

———. "Workers and Women in France Before 1914: The Debate over the Couriau Affair." *Journal of Modern History* 55 (Sept. 1983): 411–441.

Stearns, Peter. *Revolutionary Syndicalism and French Labor: Cause Without Rebels*. New Brunswick, N.J.: Rutgers University Press, 1971.

Sternhell, Zeev. *La droite révolutionnaire*. Paris: Seuil, 1978.

Thernstrom, Stephen. "Working-Class Social Mobility in Industrial America." In *Essays in Theory and History*, ed. Melvin Richter, 221–238. Cambridge, Mass.: Harvard University Press, 1970.

Thompson, E. P. *The Making of the English Working Class.* Harmondsworth, Eng.: Penguin Books, 1968.

———. "The Moral Economy of the English Crowd in the Nineteenth Century." *Past and Present* 50 (Feb. 1971): 76–106.

Thorner, Daniel, Basil Kerblay, and R.E.F. Smith, eds. *A. V. Chayanov on the Theory of Peasant Economy.* Homewood, Ill.: Richard D. Irwin, 1966.

Tilly, Charles. "The Changing Place of Collective Violence." In *Essays in Theory and History*, ed. Melvin Richter, 139–164. Cambridge, Mass.: Harvard University Press, 1970.

———. "Did the Cake of Custom Break?" In *Consciousness and Class Experience*, ed. John Merriman, 17–44. New York: Holmes & Meier, 1979.

———. "Peasants Against Capitalism and the State: A Review Essay." *Agricultural History* 52 (1978): 407–416.

———. "Proletarianization and Rural Collective Action in East Anglia and Elsewhere, 1500–1900." *Peasant Studies* 10 (Fall 1982): 5–32.

Tilly, Charles, Louise A. Tilly, and Richard Tilly. *The Rebellious Century, 1830–1960.* Cambridge, Mass.: Harvard University Press, 1975.

Tilly, Louise A. "The Family Wage Economy of a French Textile City: Roubaix, 1872–1906." *Journal of Family History* 4 (Winter 1979): 381–394.

———. "The Food Riot as a Form of Political Conflict in France." *Journal of Interdisciplinary History* 2 (Summer 1971): 23–58.

———. "Individual Lives and Family Strategies in the French Proletariat." *Journal of Family History* 4 (Summer 1979): 137–152.

———. "Paths of Proletarianization: Organization of Production, Sexual Division of Labor, and Women's Collective Action." *Signs* 7 (1981): 400–417.

Tilly, Louise, and Joan Scott. *Women, Work, and Family.* New York: Methuen, 1987.

Tilly, Louise, Joan Scott, and Miriam Cohen. "Women's Work and European Fertility Patterns." Center for Research on Social Organization, University of Michigan, Working Paper no. 95, 1974.

Toutain, J.-C. *La population de la France de 1700 à 1959.* Paris: Institut de Science Economique Appliquée, 1963.

Trempé, Rolande. *Les mineurs de Carmaux, 1848–1914.* 2 vols. Paris: Editions ouvrières, 1971.

Tudesq, André-Jean. *L'élection présidentielle de Louis-Napoléon Bonaparte.* Paris: Armand Colin, 1965.

———. "L'opposition légitimiste en Languedoc en 1840." *Annales du Midi* 68 (Oct. 1956): 391–407.

Valentin, Jean. *La révolution viticole dans l'Aude, 1789–1907.* 2 vols. Carcassonne: Centre départemental de documentation pédagogique, 1977.

Valmary, Pierre. *Familles paysannes au XVIIIe siècle en Bas-Quercy.* Paris: Presses universitaires de France, 1965.

Van de Walle, Etienne. *The Female Population of France in the Nineteenth Century.* Princeton: Princeton University Press, 1974.

———. "Marriage and Marital Fertility." *Daedalus* 97 (Spring 1968): 486–501.

Véran, Jules. "La confédération générale des vignerons: Son histoire, son but, son fonctionnement, ses résultats." *Producteur* 8 (Apr.–June 1922).

Verdejo, Xavier. "Les mutations de la vie rurale à Cuxac d'Aude aux XIXe et XXe siècles (entre 1789 et 1914)." Mémoire de maîtrise d'histoire, Université de Toulouse-Le Mirail, 1983.

Vilar, Pierre. "Géographie et histoire statistique: Histoire social et technique de production. Quelques points d'histoire de la viticulture méditerranéenne." In *Eventail de l'histoire vivante (Hommage à Lucien Febvre),* 122–135. Paris: Gallimard, 1953.

Villermé, Louis René. *Tableau de l'état physique et moral des ouvriers employés dans les manufactures de coton, de laine et de soie (1840).* Edited by Yves Tyl. Paris: Union générale des editions, Collection 10/18, 1971.

Walter, Gerard. *Histoire des paysans en France.* Paris: Flammarion, 1963.

Warner, Charles K. *The Winegrowers of France and the Government Since 1875.* New York: Columbia University Press, 1960.

Weber, Eugen. "Comment la politique vint aux paysans: A Second Look at Peasant Politics." *American Historical Review* 87 (1982): 357–389.

———. *Peasants into Frenchmen: The Modernization of Rural France, 1870–1914.* Stanford: Stanford University Press, 1976.

Willard, Claude. *Les Guesdistes. Le mouvement socialiste en France de 1893 à 1905.* Paris: Editions sociales, 1965.

Wrigley, E. A., ed. *An Introduction to English Historical Demography.* London: Widenfield & Nicholson, 1966.

———. *Nineteenth-Century Society: Essays in the Use of Quantitative Methods for the Study of Social Data.* Cambridge: Cambridge University Press, 1972.

Zeldin, Theodore. *Emile Olivier and the Liberal Empire of Napoleon III.* Oxford: Clarendon Press, 1963.

————. *France, 1848–1945*. Vol. 1: *Ambition, Love, and Politics*. Oxford: Clarendon Press, 1973.

————. *The Political System of Louis Napoleon III*. London: Macmillan, 1958.

Zylberberg-Hocquard, Marie-Hélène. *Femmes et féminisme dans le mouvement ouvrier français*. Paris: Editions ouvrières, 1981.

Index

Compositor: Keystone Typesetting, Inc.
Text: 11/13 Baskerville
Display: Baskerville
Printer: BookCrafters
Binder: BookCrafters